May 14, 2000

Dear Judi,

A very Happy 60th Birthday to You!

May you continue to be Blessed & Guided in all that you do.

Love, Anne & Dave

THE HARPERCOLLINS BOOK OF PRAYERS

THE HARPERCOLLINS
BOOK OF
PRAYERS

*A Treasury
of Prayers
Through the
Ages*

Compiled by
Robert Van de Weyer

CASTLE BOOKS
Edison, New Jersey

*To my brothers and sisters of
the Society of Christ the Sower,
with whom I pray.*

Published in 1997 by
CASTLE BOOKS
A Division of Book Sales, Inc.
114 Northfield Avenue, Edison, New Jersey 08837

Published by arrangement with HarperCollins Publishers, Inc.,
10 East 53rd Street, New York, NY 10022.

Originally published in the United Kingdom as
THE FOUNT BOOK OF PRAYER.

ISBN: 0-7858-0811-6

Library of Congress Catalog Number: 93-5978

MANUFACTURED IN THE UNITED STATES OF AMERICA.

CONTENTS

INTRODUCTION   9

THE PRAYERS   13

    Jesus Christ   15

    Adam of St Victor   17
    Aelred of Rievaulx   19
    Alcuin of York   22
    Ambrose of Milan   24
    Lancelot Andrewes   26
    Anselm of Canterbury   31
    George Appleton   36
    Juan Arias   38
    Arjuna   41
    Augustine of Hippo   43
    Aztec   46

    John Baillie   48
    Augustine Baker   50
    William Barclay   52
    Karl Barth   55
    Basil of Caesarea   57
    Richard Baxter   58
    Bede   60
    Edward Benson   61
    Bernard of Clairvaux   64
    Jacob Boehme   66
    Bonaventura   69
    Dietrich Bonhoeffer   71
    The Book of Common Prayer   74

    John Calvin   77
    Helder Camara   79
    Amy Carmichael   83
    Elizabeth Catez   84
    Catherine of Genoa   86
    Catherine of Siena   87
    Jean-Pierre de Caussade   91
    Celtic Prayers   93
    François Chagneau   98
    Richard Challoner   101
    Rex Chapman   103
    Clement of Alexandria   105

Clement of Rome	107
Columbanus	109
John Cosin	111
William Cowper	113
Thomas Cranmer	116
Richard Crashaw	118
Cyprian of Carthage	120
The Didache	121
Dimma	123
Dinka	124
John Donne	126
Edmund of Abingdon	128
Elizabeth I	129
Ephrem the Syrian	132
Erasmus	135
The Exeter Book	137
Fenelon	139
Nicholas Ferrar	141
Charles de Foucauld	143
Francis of Assisi	147
Francis of Sales	151
Johann Freylinghausen	154
Fulbert of Chartres	158
Dominic Gaisford	160
Gemma Galgani	163
The Gelasian Sacramentary	165
Paul Geres	167
Kahlil Gibran	170
Gilbert of Hoyland	172
Elizabeth Goudge	173
Gregory of Nazianzus	174
Lady Jane Grey	177
Guigo the Carthusian	179
Joseph Hall	180
Dag Hammarskjöld	183
Bernard Häring	186
George Herbert	189
Hilary of Poitiers	192
Hildegard of Bingen	194
Hippolytus	197
Henry Scott Holland	200
Michael Hollings	201
Gerard Manley Hopkins	203
Ignatius of Loyola	205

Jacopone da Todi	207
Philip Jebb	209
Jeremiah	211
John of the Cross	212
Samuel Johnson	216
Ben Jonson	218
Julian of Norwich	220
Kalahari Bushmen	221
Margery Kempe	222
Thomas Ken	226
Søren Kierkegaard	228
John Knox	230
William Laud	232
Brother Lawrence	234
The Leonine Sacramentary	235
George MacDonald	237
George MacLeod	240
Frederick Macnutt	244
Mahayana Buddhism	246
Peter Marshall	247
Mechthild of Magdeburg	250
Thomas Merton	254
Eric Milner-White	256
Mohammed	259
Thomas More	260
Mozarabic Sacramentary	263
Thomas Münzer	265
Nanak	266
John Henry Newman	268
Reinhold Niebuhr	271
Henri Nouwen	273
Huub Oosterhuis	276
Origen	280
Prayers from Papyri	281
Blaise Pascal	283
Alan Paton	286
Polycarp of Smyrna	288
Book of Psalms	289
E. B. Pusey	292
Michel Quoist	295
Rabbula of Edessa	297
Karl Rahner	298
Rahulabhadra	300

Brother Ramon 302
Walter Rauschenbusch 304
Richard Rolle 307
Christina Rossetti 311

Roger Schutz 313
John Sergieff 315
Simeon the Theodidact 319
Simon the Persian 321
Sioux 322
Rita Snowden 323
Solomon 325
Charles Haddon Spurgeon 327
Johann Starck 329
Robert Louis Stevenson 332
Henry Suso 334

Rabindranath Tagore 336
Jeremy Taylor 338
Teilhard de Chardin 341
Teresa de Ávila 344
Mother Teresa 351
Thérèse of Lisieux 354
Thomas à Kempis 358
Thomas Aquinas 362
Frank Topping 365
Thomas Traherne 367
Tychon of Zadonsk 369

Manikka Vasahar 372
Henry Vaughan 373
Atharva Veda 376
Jean-Baptiste Marie Vianney 378

Wapokomo 379
Mary Ward 380
Leslie Weatherhead 381
Charles Wesley 383
John Wesley 387
The Whole Duty of Man 390
William of Saint Thierry 392
Harry Williams 394

Count von Zinzendorf 395
Zoroaster 398

BIBLIOGRAPHY 401

INDEX OF TOPICS 407

ACKNOWLEDGEMENTS 413

INTRODUCTION

Most people who attempt to pray will say they are bad at it; almost no one claims to be good at praying. The disciples themselves were hardly confident in their communication with God, and asked Jesus to teach them the art. Yet prayer lies at the heart of religious faith, and Jesus himself constantly emphasizes its importance. And every century of the Christian era, and every Christian country, has produced countless sermons, tracts and books on how to pray.

This book is not so much an anthology of prayers, as a collection of people praying. For the present purpose I have defined prayer as a conversation with God, in which the individual addresses him directly. Of course this may be regarded as rather a narrow definition, excluding meditation in which the individual reflects upon God, and excluding also wordless contemplation. But a book for which good money is paid can hardly be filled with blank pages, conveying the spirit of silence. More importantly Jesus teaches that prayer can lead to an intimate and personal relationship with God, in which the individual talks to him as a loving father. And within a short time of Jesus' death, his followers began to regard him as divine, speaking to him as a close friend.

Most traditions of Christianity have prayer books, to be used at public worship. And most recent collections of prayers are aimed primarily at enhancing public worship, categorizing prayers according to topics, themes and festivals. But the style of praying in public is inevitably less personal and more formal than that of private prayer. The present book casts the net more widely. I have included some prayers written for public use, especially when they seem to express a deep human feeling. But the main emphasis is on devotional prayer, in which the writer is expressing his or her own needs, thoughts and emotions to God, in his or her own words. Jesus himself urges us to say our prayers in the privacy of the bed-chamber, speaking to God without inhibition in the language that comes naturally to us. This book is primarily a collection of bed-chamber prayers.

In drawing up the collection I have raided the works of all the great spiritual writers, as well as some lesser known figures. It is surprising how many masters (and mistresses) never address God directly in their published works, choosing simply to write about prayer. Others move freely from addressing the reader to addressing God and back again. There are even whole books, never intended to be read by others, which consist entirely of conversations with God. In selecting from these works, I have chosen passages in which the writers expose themselves most honestly to God. And if at times this involves confusion or even bitterness, that reflects the condition of the human soul.

There is no other way to present such a collection except by author. A brief biographical sketch is given, followed by samples of their conversations with God. I imagine that the book will be most helpful as an aid to personal prayer. Having made the collection, I myself often use it at the start of my own bed-time prayer, by picking it up, opening it at random, and allowing the person whose prayers I read to stimulate my conversation with God. But the book may also be used in a more systematic way at prayer groups, and even at public worship, when a more devotional atmosphere is appropriate. There is an index at the back if the reader wants to follow a particular theme; yet many of the prayers defy any categorization, so the index should not be relied on too heavily.

It could be feared that a book concentrating on a personal, devotional prayer could be a little monotonous. And it is noticeable that people separated by culture and era often speak to God in very similar ways. Yet equally people of the same age and nationality can address God in entirely different styles. Indeed, I can find no historical and cultural formula to distinguish the various approaches to prayer. A nineteenth-century Russian monk can sound remarkably similar to a medieval Italian gentleman; equally, two English or Spanish divines of the seventeenth-century can seem to belong to entirely different cultures. If there is a lesson to be drawn from this, it is that the Holy Spirit inspires individuals according to their particular spiritual needs, not societies or churches according to their ecclesiastical traditions.

Prayer, in the sense of speaking directly and personally to God, is a particular feature of Christianity. Indeed Jesus shocked many of his contemporaries by urging everyone to speak to God with the same intimacy that a child uses in speaking to a parent. Yet the other religions of the world at times seem to yearn for such intimacy. And for this reason the book includes Hindu, Buddhist, Sikh, Muslim, Zoroastrian and some tribal prayers. There are also prayers from the Jewish Bible – the Christian Old Testament – where the psalmists, as well as such figures as Jeremiah and Solomon, anticipate the Christian style of prayer.

Some of the prayers included here were composed in English; and in these cases I have left the language unchanged, updating only the spelling and punctuation. But most were written originally in other languages, and these are rendered in modern English. Happily the most prolific language for prayer has been Latin, which I can understand. But the other languages I have relied on published translations, some of which are themselves quite ancient. I have taken the liberty, where necessary, of updating the translations, using wherever possible two or three versions to ensure both sense and accuracy. The bibliography at the back directs the reader to the original version which is most likely to be obtainable. I must admit to a further, more dubious, liberty. At times I have felt compelled to abridge the prayers, since personal devotions can at times be unduly repetitious or verbose; but for the sake of a pleasant appearance on the page, I have not festooned the text with dots and brackets to indicate exclusions. This is a lapse of good scholarship; but since the book is intended as a companion to prayer, rather than an academic tome, I hope it is excusable.

As I am unable to master the computer or word processor, the task of imposing a coherent form on this diverse collection would have relied on numerous files and excessive amounts of glue, were it not for Carolyn Wright. She has not only typed the text, but patiently sculpted it into shape on her computer. Moreover she has an unfailing knack of spotting errors in my own hand-written scrawl. To her I owe a very large debt of gratitude. But of course all remaining errors and infelicities are entirely my own.

THE PRAYERS

Jesus Christ

1.
LORD, TEACH US TO PRAY

Our Father, who art in heaven,
hallowed be thy name;
thy kingdom come;
thy will be done, on earth as it is in heaven;
give us this day our daily bread;
and forgive us our trespasses,
as we forgive them that trespass against us;
and lead us not into temptation,
but deliver us from evil.

2.
ON THE RETURN OF HIS DISCIPLES
FROM THEIR FIRST MISSION

Father, Lord of heaven and earth,
I thank thee that thou hast hidden all this
from the wise and prudent,
and revealed it to little children;
yes, Father, for such was thy gracious will.

3.
AT THE TOMB OF LAZARUS

Father, I thank thee for hearing my prayer. For myself, I know that
thou hearest me always, but I say this for the multitude which is
standing round, that they may learn to believe it is thou who hast
sent me.

4.   ON THE NIGHT BEFORE HE DIED

Father, the hour has come; glorify thy Son that the Son may glorify
thee, since thou hast given him power over all flesh, to give eternal
life to all whom thou hast given him. And this is eternal life, that they
know thee the only true God, and Jesus Christ whom thou hast sent.
I glorified thee on earth, having accomplished the work which thou
gavest me to do, and now, Father, glorify thou me in thy own presence with the glory which I had with thee before the world was made.

I have manifested thy name to the men whom thou gavest me
out of the world; thine they were, and thou gavest them to me, and
they have kept thy word. Now they know that everything that thou
hast given me is from thee; for I have given them the words which
thou gavest me, and they have received them and know in truth
that I came from thee; and they have believed that thou didst send
me. I am praying for them; I am not praying for the world but for
those whom thou hast given me, for they are thine; all mine are
thine, and thine are mine, and I am glorified in them. And now I
am no more in the world, but they are in the world, and I am
coming to thee. Holy Father, keep them in thy name, which thou
hast given me, that they may be one, even as we are one. While I
was with them, I kept them in thy name, which thou hast given me;
I have guarded them, and none of them is lost but the son of
perdition, that the Scripture might be fulfilled. But now I am
coming to thee; and these things I speak in the world, that they
may have my joy fulfilled in themselves. I have given them thy
word; and the world has hated them because they are not of the
world, even as I am not of the world. I do not pray that thou
shouldst take them out of the world, but that thou shouldst keep
them from the evil one. They are not of the world, even as I am
not of the world. Sanctify them in the truth; thy word is truth. As
thou didst send me into the world, so I have sent them into the
world. And for their sake I consecrate myself, that they also may
be consecrated in truth.

I do not pray for these only, but also for those who believe in
me through their word, that they may all be one; even as thou,
Father, art in me, and I in thee, that they also may be in us, so that

the world may believe that thou hast sent me. The glory which thou hast given me I have given to them, that they may be one even as we are one. I in them and thou in me, that they may become perfectly one, so that the world may know that thou hast sent me and hast loved them even as thou hast loved me. Father, I desire that they also, whom thou hast given me may be with me where I am, to behold my glory which thou hast given me in thy love for me before the foundation of the world. O righteous Father, the world hast not known thee, but I have known thee; and these know that thou hast sent me. I made known to them thy name, and I will make it known, that the love with which thou hast loved me may be in them, and I in them.

5.   IN THE GARDEN OF GETHSEMANE

Father, if thou art willing, take this cup from me; yet not my will, but thine be done.

6.   ON THE CROSS

Father, forgive them; they know not what they do.

Adam of St Victor
died *c.*1177

A canon in the abbey of St Victor in Paris, he became famous for the large number of sequences he composed. These are rhythmical verses to be sung during Mass at the major festivals. They are often in the form of prayers directed at Jesus.

1.   CHRISTMAS

What is this jewel that is so precious? I can see it has been quarried not by men, but by God.

It is you, dear Jesus. You have been dug from the rocks of heaven itself to be offered to me as a gift beyond price.

You shine in the darkness. Every colour of the rainbow can be seen within you. The whole earth is bathed in your light.

Infant Jesus, by being born as man you have taken upon yourself the pain of death. But such a jewel can never be destroyed.

You are immortal. And by defying your own death, you shall deliver me from death.

2.   EASTER

I see flames of orange, yellow and red shooting upwards to the sky, piercing the whole clouds.

I see the clouds themselves chasing the flames upwards, and I feel the air itself reaching for the heavens.

Down below I see great, grey rocks beating against the earth, as if they were pushing their way down to hell.

At your resurrection that which is light and good rises up with you, and that which is heavy and evil is pushed downwards.

At your resurrection goodness breaks from evil, life breaks free from death.

3.   WHITSUN

Who is this who smothers me with the most fragrant perfume? Who is this who transforms my ugliness into perfect beauty? Who is this who gives me the sweetest wine to drink, and the finest food to eat?

It is you, Holy Spirit. You turn me into a bride fit for Jesus Christ. You give me wine and food fit for a wedding in heaven.

My heart was weary, but now it is eager for love. My soul was sad, but now it is full of joy.

Jesus gave his life for me. Now you, Holy Spirit, give me to him.

Aelred of Rievaulx
c.1110–1167

As a young man he served at the King of Scotland's court, where he was admired for his wit and good looks. But he was plagued by strong homosexual desires which horrified him. In 1134 he visited the newly-founded Cistercian abbey at Rievaulx in Yorkshire, where the rigorous austerities of monastic life captured his imagination. He joined immediately, and within just over a decade, was elected abbot. He was renowned for the sweetness and gentleness of his temperament which would resolve the most bitter disputes. Contrary to the normal practice of the times, he encouraged intimate friendships amongst the monks, recognizing that sexual feelings, even without physical expression, could be a precious element in all personal relationships. His prayers display the same intimacy towards Jesus.

1.   I EMBRACE YOU

O Lord Jesus, I will embrace you who became a little child for me. In my weakness I clasp you who became weak for me. A mere man, I embrace you who is God made man. You came a man as poor as I am, and you rode into Jerusalem seated on a humble donkey. I embrace you, O Lord, because your lowliness is my greatness, your weakness is my strength, your foolishness is my wisdom.

2.   I KISS YOUR FEET

I kiss your feet, dear Jesus, I press my lips to them, because despite
my many sins, despite the burden of guilt upon me, despite my lack
of judgement, I know that I have nothing to fear from you. I
embrace your feet, Lord Jesus; I anoint them with the oil of my
repentance. And as I crouch at your feet, I know that I am safe,
because you despise no one, reject no one, repel no one, welcome
everyone, admit everyone.

3.   THE WATER OF YOUR TEACHING

Good Jesus, the water of your teaching flows in silence. Your gospel
is not poured into our ears by an eloquent tongue, but is breathed
into our hearts by your sweet spirit. Your voice never strains nor
shouts. You do not force us to hear you. You ask only that we open
our hearts to you, and in tranquillity your love enters our souls

4.   A BED OF SPIRITUAL FLOWERS

Happy is he who opens his heart to you, good Jesus, for you enter
and rest there. You bring the midday of heavenly light to the
troubled breast, calming every emotion of the heart with the rays
of divine peace. You make a bed within the soul with fragrant
spiritual flowers, and you lie upon it, so that the soul is filled with
the knowledge of you and the joy of your sweetness.

5.   I SOMETIMES WANDER

Lord, I sometimes wander away from you. But this is not because
I am deliberately turning my back on you. It is because of the
inconstancy of my mind. I weaken in my intention to give my whole
soul to you. I fall back into thinking of myself as my own master.
But when I wander from you, my life becomes a burden, and within
me I find nothing but darkness and wretchedness, fear and anxiety.
So I come back to you, and confess that I have sinned against you.
And I know you will forgive me.

6. THE FRAGRANCE OF YOUR LOVE

Dear Lord Jesus, the fragrance of your love draws me towards you, like the perfume of the beloved attracts the lover. I shall follow you, Lord, walking with you over beautiful hills covered with sweet-smelling wild flowers. And I will not desert you when you walk to Calvary. I shall stay beside you, and follow your body when it is taken to the tomb. Let my flesh be buried with you in that tomb, because I no longer wish to live for myself, but to rise with you into the fullness of your love.

7. MY HEART DECLINES INTO DEPRESSION

Just as day declines to evening, so often after some little pleasure my heart declines into depression. Everything seems dull, every action feels like a burden. If anyone speaks, I scarcely listen. If anyone knocks, I scarcely hear. My heart is as hard as flint. Then I go out into the field to meditate, to read the holy Scriptures, and I write down my deepest thoughts in a letter to you. And suddenly your grace, dear Jesus, shatters the darkness with daylight, lifts the burden, relieves the tension. Soon tears follow sighs, and heavenly joy floods over me with the tears.

8. HASTEN TO ME

Dear Christ, hasten to me. Release me from my sins. Free my arms from the chains of evil, that I may embrace you. Lift the scales of ignorance from my eyes, that I may see you. Why do you delay? What are you waiting for? You are my God and my Lord, you are my refuge and my strength, you are my glory and my hope. In you I put my trust. Dear Christ, hasten to me.

Alcuin of York
c.735–804

After studying and teaching at the cathedral school of York, he became religious adviser to Charlemagne; later he was appointed abbot of Tours. There he composed numerous poems and prayers, which are both intimate and formal, and for many centuries were very popular in public worship.

1.   AT TABLE

Lord Christ, we ask you to spread our table with your mercy. And may you bless with your gentle hands the good things you have given us. We know that whatever we have comes from your lavish heart, for all that is good comes from you. Thus whenever we eat, we should give thanks to you. And having received from your hands, let us give with equally generous hands to those who are poor, breaking bread and sharing our bread with them. For you have told us that whatever we give to the poor, we give to you.

2.   OUR WARRIOR AND OUR PEACE

O King of glory, and Lord of valour, our warrior and our peace, may you win victories in the world through us your servants, for without you we can do nothing. May your compassion go before us and come behind us; be with us at our beginnings, and at our endings. May your will be done in everything we do, for you are our salvation, our glory and our joy.

3.   AT NIGHT

Fountain of light, source of light,
Hear our prayer.

Drive away from us the shadow of sin.
Seek us, kindly light.

You, who created us in holiness,
Who condemned our sin,
Who redeemed us from our sin,
Sustain us by your power.

The labour of the day is over,
And now we rest safely at home.
Make this home your home,
And protect us with your grace.

The sun has fallen below the earth,
And now the darkness is here.
Let your uncreated light shine
Upon our dark and weary souls.

Pour your gentle light into our dull minds.
Filling our heads with holy thoughts.
Pour your glorious light into our cold breasts,
Kindling holy love within our hearts.

From horror, lust and fear,
Guard us while we sleep.
And if we cannot sleep,
Let our eyes behold your heavenly host.

4.   WAR

Christ, why do you allow wars and massacres on earth? By what
mysterious judgement do you allow innocent people to be cruelly
slaughtered? I cannot know. I can only find assurance in the promise
that your people will find peace in heaven, where no one makes
war. As gold is purified by fire, so you purify souls by these bodily
tribulations, making them ready to be received above the stars in
your heavenly home.

5.   TIME

Dear God, here on earth you are constantly seeking to change us. At times we wish to flee into the wilderness to avoid you. But let us learn to love the lasting things of heaven, rather than the dying things of earth. We must accept that time always brings change; and we pray that by your grace the change within our souls will make us worthy of your heavenly kingdom, where all time will cease.

Ambrose of Milan
c.339–397

Having won respect as a just and honest governor of Milan, he was chosen bishop by popular acclaim only a short time after his conversion to Christianity, while he was still preparing for baptism. He became a brilliant preacher and hymn writer and many of his sermons and verses contain quick intimate prayers.

1.   CALLED TO THE PRIESTHOOD

Jesus, I wish you would let me wash your feet, since it was by walking about in me that you soiled them. I wish you would give me the task of wiping the stains from your feet, since it was my behaviour that put them there. But where can I get the running water I need to wash your feet? If I have no water, at least I have tears. Let me wash your feet with my tears, and wash myself at the same time.

Jesus, you called me to the priesthood from the noisy wranglings of the law courts and the daunting responsibilities of public administration. In my former life I pursued my own interests, without thought of you. But you decided that you could re-shape me to be of service to you and your Church. You forgave my sins, and made me what I am. I was a lost soul when you called me; help me not to become a lost priest as well.

As a priest let me always remember the depth of sin in which I used to dwell; and in this way let me sympathize with those who still dwell in sin, and so help to draw them up to your love. May I show compassion to anyone who falls into sin. Instead of reproving him, may I grieve and lament with him. Instead of looking upon him with contempt, may I weep for him, that through me he may know your mercy.

2. ## FRIENDSHIP AFTER DEATH

Since no one, Lord, can desire more for another man than he wishes for himself, I ask you not to separate me when I am dead from those who were so dear to me while I lived. I beg that where I am, they too may be with me. As I have not been able to see much of them here on earth, let me enjoy their company in heaven for ever. I beseech you, God most high, to grant a speedy resurrection to these children whom I love so much.

3. ## FOR THE DEAD

You watch over the insignificant, Lord, and keep them humble. Protect all who put their trust in you. Give rest to all who die in faith, returning their souls whence they came. May they not feel the sting of death. Instead let them know that death is the death of sin, and thence the beginning of eternal life.

4. ## AT DAWN

Jesus, a look from you can draw us from our slumbers, and set us firmly on our feet. Sin shudders and falters at your glance, and guilt dissolves into tears of repentance. Shine, then, on our torpid minds and set our dormant thoughts astir. May we leave sin behind us, and may our first action be to turn to you in repentant prayer.

5. AT NIGHT

Jesus, a look from you can embrace us with peaceful sleep, and ensure that our dreams are pure and holy. Sin shudders and falters at your glance, and guilt dissolves into tears of repentance. Bring peace, Lord, to our weary minds, and give rest to our tired limbs. May we leave sin behind us, and may our final reflections before sleep be prayers for your mercy.

6. THE SINNER'S BANQUET

Lord Jesus, you have invited me to your banquet table, though I deserve to be thrown into the dungeon. So I accept your invitation in fear and trembling, encouraged only by your mercy and goodness.

My soul and body are defiled by so many sinful deeds. My tongue and my heart have run wild without restraint, causing misery to others and shame to myself. My soul bleeds with the wounds of wrongdoing, and my body is like a temple of Satan. If I was to come before you as my judge, you could only condemn me to eternal torment, for that is what I deserve.

Yet I come before you, not as a judge, but as a saviour. I depend not on your justice, but on your mercy. As you look upon the wretched creature that I am, I ask that your eyes be filled with compassion and forgiveness. And as I sit at your table, I beg you to renew within me a spirit of holiness, that I may be worthy to share your supper.

Lancelot Andrewes
1555–1626

As one of the main translators of the Authorized Version of the Bible, Lancelot Andrewes was a master of language. He was also a master of prayer, composing for himself a book of private devotion which he used daily. Despite a busy life as bishop of Ely and then Winchester, it is said that he spent five hours each day in prayer; and his worn copy of his Private Prayers *was "watered by penitential tears". His pattern both in the morning and the evening included confession, profession of faith, intercession, and thanksgiving. He also composed an horology of short prayers to be said at each hour through the day.*

1.   CONFESSION

Essence beyond essence, Nature uncreate, framer of the universe, I set thee, Lord, before my face, and I lift up my soul unto thee. I worship thee on my knees, and humble myself under thy mighty hand. I stretch forth my hands unto thee, my soul gaspeth unto thee as a thirsty land. I smite on my breast, and say with the publican, God be merciful to me, a sinner, the chief of sinners; to the sinner above the publican, be merciful as to the publican. Father of mercies, I beseech thy fatherly affection, despise me not, an unclean worm, a dead dog, a putrid corpse; despise not thou the work of thine own hands; despise not thine own image though branded by sin. Lord, if thou wilt, thou canst make me clean; Lord, only say the word, and I shall be cleansed.

And thou, my Saviour Christ, Christ my Saviour, Saviour of sinners, of whom I am chief, despise me not; despise me not, O Lord, despise not the cost of thy blood, who am called by thy name; but look upon me with those eyes with which thou didst look upon Magdalene at the feast, Peter in the hall, the thief on the wood; that with the thief I may call on thee humbly, "Remember me, Lord, in thy kingdom"; that with Peter I may bitterly weep and say, "O that mine eyes were a fountain of tears, that I might weep day and night"; that with Magdalene I may hear thee say, "Thy sins be forgiven thee"; and with her may love much, for many sins, yea manifold, have been forgiven me.

And thou, all-holy, good and life-giving Spirit, despise me not, thy breath, despise not thine own holy things; but turn thee again, O Lord, at the last, and be gracious unto thy servant.

2.   PROFESSION

I believe, O Lord, in thee, Father, Word, Spirit, one God; that by thy
fatherly love and power all things were created; that by thy goodness
and love to man all things have begun anew in thy Word; who for us
men and for our salvation was made flesh, was conceived and born,
suffered and was crucified, died and was buried, descended and rose
again, ascended and sat down, will return and will repay; that by the
shining forth and working of thy Holy Spirit hath been called out of
the whole world a peculiar people into a polity, in belief of the truth
and sanctity of living; that in it we are partakers of the communion of
saints and forgiveness of sins in this world; that in it we are waiting
for resurrection of the flesh and life everlasting in the world to come.
This most holy faith which was once delivered to the saints, I believe,
O Lord; help thou mine unbelief, and vouchsafe to me to love the
Father for his fatherly love, to reverence the Almighty for his power,
as a faithful Creator to commit my soul to him in well-doing.

Vouchsafe to me to partake from Jesus of salvation, from Christ
of anointing, from the only-begotten of adoption. To worship the
Lord for his conception, in faith; for his birth, in humility; for his
sufferings, in patience and hatred of sin; for his cross, to crucify
beginnings; for his death, to mortify the flesh; for his burial, to
bury evil thoughts in good works; for his descent, to meditate upon
hell; for his resurrection, upon newness of life; for his ascension, to
mind things above; for his sitting on high, to mind the good things
on his right; for his return, to fear his second appearance; for his
judgement, to judge myself ere I be judged.

From the Spirit vouchsafe to me the breath of salutary grace. In
the holy and catholic Church to have my own calling, and holiness,
and portion, and a fellowship of her sacred rites, prayers, fastings,
groans, vigils, tears and sufferings, for assurance of remission of
sins, for hope of resurrection and translation to eternal life.

3.   INTERCESSION

O God of truth, the Prince of peace, let there be peace and truth
in our days; let all that believe be of one heart and of one soul.

O thou who breakest not the bruised reed, who quenchest not the smoking flax, establish all them that stand in truth and grace, restore them that are falling through error or sin.

I beseech thee, Lord, of thy mercy, let thine anger be turned away from this city and from this house; for we have sinned against thee. Be thou pleased favourably to regard this place and all this land, tempering justice with mercy.

Grant that I may love them that love me, even though unknown to me; and bring them, as me, into thy heavenly kingdom, and grant that I may show them the mercy of God, by remembering them in my prayers; that I, with those for whom I have prayed, and those for whom I am in any way bound to pray, and with all the people of God, may have an entrance into thy kingdom, there to appear in righteousness and be satisfied with glory.

4.   THANKSGIVING

Blessed art thou, O Lord, who has created and brought me forth into this life, and hast ordered that I should be a living soul and not senseless matter; a man, not a brute; civilized, not savage; free, not a slave; legitimate, not spurious; of good parentage, not of vile extraction and as vile myself; endued with sense, not an idiot; sound in sense, not blind nor deaf; sound in limbs, not halt nor maimed; educated, not neglected; a Christian, not a pagan; preserved from dangers and infamy, not overwhelmed thereby in the days of peace, not tossed in tempestuous struggles; of competent fortune, so that I need neither to flatter nor to borrow; set free from many sins; endued with the gifts of grace, in redemption and calling; with the gifts of nature and fortune, who according to thine abundant mercy hath begotten us again into a lively hope by the resurrection of Jesus Christ from the dead, to an inheritance incorruptible and undefiled, and that fadeth not away, reserved in heaven for us; who hast blessed me with all spiritual blessings in heavenly things in Christ; who comfortest me in all my tribulation, that, as the sufferings of Christ abound in me, so my consolation also aboundeth in Christ. To thee, O God of my fathers, I give thanks; thee I praise, who hast in some measure endued me with wisdom and might, and hast made known unto me that which I desired of thee, and hast made known to me the King's matter; who hast made me the work of thine hands, the price of thy blood, the image of thy countenance, the servant of thy purchase, the seal of thy name, the child of thy adoption, a temple of thy spirit, a member of thy Church.

5.   AN HOROLOGY

O thou that hast put in thine own power the times and the seasons, give us grace that we may pray to thee in a convenient and opportune season; and save us.

O thou that for us men and for our salvation wast born in the depth of night, grant us to be renewed daily by the Holy Ghost, until Christ himself be formed in us, to a perfect man; and save us.

O thou that very early in the morning, at the rising of the sun, didst rise again from the dead, raise us also daily to newness of life, suggesting to us, for thou knowest them, habits meet for repentance; and save us.

O thou that at the third hour didst send down thy Holy Ghost on the apostles, take not that same Holy Spirit from us, but renew him every day in our hearts; and save us.

O thou that at the sixth hour of the sixth day didst nail together with thyself upon the cross the sins of the world, blot out the handwriting of our sins that is against us, and taking it away, save us.

Thou that at the seventh hour didst command the fever to leave the nobleman's son, if there be any fever in our hearts, if any sickness, remove it from us also; and save us.

Thou that at the ninth hour for us sinners and for our sins, didst taste of death, mortify our members which are upon earth, and whatsoever is contrary to thy will; and save us.

Thou that at the tenth hour didst grant unto thine apostle to discover thy Son and to cry out with great gladness, "we have found the Messiah", grant to us also, in like manner, to find the same Messiah and having found him to rejoice in like manner; and save us.

Thou that didst even at the eleventh hour of the day of thy goodness send into thy vineyard those that had stood all the day idle, promising them a reward, give us the like grace, and though it be late, even as it were about the eleventh hour, favourably receive us who return to thee; and save us.

Thou that at the sacred hour of the Supper wast pleased to institute the mysteries of thy Body and Blood, render us mindful and partakers of the same; yet never to condemnation, but to the remission of sin, and to the acquiring of the promises of the New Testament; and save us.

Thou that at eventide wast pleased to be taken down from the cross and laid in the grave, take away from us, and bury in thy sepulchre, our sins, covering whatever evil we have committed with good works; and save us.

Thou that hast made the evening the end of the day, so that thou mightest bring the evening of life to our minds, grant us always to reflect that our life passeth away like a day; to remember the days of darkness that they are many; that the night cometh wherein no man can work; by good works to prevent the darkness, lest we be cast out into outer darkness; and continually to cry unto thee, "Abide with us, O Lord, for it draweth towards evening and the day of our life is now far spent".

Anselm of Canterbury
c.1033–1109

The son of a Lombard nobleman, he rejected the political career which his father had planned for him and joined the monastery at Bec in Normandy. His warm personality attracted both fellow monks and lay people to come to him for spiritual advice, and he found the most common problem was boredom and dryness in prayer. So he began to compose meditations for people to use privately, in which the whole range of human emotions, positive and negative, are laid bare before God.

His meditation on the relationship between belief

*and understanding has been used by theologians
as propounding the "ontological proof" of God's
existence – that God must exist because we can
conceive nothing greater.*

*In 1093 King William I, whom he had known
as Duke of Normandy, summoned him to England
as Archbishop of Canterbury.*

1.

I AM DESPERATE

I am desperate for your love, Lord.
My heart is aflame with fervent passion.
When I remember the good things you have done,
My heart burns with desire to embrace you.
I thirst for you,
I hunger for you,
I long for you,
I sigh for you.
I am jealous of your love.
What shall I say to you? What can I do for you?
Where shall I seek you?
I am sick for your love.
The joy of my heart turns to dust.
My happy laughter is reduced to ashes.
I want you.
I hope for you.
My soul is like a widow, bereft of you.
Turn to me, and see my tears.
I will weep until you come to me.
Come now, Lord, and I will be comforted.
Show me your face, and I shall be saved.
Enter my room, and I shall be satisfied.
Reveal your beauty, and my joy will be complete.

2.

I AM FRIGHTENED

I am frightened of living, Lord.
My whole life seems sinful or sterile.

Any fruits I bear are either false or rotten.
Nothing I do seems pleasing to you.
I am a barren tree that deserves
To be chopped down, cut up and burnt.
I bear only the sharp and bitter thorns of sin.
If only those thorns could prick me into repentance.
Inside me my conscience burns.
I dare not show myself, yet I have nowhere to hide.
What will happen to me?
Who will protect me from your wrath?
Where can I find safety?
Lord, you are my judge in whose hands I tremble.
Yet you also are the one who can save me.
Though I fear you, I trust you.
Though I want to flee from you, I flee towards you.
Jesus, Jesus, deal with me according to your love.
Jesus, Jesus, forget the sin by which I have provoked you,
   And see only the misery which invokes you.
Most kind Lord,
Confirm in me all that belongs to you,
And cast away all that is alien to you.

3.   BEFORE RECEIVING COMMUNION

Lord, I acknowledge that I am far from worthy
To approach and touch this sacrament.
But I trust in that mercy
Which caused you to lay down your life for sinners,
That they might be saved from sin.
So I, a sinner, presume to receive these gifts.
Make me, O Lord, so to receive with lips and heart
And know by faith and by love,
That by virtue of this sacrament
I may die to sin as you died,
And rise to fullness of life as you rose.
May I be made worthy
To become a member of your holy body,
A stone in your living temple,

And let me rejoice forever
In your eternal love.

4.   FOR FRIENDS

My good Lord,
I long to pray to you for my friends,
But I am held back by my sins.
Since I stand in such need of grace myself,
How can I dare ask for grace for others?
I anxiously seek intercession on my own behalf.
Yet even so I shall be so bold
As to intercede for others.
You commend me to pray for my friends,
And love prompts me to do so.
So I pray to you, good and gracious God,
For those who love me for your sake
And whom I love in you.
If my prayer does not deserve to be answered,
Please love them for their own sakes,
For you are the source of all love.
And make them love you with all their hearts
So that they will speak and do
Only that which pleases you.
My prayer is but a cold affair, Lord,
Because my love burns with such a small flame.
Yet you who are rich in mercy
Will bestow your grace not according to my prayers
But according to the infinite warmth of your love.

5.   FOR ENEMIES

Almighty and tender Lord Jesus Christ,
Just as I have asked you to love my friends
So I ask the same for my enemies.
You alone, Lord, are mighty.
You alone are merciful.
Whatever you make me desire for my enemies,

Give it to them.
And give the same back to me.
If I ever ask for them anything
Which is outside your perfect rule of love,
Whether through weakness, ignorance or malice,
Good Lord, do not give it to them
And do not give it back to me.
You who are the true light, lighten their darkness.
You who are the whole truth, correct their errors.
You who are the incarnate word, give life to their souls.
Tender Lord Jesus.
Let me not be a stumbling block to them
Nor a rock of offence.
My sin is sufficient to me, without harming others.
I, a slave to sin,
Beg your mercy on my fellow slaves.
Let them be reconciled with you,
And through you reconciled to me.

6.   FROM BELIEF TO UNDERSTANDING

Since, Lord, it is you who gives understanding to our faith, grant
me to understand, as far as you think fit, that you are as we believe,
and that you are what we believe you to be.

Our position seems like that of a painter. When a painter first
conceives of what he is going to create, he has seen it in his imagination, but does not yet understand it because he has not painted it.
But when he has finished the picture, he both understands it and
possesses it. Likewise even a fool can conceive that something exists
above which nothing greater can exist, even though he does not
understand it. And this belief brings understanding.

Thus, Lord, you are that of which nothing greater can be conceived. And whoever truly understands this will also understand
that you must exist, because to imagine your existence proves your
reality.

Thank you, good Lord, for the gift of belief, because this has
given me the light of understanding. It is because I first believed
that you exist that I can now understand it.

George Appleton
1902–

He served as an Anglican priest in London, Burma and India, learning to rejoice in the wisdom of others' faiths; and for a year was chaplain to a Jewish Lord Mayor of London. In 1963 he became Archbishop of Western Australia, and five years later was appointed Anglican Archbishop in Jerusalem, where he sought to build bridges between the Christian, Jewish and Muslim communities. His numerous prayers touch on the deepest human feelings.

1.   RENEWAL

O my God,
grant that I may so wait upon thee,
that when quick decision and action are needed
I may mount up with wings as an eagle;
and when under direction of thy will
and the needs of people
I have to keep going under pressure,
I may run and not be weary;
and in times of routine and humble duty,
I may walk and not faint.
For all my fresh springs are in thee,
O God of my strength.

2.   MOODS

O my Lord, when moods
of depression, anxiety, or resentment

take possession of me,
let me ask, "Why art thou so heavy, O my soul,
and why art thou so disquieted within me?"
And let the answer show me
the cause of my mood and dispel it,
so that I forget my hurts and want only thee.

3.

FOR THE SICK IN MIND

O Holy Spirit who dost delve into all things,
even the deep things of God
and the deep things of man,
we pray thee to penetrate the springs of personality
of all who are sick in mind,
to bring them cleansing, healing, and unity.
Sanctify all memory, dispel all fear,
bring them to love thee
with all their mind and will,
that they may be made whole
and glorify thee for ever.
We ask this in the name of him
who cast out devils and healed men's minds,
even Jesus Christ our Lord.

4.

GROWING OLD

Lord, I am growing old. I am slower than I used to be. My memory
is not so good. The disabilities and irritations of old age come upon
me. I find myself telling the same old jokes. Loved ones and friends
pass on across the frontier of this life and the next. Lord God, I
dare to ask if in prayer I may keep in touch with them and they
with me. May your beloved Son, who brings love to us, take our
love to them, for he still spans this world of creation and the world
of full life.

5.   DEATH

O God, we thy creatures try to evade the fact of death, and to keep
it out of mind, yet in our deeper moments we know it is a warning
note, urging us so to die every day to all selfishness and sin, that
when the times comes for our final migration, we may take death
in our stride because life is so strong within us, as it was in him who
was so manifestly thy true Son and so convincingly the prototype of
thy finished humanity, even Jesus Christ, thy Son, our brother.

Juan Arias

A Roman Catholic priest in Spain, his collection
Prayer Without Frills *had a major impact
throughout Europe, because his prayers express to
God, with both rage and joy, the needs of those who
normally find no place in Christian worship.*

1   THE DESPISED

Today we come to you, Lord, we, the despised. We are not a
sorry procession, but a repugnant one. We do not even arouse
compassion or hatred, tenderness or sympathy. We are simply
despised; we disgust people. The leper arouses compassion. The
fiercest criminal stirs up hatred or terror. The mentally ill or the
retarded inspire pity or protectiveness. But there is no place
reserved for us in the catalogue of the works of mercy.

I, Lord, am a drug addict; for all practical purposes, I have resigned
from the human race. I have lost all hope of regaining my self-
control, of becoming myself again. There are other people who
have drugged, not their bodies, but their consciences and hearts.
But nobody despises them. At worst, they are feared.

I, Lord, am a homosexual. I don't like women. Now and then, I go with another man. I commit fewer sins than my brother who certainly does like women and who even takes up with other men's wives. But no one at home or outside turns their nose up at him; they don't find him repugnant; on the contrary, sometimes they even admire him. But everyone, both men and women, shy away from me. And I am acceptable only to someone who, like me, also feels that he is cast off by normal society.

I, Lord, am a drunkard, but a poor one. I've been on the bottle for many years. They don't want me at home because they're ashamed of me, and so I'm left to stagger around the streets like a sick dog. When people see me coming, they hastily cross to the other side of the street. Even a beggar occasionally has the consolation of having someone approach him and, although hurriedly, put a small coin in his hand, which, as you yourself have told us, is also in your hand. But nobody comes near me; except perhaps a policeman to hustle me off to jail.

Yet, Lord, there are others who also get drunk but they do it at exclusive parties in the suburbs and, because they are influential, people only laugh good-naturedly at their drunken antics. They are readily forgiven and, if necessary, excuses are found for them by their hangers-on, who cover up for them. No policeman ever lays a finger on them.

I wonder – am I more repugnant when drunk than they are, just because I get loaded on cheap wine, while they do it on expensive whiskey, vodka and gin?

I, Lord, am a prostitute. I can't claim to be one of the girls, not any more. Because now I'm old and fat and tired. I have no one now to pay the rent of an apartment for me and buy me nice things. I am one of those who have to be satisfied with what the "customers" feel like giving them. I no longer have a nice apartment to entertain my clients in, and I don't have the money to advertise in the newspapers as a "masseuse". I have to be satisfied with hanging around cheap bars in the slums or on street corners in the cold and the rain, hoping that some poor wretch will be willing to pay me a few coins for the remnants of my favours.

People passing in their cars look down their noses at me and
quickly turn away so as not to meet my eyes. I am despised even
by the high-class call girls who, glittering with jewels and wrapped
in furs, glide by in big cars driven by their so-very-respectable
"patrons".

We and so many others whom society does not even pity; we, the
despised of the earth, who arouse neither hatred nor pity nor fear,
but only disgust, today we come to you, who are sinless, because
we believe that, if you do exist, you will not despise but will even
forgive us.

We aren't trying to hide or make excuses for the sins that have
caused us to be cast off by society. We only hope that perhaps you,
who not only forgive but also excuse, will be able to avoid humiliat-
ing us further and to tell us, as once you told the man possessed by
the devil, that saving us will let others see your glory and mercy in
us. Remember, you said you came to save what was lost. And who
is more lost than we who do not even arouse pity? Sometimes a ray
of hope lets us dream for a moment that perhaps you may bring
yourself to love even us.

2.   THE ATHEIST

I am an atheist. This does not mean that I believe in nothing, but
that I don't believe in any Totality. For me, God is a lovely dream
or a beautiful poem. I'm speaking now about a God whom I could
love, because there is another God, the God of the despoilers of
history, whom I would like to murder with my own hands. I am an
atheist and therefore I cannot pray to anyone because I do not
believe in the existence of Someone who is different from me and
to whom I can pray. Nevertheless, I have to confess that at times I
feel very keenly the anguish of utter solitude. Sometimes I would
like to be able to cry out to someone all my thirst for I-know-not-
what, and to ask him so many questions that now have no answers.
But that would be like shouting into the wind.

Therefore I know that I must accept myself as I am, that I must
just plod along through the darkness of the world, that I must not
look for a definite answer to the problem of my very existence. It

seems to me that people who believe in God are crazy, although at times I catch myself wondering if I am not the one who's crazy.

God, God, God! Are you a beautiful invention of the poets? Are you merely the echo of those who mistakenly think that they have found something to hope for? Are you a cynical creation which the exploiters of mankind use as an alibi? Are you the unconscious projection of man's need to be protected? Of course, you could also be the one true reality that makes sense of men and things. But what if you are only the product of a great illusion, of man's urge to make divine what is merely earthly? Accordingly, I shall continue to shout my prayer into the wind.

Arjuna
c.8th century BC

He was the son of Padu, one of the ancient kings of northern India. A great warrior, he led his father's army to many victories. He is a major character in the Mahabharata, *one of the great Indian epic poems, and these prayers are taken from his conversation with Krishna, who was an incarnation of God. This conversation, which took place immediately prior to a great battle, is known as the Bhagavad Gita.*

1.   THE TRUTH OF GOD

Supreme God, your light is brighter than the sun, your purity whiter than mountain snow, you are present wherever I go.

All people of wisdom praise you. So I too put faith in all your words, knowing that everything you teach is true. Neither the

angels in heaven nor the demons in hell can know the perfection
of your wisdom, for it is beyond all understanding.

Only your Spirit knows you; only you can know your true self.
You are the source of all being, the power of all power, the ruler
of all creatures. So you alone understand what you are.

In your mercy reveal to me all that I need to know, in order to
find peace and joy. Tell me the truths that are necessary for the
world in which I live.

Show me how I can meditate upon you, learning from you the
wisdom that I need. I am never tired of hearing you, because your
words bring life.

2.   THE INFINITY OF GOD

I see you in all things, O my God. Infinity itself is your creation.
And all around are the signs of your infinity: the bursting life of
countless plants; the unending song of innumerable birds; the tireless movement of animals and insects. Nowhere can I see a beginning or an end of your creation.

I see the infinite beauty which infuses the entire universe. You
are the king of the universe, and its beauty is your crown and
sceptre. I bow down in homage and adoration.

You are immortal, imperishable, the summit of all knowledge,
the power behind all movement. You designed all things, and set
them in motion.

The sun is your eye during the day, and the moon your eye at
night. The wind is your breath, and the fertile brown earth is your
heart.

By your power all things are created, and by your power they are
destroyed. Birth and death are in your hands. I tremble with awe
and wonder when I contemplate your power.

As the waters of a river flow to the sea, the path determined by
the line of the valley, so we pass through life to death, our destiny
mapped out by your will.

Lord, reveal yourself to me. Show me that love, not hatred,
inspires your creation. Show me that mercy, not anger, guides my
life. I do not ask to understand the mystery of your works; I want
only to be assured of your goodness.

Augustine of Hippo
354–430

The son of a Christian mother and pagan father, he spent the early years of his life seeking inner peace through philosophical knowledge, despising the simplicity of Christianity. He was deeply disturbed by his sexual passions, and kept a mistress who bore him a son. His Confessions *describes his eventual conversion to Christianity in the most vivid and agonizing details. Large parts of it are in the form of outpourings to God. He went on to be a bishop in his native region of north Africa, as well as a prolific theologian whose ideas deeply influenced the Protestant Reformation.*

1. OUR HEARTS ARE RESTLESS

You are great, Lord, and greatly to be praised. Great is your power, and of your wisdom there is no end. And man, who is part of what you have created, desires to praise you. Yes, even though he carries his mortality wherever he goes, as the proof of his sin and testimony of your justice, man desires to praise you. For you have stirred up his heart so that he takes pleasure in praising you. You have created us for yourself, and our hearts are restless until they rest in you.

2. CALLING, PRAISING, KNOWING

Grant, O God, that I may know and understand which of these should be first: to call upon you, or to praise you. And again: to know you, or to call upon you. For who can call upon you without knowing you, because a person that does not know you may call on some other being? Or are you to be called on in order that you might be known? Yet how can people call on him in whom they have not believed, and how can they believe without a preacher?

Those who seek the Lord shall praise him. For those who seek shall find him, and in finding him they shall praise him. Thus I will seek you, O Lord, calling upon you, because you have preached to us. My faith, O God, which you have given me, and with which you have inspired me by the humanity of your son and by his ministry as your preacher, calls upon you.

3.   HOW SHALL I CALL UPON YOU?

How shall I call upon my Lord and my God? When I call him, I am asking him to come into myself; and yet what place is there in me that can contain God, who created heaven and earth? Is there, Lord, anything in me that can contain you? Do heaven and earth, which you have made and in which you have made me, contain you? Or, since without you nothing could exist, does everything contain you? Since, then, I exist, why do I desire that you may come into me? I would not exist at all unless you were already in me.

4.   LORD, I SEEK YOU

Lord, I seek you with all my heart, with all the strength you have given me. I long to understand that which I believe.

You are my only hope; please listen to me. Do not let my weariness lessen my desire to find you, to see your face.

You created me in order to find you; you gave me strength to seek you. My strength and my weakness are in your hands: preserve my strength, and help my weakness. Where you have already opened the door, let me come in; where it is shut, open at my knocking.

Let me always remember you, love you, meditate upon you, and pray to you, until you restore me to your perfect pattern.

5.   WHAT ARE YOU, MY GOD?

What are you, my God? What are you, but the Lord God himself? You are the highest, the most righteous and the most powerful being. You are the most merciful, and yet the most just. You are the most mysterious, and yet the most present. You are the most beautiful, and yet the strongest. You are stable, yet incomprehensible. You are unchanging, yet changing all things. You are never new and never old, yet you are constantly renewing all things. You are always working, yet always at rest. You create great riches on earth, yet you need nothing yourself. You support, nourish and protect all.

You love, and yet you are without passion. You are jealous, and yet have no fear. You recoil at our sin, and yet you do not grieve. You are angry, yet remain serene. You alter your plans in response to our actions, yet your law and purpose remain firm. You take as you find, yet never lose. You have no needs, yet you rejoice in all goodness. You have no envy, yet you require us to multiply the talents you have bestowed. You pay debts, yet owe nothing; you forgive debts, yet lose nothing.

What shall I say, O my God, my life, my holy joy? What can any man say when he speaks of you? Silence offers the greatest eloquence, yet woe to him who does not sing your praise.

6.   YOUR RIGHT HAND REACHED DOWN TO ME

What evil have I not done by my actions; and if not by my actions, then by my words; and if not by my words, then by my will? But you, O Lord, are gracious and merciful. Your right hand reached down to me in the depths of sin, and from the bottom of my heart you drew out the faith of my corruption. And this deliverance was not according to my will; rather your will began to make me will such a deliverance.

But where had that free will of mine remained for so long, and from what deep and secret corner did you call it forth? How did I come to submit my neck to your easy yoke, and allow my shoulders to carry your light burden? Instantly your yoke and burden, dear Christ, felt wonderfully sweet, so much sweeter than those vain delights which I had forsaken. Indeed it was a joy to me to be deprived of those joys which earlier I had feared to lose. For you, O Lord, cast them away from me, and in their place you yourself entered me, bringing joy which is sweeter than any earthly pleasure. Your joy is clearer than any light, yet it is more mysterious than any secret; it is higher than the highest honour, but does not flatter our pride.

Thus my mind became free from the biting cares of worldly honour and riches, it became free of spiritual filth, and I no longer felt the insatiable itch of lust. I prattled like a child to you, my tongue speaking freely to you – you who are my light, my wealth, my salvation, my Lord and my God.

7.   WITHOUT YOU I AM NOTHING

I call upon you, O God – you who created me, and who did not forget me when I forgot you. Let me know you – you who are the only one who truly knows me. Come into my soul, because you are the power that makes my soul live. Make me fit to belong to you, because that is my only hope. Enter my heart, because by inspiring me to long for you, you make me ready to be your bride.

When I was far from you, you persuaded me to listen to your voice and turn back to you. I called to you for help, but all the time you were calling me to yourself. You blotted out all my sins, instead of punishing me as I deserved.

I was nothing. You had no need of me. Even now my service has not even the value of a labourer tilling his master's land, because even if I did not work, you would bring forth the same harvest. I can only serve you and worship you with the good that comes from you. It is from you alone that I receive strength, and without you I am nothing.

Aztec
*c.*15th century

For two centuries prior to the arrival of the Spanish conquerors, the Aztec tribe formed a great empire and civilization. At the heart of their success was their religion, in which the sun was regarded as the symbol of a Supreme Deity. They believed in divine guidance over every aspect of their lives, including war, which was regarded as a religious obligation.

1.   IN THE TIME OF WAR

Most powerful Lord, under whose empire we live, you are invisible and untouchable, like the night and like the air. The ground is now shaking, as warriors stamp their feet in fury at their enemy. The earth is opening her throat, ready to receive the blood which is spilt in the heat of battle. Even the wild animals run away, terrified of the coming slaughter.

Lord, you alone know who will die and who will live, who will collapse in defeat and who will rise in victory. We pray that those who fall in battle may die with honour, and ascend to you to live among the heroes. May they share in your eternal glory and savour your eternal sweetness.

2.   IN TIME OF SICKNESS

Most powerful Lord, beneath whose wings we find protection and shelter, you are invisible and untouchable, like the night and like the air. I appear before you, stammering with nervous uncertainty, as one who has stumbled and lost his way. I am afraid that my wrong-doing has provoked your wrath and aroused your indignation against me. For that is the only explanation I can find for the terrible sickness that has fallen upon my family. The misery of my children is surely the consequence of my wickedness.

Lord, do with my body whatever pleases. Heap upon me whatever diseases I deserve. Do not spare me any suffering or any indignity. Let me bear the punishment for my own actions. And so let my children be restored to health and happiness, that they may stand upright and follow your path of righteousness. Let me die, that they may live.

John Baillie
1886–1960

A Scottish theologian who also taught extensively in North America, he was a prolific writer. He served as president of the World Council of Churches, and throughout his life worked for close relations between Christian denominations. His most popular work, published in 1936, is A Diary of Private Prayer, *which contains a monthly cycle of morning and evening prayers.*

1.   FOR THE MORNING

Eternal Father of my soul, let my first thought today be of thee, let my first impulse be to worship thee, let my first speech be thy name, let my first action be to kneel before thee in prayer.

> For thy perfect wisdom and perfect goodness:
> For the love wherewith thou lovest mankind:
> For the love wherewith thou lovest me:
> For the great and mysterious opportunity of my life:
> For the indwelling of thy Spirit in my heart:
> For the sevenfold gifts of thy Spirit:
>   I praise and worship thee, O Lord.

Yet let me not, when this morning prayer is said, think my worship ended and spend the day in forgetfulness of thee. Rather from these moments of quietness let light go forth, and joy, and power, that will remain with me through all the hours of the day;

> Keeping me chaste in thought:
> Keeping me temperate and truthful in speech:
> Keeping me faithful and diligent in my work:
> Keeping me humble in my estimation of myself:

Keeping me honourable and generous in my dealings with
    others:
Keeping me loyal to every hallowed memory of the past:
Keeping me mindful of my eternal destiny as a child of
    thine.

O God, who hast been the refuge of my fathers through many
generations, be my refuge today in every time and circumstance of
need. Be my guide through all that is dark and doubtful. Be my
guard against all that threatens my spirit's welfare. Be my strength
in time of testing. Gladden my heart with thy peace.

2.   FOR THE EVENING

O thou in whose boundless being are laid up all treasures of wisdom
and truth, and holiness, grant that through constant fellowship with
thee the true graces of Christian character may more and more take
shape within my soul:

The grace of a thankful and uncomplaining heart:
The grace to await thy leisure patiently and to answer thy
    call promptly:
The grace of courage, whether in suffering or in danger:
The grace to endure hardness as a good soldier of Jesus
    Christ:
The grace of boldness in standing for what is right:
The grace of preparedness, lest I enter into temptation:
The grace of bodily discipline:
The grace of strict truthfulness:
The grace to treat others as I would have others treat me:
The grace of charity, that I may refrain from hasty
    judgement:
The grace of silence, that I may refrain from hasty speech:
The grace of forgiveness towards all who have wronged
    me:
The grace of tenderness towards all who are weaker than
    myself:
The grace of steadfastness in continuing to desire that
    thou wilt do as now I pray.

And now, O God, give me a quiet mind, as I lie down to rest. Dwell in my thoughts until sleep overtake me. Let me not be fretted by any anxiety over the lesser interests of life. Let no troubled dreams disturb me, so that I may awake refreshed and ready for the tasks of another day.

Augustine Baker
1575–1641

Brought up as a Protestant in Wales, he changed to Roman Catholicism in his late twenties, becoming a Benedictine monk at Douai in England. Holy Wisdom *is a collection (made after his death) of his spiritual writings. It contains a series of spiritual exercises which many continue to practise, focusing on the various aspects of the individual's relationship with God.*

1.   EXERCISES OF CONTRITION

Thou hast made me, O Lord, when I was not, and that according to thine own image.

Thou from the very first instant of my being hast been
> My God,
> My Father,
> My Deliverer, and
> All my Good.

Thou, with the benefits of thy providence, hast preserved my life even till this present. O, let it be spent in thy service!

But because these things, O gracious Lord, cost thee nothing, to bind me more fast to thee, thou wouldst need give me a present bought by thee most dearly.

Thou hast come down from heaven, to seek me in all those ways in which I had lost myself. O, draw up my soul unto thee!

Bestow on me, O Lord, thy fear, compunction of heart, humility, and a conscience free from all sin.

Grant me grace, O Lord, that I may be always able to live in charity with my brethren; not forgetting my own sins, or prying into the sins or doings of other men.

> Visit me weakened;
> Cure me diseased;
> Refresh me wearied;
> Raise me dead.

Grant me, O Lord, a heart that may fear thee, a mind that may love thee, a sense that may conceive thee, eyes that may see thee.

Give me, O Lord, discretion to be able to discern betwixt good and evil, and endue me with an understanding ever watchful.

2. ### EXERCISES OF LOVE

O my God, I love and desire to love thee, with a love pure and free from all respect of proper commodity and self-interest.

I love thee, my Lord, with a perseverant love, purposing by the help of thy holy grace and assistance never to be separated from thee by sin.

And if I were to live for millions of years, yet would I ever remain thy faithful servant and lover.

I wish all creatures would adore and serve thee, and that infidels may be converted to thy faith, and all sinners to a good life; and all this only for thy supreme honour and glory.

I congratulate with thee, O my God, for the blessedness and all the perfections that are in thee, and which for all eternity thou hast ever had; as thy omnipotence and wisdom.

I congratulate with thee also, and am glad that thou hast need of no extrinsical thing, but art in thyself most rich and fully sufficient both for thyself and all creatures.

I likewise with thee, O my Lord, rejoice in the sweet ordinance and disposition of heaven and earth, and for all the things which are in the marvellous creation of this world, and for all the works which thou hast made, or shalt yet make unto the end of the world.

3.   EXERCISES OF WILL

From this hour my purpose, through thy grace, is to accept and welcome all occurrences, whether pleasing or distasteful to sense, as coming from thy heavenly providence: this shall be my comfort and stay in all my afflictions; in dangers, security; and perfect rest of mind in expectation of future events.

Thou alone, O my God, provide, determine, will and choose for me.

Hast not thou, O my God, provided for me thine own kingdom? What, then, can make me dejected?

I offer unto thee my understanding, firmly to adhere to all divine verities revealed by thee to thy Church, renouncing all doubt or questioning of any of them; and herein my purpose irrevocable is, through thy grace, to live and die.

O that it would please thee that all mankind might know thee, and with a firm faith confess thee!

My God, I do willingly offer unto thee my blood to seal this my faith, whensoever by thy providence an occasion shall be presented, hoping that then thou wilt be my strength and my salvation; and being assured that, whilst I hope in thee, I shall not be weakened.

William Barclay
1907–1978

After thirteen years as minister of a poor industrial parish on Clydeside, in 1946 he went to teach Biblical studies at Glasgow University. There is a profound simplicity in his Bible commentaries and his prayers which won him readers throughout the world.

1. FOR EACH ONE'S NEED

O God, our Father, there are no two of us here with the same need. You know our needs. Bless us as each one of us needs. Specially bless those who are in the middle of some specially difficult time:

> Those who have some specially difficult task to face or some specially difficult examination to sit;
> Those who have some specially difficult problem to solve;
> Those who have some specially difficult decision to take;
> Those who have some specially difficult temptation to resist;
> Those who have some specially baffling doubt through which to think their way.

Speak to those who are

> Evading some decision;
> Shirking some task;
> Putting off some duty;
> Playing with fire;
> Wasting their time;
> Throwing away their opportunities.

Tell them that they dare not bring shame to themselves and disappointment to those who love them.

Speak to those who are successful, that they may be kept from all pride and self-conceit; speak to those who are too self-confident, that they may not be riding for a fall; speak to those who are too sure that they are right and too sure that everyone else is wrong, that they may be kept from intolerance. Help those who are shy. Remember those who are in disgrace and in prison, and keep them from despair.

2. DIFFICULT TO LIVE WITH

O God, forgive us for the faults which make us difficult to live with.

> If we behave as if we were the only people for whom life is difficult;

If we behave as if we were far harder worked than anyone
    else;
If we behave as if we were the only people who were ever
    disappointed, or the only people who ever got a raw deal;
If we are far too self-centred and far too full of self-pity:
           Forgive us, O God.

If we are too impatient to finish the work we have begun;
If we are too impatient to listen to someone who wants to
    talk to us, or to give someone a helping hand;
If we think that other people are fools, and make no
    attempt to conceal our contempt for them:
           Forgive us, O God.

If we too often rub people the wrong way;
If we spoil a good case by trying to ram it down someone's
    throat;
If we do things that get on people's nerves, and go on
    doing them, even when we are asked not to:
           Forgive us, O God.

Help us to take the selfishness and the ugliness out of life and to
do better in the days to come.

3.   IMPORTANT AND UNIMPORTANT

O God, our Father, forgive us that we so often give our best to the
wrong things.

Sometimes we put far more enthusiasm and thought and effort
into our pleasures and our games and our amusement than we do
into our work.

Sometimes we keep our best behaviour for strangers and our
worst behaviour for our own homes; and often we treat our nearest
and dearest with a discourtesy and disregard we would never show
to strangers.

Sometimes we get irritated and annoyed and angry about things
which in our calmer moments we know do not matter.

Sometimes we lose our temper in an argument about trifles.

Sometimes we allow very little things to cause a quarrel with a friend.

Help us to see what is important and what is unimportant, so that we may never forget the things that matter, and so that we may never allow the things which do not matter to matter too much.

Karl Barth
1886–1968

The most prominent Protestant theologian of his time, he asserted that the supremacy of God, revealed in Jesus Christ, was far above the grasp of human reason. Most of his life was devoted to his academic work and to resisting the Nazi movement. But in his mellow old age he preached a series of poignant sermons at Basle prison in his native Switzerland, each of which concluded with a prayer.

1.   CHRISTMAS

O Lord, our King and our Saviour! Let us celebrate this festival without false ideas, but with our hearts open to receive your Word, your promise, your commandment. Our grumbles and doubts, our errors and mistakes, our stubbornness and defiance, should trouble us even during these days of joy, because they trouble you. But as we rejoice at your birth in the world, we ask you to accept us and uplift us as we are. And we pray that, in your strength, we shall be willing to be counted amongst the poor and the humble, as you counted yourself.

So we remember before you all our brothers and sisters who are troubled and confused, who are sick in body or in mind, who lack the material means of survival. And we trust that in you the gospel of freedom may be proclaimed more cheerfully and joyfully by both

Catholics and Protestants alike, that they become the salt for which the world longs.

And now may we have a good Christmas. Let us look forward beyond the bright lights of our Christmas decorations towards the dawning of your eternal light.

2.   NEW YEAR'S EVE

O Lord, our Father! We have gathered here at the turn of the year because we do not want to be alone but want to be with each other, and together be united with you. Our hearts are filled with sombre thoughts as we reflect on our misdeeds of the past year. And our ears are deafened by the voices of the radio and in the newspapers, with their numerous predictions for the coming year. Instead we want to hear your word, your voice, your assurance, your guidance. We know that you are in our midst, and are eager to give us all that we need, whether we ask or not. On this night we ask for one thing only: that you collect our scattered thoughts, getting rid of the confused and defiant thoughts that may distract us, and thus enable us to concentrate on your limitless generosity to us. You were abundantly generous to us last year, and will be no less generous to us next year, and in every year to come. Fill us with gratitude to you.

3.   EASTER

O Lord God, our Father. You are the light that can never be put out; and now you give us a light that shall drive away all darkness. You are love without coldness, and you have given us such warmth in our hearts that we can love all when we meet. You are the life that defies death, and you have opened for us the way that leads to eternal life.

None of us is a great Christian; we are all humble and ordinary. But your grace is enough for us. Arouse in us that small degree of joy and thankfulness of which we are capable, to the timid faith which we can muster, to the cautious obedience which we cannot refuse, and thus to the wholeness of life which you have prepared for all of us through the death and resurrection of your Son. Do not allow any of us to remain apathetic or indifferent to the wondrous glory of Easter, but let the light of our risen Lord reach every corner of our dull hearts.

Basil of Caesarea
c.330–379

A cultured man, well-versed in both pagan and Christian philosophy, he gave up a glittering career to become a hermit near Caesarea. Others soon joined him, and he composed a monastic rule which remains the basis of religious life in the Eastern Church. But his reputation for piety and wisdom was such that the people of Caesarea begged him to become their bishop, and for the remainder of his life he was a staunch defender of orthodoxy against various popular heresies. His numerous compositions include several vivid personal prayers.

1. ### THE SHIP OF LIFE

Steer the ship of my life, good Lord, to your quiet harbour, where I can be safe from the storms of sin and conflict. Show me the course I should take. Renew in me the gift of discernment, so that I can always see the right direction in which I should go. And give me the strength and the courage to choose the right course, even when the sea is rough and the waves are high, knowing that through enduring hardship and danger in your name we shall find comfort and peace.

2.   RECEIVING THE SINNER

O Lord and Master, I am unworthy both of heaven and of earth, because I have surrendered myself to sin, and become the slave of worldly pleasures. Yet, since you created me, and since you can shape me as you want, I do not despair of salvation; but made bold by your compassionate love, I come before you. Receive me, dear Lord, as you received the harlot, the thief, the tax collector and even the prodigal son. You love all people, so pour out your love upon me. Lift from me the heavy burden of sin, cleanse every stain of unrighteousness from me, and wash me white with the waters of holiness.

3.   BREAD AND WATER OF ETERNITY

You, Lord, are the bread of life and the well of holiness. Just as you feed me day by day with the food that sustains my body, keeping me alive on earth, I pray that you will feed my soul with the spiritual bread of eternity, making me ready for heaven. Just as you satisfy my bodily thirst with cool water from the rivers and streams, I pray that you will pour the water of holiness into my soul, making my every word and action a joyful sign of your love.

Richard Baxter
1615–1691

A strict Puritan, he served for twenty years as incumbent at Kidderminster where, despite his long and impenetrable sermons, his tireless devotion to his people attracted a huge congregation. Although an admirer of Cromwell, he publicly opposed the execution of King Charles I, believing that monarchy was divinely instituted. Yet he also refused a bishopric under King Charles II, objecting that bishops were acquiring excessive wealth and power. His short book Instructions for a Holy Life *contains a number of prayers which are redolent of the Puritan spirit.*

1.

LORD, BLESS THE WORLD

Lord, bless the world, and specially these kingdoms, with wise godly, just and peaceable princes and inferior judges and magistrates; and guide, protect and perfect them for the common good and the promoting of godliness and suppressing of sin. And bless all churches with able, godly, faithful pastors, that are zealous lovers of God and goodness and the people's souls. And save the nations and churches from oppressing tyrants and deceivers, and from malignant enemies to serious piety. And cause subjects to live in just obedience and in love and peace. Bless families with wise, religious governors, who will carefully instruct their children and servants and restrain them from sin and keep them from temptation. Teach children and servants to fear God and honour and obey their governors.

2.

BEFORE A MEAL

Most gracious God, who hast given us Christ and with him all that is necessary to life and godliness: we thankfully take this our food as the gift of thy bounty, procured by his merits. Bless it to the nourishment and strength of our frail bodies to fit us for thy cheerful service.

3.

AFTER A MEAL

Most merciful Father, accept of our thanks for these and all thy mercies; and give us yet more thankful hearts. O give us more of the great mercies proper to thy children, even thy sanctifying and comforting Spirit and assurance of thy love through Christ.

Bede
c.673–735

The greatest scholar of the early English Church, he spent his whole adult life as a monk in Jarrow, on the Northumbrian coast. His Life of St Cuthbert *continues to inspire readers, while his* History of the English Church *combines meticulous historical research with gentle spiritual interpretation.*

1.   LIFE AND DEATH

I beseech you, good Jesus, that as you have graciously granted to me here on earth to enjoy the sweetness of your wisdom and truth, so at death you will bring me into your presence, that I may see the beauty of your face, and listen to your voice which is the source of all wisdom and truth.

2.   THE SPIRIT'S GRACE

Lord God, open my heart and pour into it the grace of your Holy Spirit. By this grace may I always seek to do what is pleasing to you; may my thoughts always reflect your thoughts; and may my affections be solely directed towards the unending joys of heaven. Thus may I on earth fulfil your commandments, that I may be worthy of your everlasting reward.

3.   STUDYING SCRIPTURES

May your Spirit, O Christ, lead me in the right way, keeping me safe from all forces of evil and destruction. And, free from all malice, may I search diligently in your Holy Word to discover with the

eyes of my mind your commandments. Finally, give me the strength
of will to put those commandments into practice through all the
days of my life.

4.   FOR PROTECTION

O God, who are the only hope of the world, the only refuge for
unhappy men, abiding in the perfect harmony of heaven, give me
courage and strength amidst the conflicts here on earth. Protect
me from the utter ruin that would befall me if my weak faith gave
way under the many blows which assail me. Remember that I am
mere dust and wind and shadow, whose life is as fleeting as that of
a wild flower in the grass. But may your eternal mercy, which has
shone since time began, rescue me from the jaws of evil.

Edward Benson
1829–1896

*A magisterial and somewhat forbidding Archbishop
of Canterbury, he revealed a humbler and more
self-critical side of himself in his private prayers, in
which he grapples with his episcopal ministry. These
prayers were edited and published by his widow
three years after his death.*

1.   A BISHOP'S MINISTRY

O Father, who calledst me with a holy calling,
not according to my works, but according to
thine own purpose and eternal grace given unto us
in Christ Jesus before times eternal,
furnish me as a man of God
to flee all worldly lusts,
to follow after righteousness, godliness,

faith, love, patience,
to fight the good fight of faith,
to lay hold on the true life.
Thou who didst abound in grace exceedingly
with faith and love,
give me understanding in all things.
Thou then who didst set me at the good work of a
    bishop
and to take care of the Church of God,
grant that I may stir up the gift that was given me
with the laying on of the hands of the presbytery
and not to neglect it,
since thou, O God, didst not give us a spirit of
    fearfulness
but of love and power and discipline.
Let me not, being puffed up,
fall into the condemnation of the devil,
but be blameless,
temperate, sober-minded, orderly,
a lover of strangers, a lover of good men,
apt to teach,
forbearing, gentle, courteous,
not contentious, no lover of money;
to rule mine own house well.

2.   A BISHOP'S SOUL

O Word of God, living and active,
pierce me even to the dividing of soul and spirit,
of both joints and marrow,
and be thou quick to discern the thoughts
and intents of my heart;
that I may not desire to make a fair show in the flesh,
to appear comely, outwardly righteous.
O, that I might not glory save in the cross,
through it to have been crucified to the world!
that I might not deceive myself,
thinking myself to be something,

when I am nothing!
Teach thou me to prove mine own work;
by well-doing to put to silence the ignorance of
foolish men;
by doing good to lay hold on the life which is
life indeed:
not to tire in well-doing, not to faint,
not to wax weary in soul;
to show my works by my good life
in meekness of wisdom;
to be wise and understanding in the wisdom
that is from above, which is first pure,
then peaceable, gentle, easy to be entreated,
full of mercy and good fruits,
without variance, without hypocrisy:
by making peace to sow in peace the fruit
of righteousness;
to consider others to provoke to love
and good works;
not to be a men-pleaser, not double-speaking,
not double-tongued,
in no wise, in no place, willingly, unwillingly,
knowingly, ignorantly,
to corrupt the word;
nourished in the good and sound doctrine;
to give heed to reading, to exhortation;
to exercise myself unto godliness;
to determine unceasingly not to know anything
among the people
save Christ Jesus
and him crucified.

Bernard of Clairvaux
1090–1153

The main inspiration of the Cistercian Order of monks, renowned for its strict austerities, he was a leading proponent of the Crusades as well as a ruthless opponent of heretics. But behind his forceful exterior was a more tranquil, mystical spirit whose sermons and prayers written for the major Christian festivals were widely disseminated.

1.   CHRISTMAS

Let your goodness, Lord, appear to us, that we, made in your image, conform ourselves to it. In our own strength we cannot imitate your majesty, power and wonder; nor is it fitting for us to try. But your mercy reaches from the heavens, through the clouds, to the earth below. You have come to us as a small child, but you have brought us the greatest of all gifts, the gift of eternal love. Caress us with your tiny hands, embrace us with your tiny arms, and pierce our hearts with your soft, sweet cries.

2.   LENT

Let me hold fast to you, beautiful Lord, whom the angels themselves yearn to look upon. Wherever you go, I will follow you. If you pass through fire, I will not flinch, I fear no evil when you are with me. You carry my griefs, because you grieve for my sake. You passed through the narrow doorway from death to life, to make it wide enough for all to follow. Nothing can ever now separate me from your love.

3.
HOLY WEEK

You taught us, Lord, that the greatest love a man can show is to lay down his life for his friends. But your love was greater still, because you laid down your life for your enemies. It was while we were still enemies that you reconciled us to yourself by your death. What other love has ever been, or could ever be, like yours? You suffered unjustly for the sake of the unjust. You died at the hands of sinners for the sake of the sinful. You became a slave to tyrants, to set the oppressed free.

4.
EASTER

Lord, you have passed over into new life, and you now invite us to pass over also. In these past days we have grieved at your suffering and mourned at your death. We have given ourselves over to repentance and prayer, to abstinence and gravity. Now at Easter you tell us that we have died to sin. Yet, if this is true, how can we remain on earth? How can we pass over to your risen life, while we are still in this world. Will we not be just as meddlesome, just as lazy, just as selfish as before? Will we not still be bad-tempered and stubborn, enmeshed in all the vices of the past. We pray that as we pass over with you, our faces will never look back. Instead, let us, like you, make heaven on earth.

5.
ASCENSION

To complete your seamless robe, and so to complete our faith, you ascended through the air into the heavens, before the very eyes of the apostles. In this way you showed that you are Lord of all, and are the fulfilment of all creation. Thus from that moment every human and every living creature should bow at your name. And, in the eyes of faith, we can see that all creation proclaims your greatness.

6.   THE LORD'S RETURN

What use to me, O Lord, are all the solemnities and rituals of
worship? I did not see you hanging on the cross. I did not suffer with
you, nor follow you to the grave, my tears bathing your wounds. I
did not see you rise into the heavens. On earth you never greeted
me, and when you ascended to the heavens, you never bid me
farewell. I missed your first coming, and my soul is bitter and sad.
But your angels comfort me when they promise that you shall
return in the same manner that you left, as King of kings. When
you first came to Bethlehem you were humble and lowly. When
you return the fullness of your glory and power shall be revealed.

7.   THE SWEETNESS OF DIVINE LOVE

Jesus, how sweet is the very thought of you! You fill my heart with
joy. The sweetness of your love surpasses the sweetness of honey.
Nothing sweeter than you can be described; no words can express
the joy of your love. Only those who have tasted your love for
themselves can comprehend it. In your love you listen to all my
prayers, even when my wishes are childish, my words confused, and
my thoughts foolish. And you answer my prayers, not according to
my own misdirected desires, which would bring only bitter misery,
but according to my real needs, which brings me sweet joy. Thank
you, Jesus, for giving yourself to me.

Jacob Boehme
1575–1624

*A humble shoemaker in Germany, he rebelled
against the strict teaching and formal worship of the
Lutheran Church, desiring direct divine illumina-
tions. The fervour of his writings, though often
obscure and crude in composition, helped to inspire*

the Evangelical revival in Britain, while his meta-
physical speculations appealed to philosophers such as
Newton and Hegel. He composed for his own use a set
of simple, direct prayers to be used through the day.

1.   ON WAKING

Living Lord, you have watched over me, and put your hand on my
head, during the long, dark hours of night. Your holy angels have
protected me from all harm and pain. To you, Lord, I owe life itself.
Continue to watch over me and bless me during the hours of day.

2.   ON RISING

Rule over me this day, O God, leading me on the path of righteousness. Put your Word in my mind and your Truth in my heart, that
this day I neither think nor feel anything except what is good and
honest. Protect me from all lies and falsehood, helping me to discern deception wherever I meet it. Let my eyes always look straight
ahead on the road you wish me to tread, that I might not be tempted
by any distraction. And make my eyes pure, that no false desires
may be awakened within me.

3.   ON DRESSING

Merciful God, you clothed your Word with the pure and perfect
body of our Lord Jesus. Clothe my soul with that same purity, that
I may share his perfection. Yet at his passion our Lord Jesus was
stripped, and on the cross his earthly body killed. Thus my own
body can only be clothed in purity if my sins are stripped and laid
bare, and then nailed to the cross. Dear God, destroy my sins, and
so make me ready to put on the cloak of eternal life.

4.   ON GOING TO WORK

Give me, dear Lord, a pure heart and a wise mind, that I may carry
out my work according to your will. Save me from all false desires,
from pride, greed, envy and anger, and let me accept joyfully every

task you set before me. Let me seek to serve the poor, the sad and those unable to work. Help me to discern honestly my own gifts that I may do the things of which I am capable, and happily and humbly leave the rest to others. Above all, remind me constantly that I have nothing except what you give me, and can do nothing except what you enable me to do.

5.   AT NOON

O God, the source of eternal light, you provide temporal light for the earth, ruling over the sun and the moon that all creatures may live and thrive. The warmth and brightness of the sun makes the flowers bloom and the crops grow. And the gentle beams of the moon and stars remind us that your Word is alive and active even when we can see only dimly. Guide me to find my rightful place in your creation, that in some small way I may add to the beauty of your handiwork. And may your eternal light shine in the darkest corners of my soul, that all shadow of sin may be expelled.

6.   AT EVENING

I thank you, O God, for your care and protection this day, keeping me from physical harm and spiritual corruption. I now place the work of the day into your hands, trusting that you will redeem my errors and turn my achievements to your glory. And I now ask you to work within me, trusting that you will use the hours of rest to create in me a new heart and new soul. Let my mind, which through the day has been directed to my work, through the evening be wholly directed at you.

7.   AT BED-TIME

As I take off my dusty, dirty clothes, let me also be stripped of the sins I have committed this day. I confess, dear Lord, that in so many ways my thoughts and actions have been impure. Now I come before you, naked in body and bare in soul, to be washed clean. Let me rest tonight in your arms, and so may the dreams that pass through my mind be holy. And let me awake tomorrow, strong and eager to serve you.

Bonaventura
1217–1274

As leader of the Franciscans after the death of their founder, he settled many internal disputes and gave theological form to the teachings of Francis. Yet, despite his high learning and political skill, his spirituality was infused with the same warm, intimate love of Jesus that had inspired Francis. As his prayers express, he saw the Christian life as the direct reflection of the passion and resurrection of Jesus.

1.   GETHSEMANE

Lord Jesus, you have shaped our faith, by making us believe you shared our mortal nature. In Gethsemane real drops of sweat fell from your body.

Lord Jesus, you have given us hope, because you endured all the spiritual and physical hardships which mortal nature can suffer. In Gethsemane your soul was in torment, and your heart shook at the prospect of the physical pain to come.

You showed all the natural weaknesses of the flesh, that we might know that you have truly borne our sorrows.

2.   TRIAL

Sweet Jesus, what soul can be so hardened as not to cry out at your plight?

Sweet Jesus, what heart can be so hardened as not to groan with compassion for you?

Sweet Jesus, my ears can hardly bear to hear those horrible shouts:

"Away with him. Away with him. Crucify him."

3.   CRUCIFIXION

O Lord, holy Father, show us what kind of man it is who is hanging for our sakes on the cross, whose suffering causes the rocks themselves to crack and crumble with compassion, whose death brings the dead back to life.

Let my heart crack and crumble at the sight of him. Let my soul break apart with compassion for his suffering. Let it be shattered with grief at my sins for which he dies. And finally let it be softened with devoted love for him.

4.   BURIAL

O my God, Jesus, I am in every way unworthy of you. Yet, like Joseph of Arimathea, I want to offer a space for you. He offered his own tomb; I offer my heart.

Enter the darkness of my heart, as your body entered the darkness of Joseph's tomb. And make me worthy to receive you, driving out all sin that I may be filled with your spiritual light.

5.   RESURRECTION

Rise, beloved Christ, like a dove rising high in the sky, its white feathers glistening in the sun. Let us see your purity of soul.

Like a sparrow keeping constant watch over its nest of little ones, watch over us day and night, guarding us against all physical and spiritual danger.

Like a turtledove hiding its offspring from all attackers, hide us from the attacks of the Devil.

Like a swallow, swooping down towards the earth, swoop down upon us and touch us with your life-giving Spirit.

6. ASCENSION

Lord Jesus, I put my faith in you. I place my hope in you, and I love you with my whole mind and my whole strength. When you rise up to heaven, I long to be carried up to heaven, that my faith may be vindicated, my hope fulfilled, and my love rewarded.

Lord Jesus, as you sit upon your throne in heaven, redeem those who are lost, sanctify those who are redeemed, and give joy to those who are sanctified.

7. FOR THE SEVEN GIFTS OF THE SPIRIT

Lord Jesus, as God's Spirit came down and rested upon you, may the same Spirit rest upon us, bestowing his sevenfold gifts.

First, grant us the gift of understanding, by which your precepts may enlighten our minds.

Second, grant us counsel, by which we may follow in your footsteps on the path of righteousness.

Third, grant us courage, by which we may ward off the Enemy's attacks.

Fourth, grant us knowledge, by which we can distinguish good from evil.

Fifth, grant us piety, by which we may acquire compassionate hearts.

Sixth, grant us fear, by which we may draw back from evil and submit to what is good.

Seventh, grant us wisdom, that we may taste fully the life-giving sweetness of your love.

Dietrich Bonhoeffer
1906–1945

A German Lutheran pastor, he publicly opposed the Nazi movement. At the outbreak of war he tried to forge a link between Germans opposed to Hitler

*and the British government. In 1943 he was impli-
cated in a plot to assassinate Hitler, and after two
years in prison he was hanged. In addition to the
more famous letters and papers, he wrote in prison
a number of prayers which express both his bitter
anguish and unquenchable faith.*

1.   THE CHURCH'S FAILURE

We come before you, source of all being,
As sinners.
We have betrayed you.
We saw a great lie raise its head,
And we did not honour the truth.
We saw our brethren in direst need,
And we feared only for our own safety.

We come before you, source of all mercy,
As confessors of our sins.
After the ferment of these terrible times,
Send us times of assurance.
After wandering so long in darkness,
Let us walk in the light of the sun.
After the falsehood of the current way,
Build a road for us by your Word.

And until you wipe out our guilt,
Lord, make us patient.

2.   ON WAKING IN PRISON

O God, early in the morning I cry to you.
Help me to pray, and to think only of you.
I cannot pray alone.

In me there is darkness,
But with you there is light.
I am lonely, but you never leave me.

I am feeble in heart, but you are always strong.
I am restless, but in you there is peace.
In me there is bitterness, but with you patience.
Your ways are beyond my understanding,
But you know the way for me.

Lord Jesus Christ,
You were poor and wretched,
You were a captive as I am,
Cut off from your friends as I am.
You know all men's distress.
You abide in me, in my isolation.
You do not forget me, but seek me out.
You desire that I should know and love you.
Lord, I hear your call and follow you.

Holy Spirit,
Grant me the faith that will protect me from despair.
Pour into me such love for you and for all men,
That any hatred and bitterness may be blotted out.
Grant me the faith that will deliver me from fear.

3. CONDEMNED TO DEATH

O Lord God,
Great is the misery that has come upon me.
My cares overwhelm me: I am at a loss.
O God, comfort and help me.
Give me strength to bear what you send,
And do not let fear rule over me.
As a loving Father, take care of my loved ones,
My wife and my children.

O merciful God,
Forgive all the sins I have committed
Against you and against my fellow men.
I put my trust in your grace,
And commit my life wholly into your hands.

Do with me as is best for you,
For that will be best for me too.
Whether I live or die, I am with you,
And you are with me.
Lord, I wait for your salvation
And for your kingdom.

The Book of Common Prayer
1549

Thomas Cranmer plundered the ancient prayer books of both the western and the eastern churches in compiling the English Prayer Book. He translated and adapted the best of the old prayers, to produce collects which for four centuries have nourished millions of English-speaking Christians. His most favoured source was the medieval Sarum Missal, *but this in turn was based on older liturgies. In addition to the prayers in the regular services, he wrote collects for every Sunday of the year. Until the 1960s the* Book of Common Prayer *was the official prayer book for the whole Anglican Communion, uniting all wings of the church, and it is still widely used.*

1.   FOR PEACE

O God, who art the author of peace, and lover of concord, in knowledge of whom standeth our eternal life, whose service is perfect freedom: Defend us, thy humble servants, in all assaults of our enemies; that we, surely trusting in thy defence, may not fear the power of any adversaries.

2. ## FOR GRACE

O Lord, our heavenly Father, Almighty and everlasting God, who hast safely brought us to the beginning of this day: Defend us in the same with thy mighty power; and grant that this day we fall into no sin, neither run into any kind of danger; but that all our doings may be ordered by thy governance, to do always that is righteous in thy sight.

3. ## FOR REST AND QUIETNESS

O God, from whom all holy desires, all good counsels, and all just works do proceed: Give unto thy servants that peace which the world cannot give; that both our hearts may be set to obey thy commandments, and also that by thee we, being defended from the fear of our enemies, may pass our time in rest and quietness.

4. ## FOR PURITY

Almighty God, unto whom all hearts be open, all desires known, and from whom no secrets are hid: Cleanse the thoughts of our hearts, by the inspiration of thy Holy Spirit: that we may perfectly love thee, and worthily magnify thy holy name.

5. ## BEFORE HOLY COMMUNION

We do not presume to come to this thy table, O merciful Lord, trusting in our own righteousness, but in thy manifold and great mercies. We are not worthy so much as to gather up the crumbs under thy table. But thou art the same Lord whose property is always to have mercy: Grant us therefore, gracious Lord, so to eat the flesh of thy dear Son Jesus Christ, and to drink his blood, that our sinful bodies may be made clean by his body, and our souls washed through his most precious blood.

6.   QUINQUAGESIMA

O Lord, who hast taught us that all our doings without charity
are nothing worth: Send thy Holy Ghost, and pour into our hearts
that most excellent gift of charity, the very bond of peace and all
virtues, without which, whosoever liveth is counted dead before
thee.

7.   FOURTH SUNDAY AFTER EASTER

O Almighty God, who alone canst order the unruly wills and affections of sinful men: Grant unto thy people, that they may love the
thing which thou commandest, and desire that which thou dost
promise: that so among the sundry and manifold changes of the
world, our hearts may surely there be fixed, where true joys are to
be found.

8.   FIFTH SUNDAY AFTER EASTER

O Lord, from whom all good things do come: Grant to us thy
humble servants, that by thy holy inspiration we may think those
things that be good, and by thy merciful guiding may perform the
same.

9.   SIXTH SUNDAY AFTER TRINITY SUNDAY

O God, who hast prepared for them that love thee, such good
things as pass man's understanding: Pour into our hearts such love
toward thee, that we, loving thee above all things, may obtain thy
promises, which exceed all that we can desire.

John Calvin
1509–1564

*He inspired the Protestant reformation in Geneva,
governing both the religious and the political efforts
of the city according to biblical principles, as he
interpreted them. His influence quickly spread to
other countries such as Holland and Scotland, while
the Puritans in England largely adopted his teachings. His daily prayers, which he composed for the
ordinary people of Geneva, reflect his conviction
that spiritual faith is worthless without practical
application.*

1. ## IN THE MORNING

My God, Father and Preserver, who in your goodness has watched
over me in this past night and brought me to this day, grant that I
may spend the day wholly in your service. Let me not think or say
or do a single thing that is not in obedience to your will; but rather
let all my actions be directed to your glory and the salvation of my
brethren. Let me attempt nothing that is not pleasing to you; but
rather let me seek happiness only in your grace and goodness. Grant
also, that as I labour for the goods and clothing necessary for this
life, I may constantly raise my mind upwards to the heavenly life
which you promise to all your children.

2. ## GOING TO WORK

My God, Father and Saviour, since you have commanded us to
work in order to meet our needs, sanctify our labour that it may
bring nourishment to our souls as well as to our bodies. Make us
constantly aware that our efforts are worthless unless guided by

your light and strengthened by your hand. Make us faithful to the particular tasks for which you have bestowed upon us the necessary gifts, taking from us any envy or jealousy at the vocations of others.

Give us a good heart to supply the needs of the poor, saving us from any desire to exalt ourselves over those who receive our bounty. And if you should call us into greater poverty than we humanly desire, save us from any spirit of defiance or resentment, but rather let us graciously and humbly receive the bounty of others. Above all may every temporal grace be matched by spiritual grace, that in both body and soul we may live to your glory.

3.   GOING TO SCHOOL

O Lord, who is the fountain of all wisdom and learning, you have given me the years of my youth to learn the arts and skills necessary for an honest and holy life. Enlighten my mind, that I may acquire knowledge. Strengthen my memory that I may retain what I have learnt. Govern my heart, that I may always be eager and diligent in my studies. And let your Spirit of truth, judgement and prudence guide my understanding, that I may perceive how everything I learn fits into your holy plan for the world.

4.   BEFORE A MEAL

O Lord, who is the giver of all good things, fill our hearts with gratitude for the food and drink laid before us. And as we fill our bellies, may we be sober and frugal in our eating, taking only that which is necessary to refresh ourselves for your service. Let the pleasure we take in the bread which nourishes our earthly bodies, be as nothing to the joy we take in the spiritual bread of your truth, which nourishes the soul.

5.   AFTER A MEAL

We give thanks, O God and Father, for the many mercies which you constantly bestow upon us. In supplying the food and drink necessary to sustain our present life, you show how much you care for our mortal bodies. And in supplying the life and the teachings of your Son, you reveal how much you love our immortal souls. Let the meal which we have enjoyed be a reminder to us of the eternal joy you promise to all who feed on your holy Word.

6. AT NIGHT

O Lord God, who has given us the night for rest, I pray that in my sleep my soul may remain awake to you, steadfastly adhering to your love. As I lay aside my cares to relax and relieve my mind, may I not forget your infinite and unresting care for me. And in this way, let my conscience be at peace, so that when I rise tomorrow, I am refreshed in body, mind and soul.

Helder Camara
1909–

A Roman Catholic priest, he served as Archbishop of Olinda and Recife in north-east Brazil, the poorest and least developed part of the country. His collection of meditations, Into Your Hands, Lord, *expresses the unconditional love he showed for the weak and vulnerable in his ministry.*

1. GOD IS LOVE

A name is not,
cannot, must not be
a label stuck
on persons or on things.

The name comes from within
the things and persons
and must on no account ring false.
It has to express

The essence of the essence,
the real reason
for the being, the existence
of the thing or person *named*.

Your name
is and only can be
Love.

2.   ENROL US IN YOUR SCHOOL OF LOVE

Teach us to love and be loved
in perfect transparency.

Let our love be diaphanous,
lest we project
the mote in our eye
into the eye of another,
and make it a beam besides!

Let our love be transparent
lest we ever play host
to a love that is false.
Love that springs from aught but you,
love that lives in aught but you,
love that returns not to you,
is not love.

Teach us to love each and every person
as if he or she
were the only person on earth.
After all,
this is how you love:
uniquely, truly, robustly;
it's perfect, your way.

But our way,
in this poor human clay,

love creates incredible problems,
given the machismo
common to the three sexes
and most particularly
to the unlucky third . . . .

3.   AREN'T YOU GOING TOO FAR, LORD . . .

. . . with your respect for human freedom?
Your love extends to all creatures.

But you reserve your special love
for the small, the simple, the poor.
Then how can you bear to see
these millions
of your sons and daughters
living in subhuman conditions
owing to the selfishness
and ambition
of unjust and oppressive minorities?

By now you must have realized
that your cataclysms –
floods and droughts,
volcanic eruptions,
typhoons,
earthquakes –
affect the little ones most of all,
whose life is already
subhuman.

Isn't it bad enough
for them to be crushed
by diseases or human weakness?

How are we to explain
what comes from you?
Is it sufficient to say

that you have given us brains
and teach us how to overcome
natural disasters?

4.   THE BABY

The baby with her tiny steps
needs to scamper a bit
from time to time
to keep pace
with grownups . . . .

Just so, my God –
how often you take me in your arms
to spare me the embarrassment
of looking like a turtle!

5.   AFTER THE TURBULENCE OF THE DAY

After the turbulence of the day,
thank you for sending the peacefulness of the
    night.
How blessed the peace of the night,
so still
that the very tones
of mountain and skyscraper
lose their jutty, harsh aspect
and bathe in thrilling stillness.

Let us not ruminate upon
the disagreeable scenes of the day.
Let us not rehearse
injustices,
bitter, hard words,
coarse actions.

Mindful, Father,
of your infinite patience with us,

your infinite goodness,
we ask you to help us
never to harbour a single drop
of hatred, or resentment,
or bitterness
against anyone.

Fill us
with your limitless mercy.

Amy Carmichael
1867–1951

For over half a century she was a missionary in India, founding a children's home in Tinnevelly. After her enforced retirement due to arthritis, she gained wide popularity through her devotional books. Embedded within these are a few simple prayers of great depth.

1. ### THOU HAST CALLED ME

Thou hast called me – I cannot tell why.
Thou wilt justify me – I cannot tell how.
Thou wilt glorify me – I cannot tell when.

2. ### MAKING POSSIBLE

May thy grace, O Lord, make that possible to me which seems impossible to me by nature.

3.   FOR LOVE, FOR LOVE

Father of spirits, this my sovereign plea
I bring again and yet again to thee.

Fulfil me now with love, that I may know
A daily inflow, daily overflow.

For love, for love, my Lord was crucified,
With cords of love he bound me to his side.

Pour through me now; I yield myself to thee,
O Love that led my Lord to Calvary.

4.   KEEP ALL MY CHILDREN

Lord, keep all my children free to love. Never let the slightest shade
of suspicion shadow any heart. Help each to think the best of every
other. Through all the chances and changes of life, hold all together
in tender love. Let nothing quench love. Let nothing cool it. Keep
every thread of the gold cord unbroken, unweakened, even unto the
end. O my Lord, thou Loving One, keep my beloveds close together
in thy love for ever.

Elizabeth Catez
1880–1906

*As a teenage girl she tried to live like a nun. Then at
the age of twenty-one she entered a Carmelite community near Dijon in France. She believed that the
total devotion to Christ which a nun could enjoy
would radiate love into the world, giving light to
dark and lonely lives.*

1.   TRINITY, MY ALL

O beloved Father, whom I adore, help me to forget myself entirely that I may think only of you, and so be as peaceful as if I were already in eternity. May nothing trouble my peace or make me leave you, O unchanging One, but may each minute carry me further into the depths of your mystery. Make my soul your heaven, your dwelling, and your bed. May I never leave you there alone but be wholly present, wholly faithful, wholly vigilant, wholly adoring, and wholly surrendered to you.

O beloved Christ, crucified by love, I wish to be a bride of your heart. I wish to cover you with glory. I wish to love you, even to die for you. But I can feel my weakness, so I beg you to clothe me with yourself, to overwhelm me, to possess me, to substitute yourself for me that my life may be your life. May every action of mine be movements of your soul. Come to me as adorer, as restorer, as saviour. Eternal Word, I want to spend every day listening to you, learning from you. Then every night I want to gaze on you and bask in your radiant light.

O Spirit of love, consuming fire, come upon me and re-create me as another incarnation of the eternal Word. Thus my humanity may be Christ's humanity, revealing to the world the mystery of the Father. And when you, Spirit, have transformed me into the human image of Christ, then his Father will have become my Father.

O Trinity, my all, you are the immensity in which I can lose myself, the almighty power to which I can surrender, the holy ground in which I can bury myself, the infinitely beautiful light which I can contemplate for all eternity.

Catherine of Genoa
1447–1510

*The daughter of a Genoese aristocrat, at the age of
sixteen she was forced into a miserable marriage.
Ten years later she, along with her husband,
underwent a religious conversion. They moved to a
poor area of the city, where she devoted herself to
nursing the sick in a filthy, dilapidated hospital. She
soon took over the female wards, which quickly
became famous for their cleanliness and also for the
joyfulness of patients and staff alike. Her prayers
reveal a restless, uncertain soul whose faith is mixed
with deep anguish.*

1.   A RESTLESS SOUL

Lord, why did you enlighten a soul so dark? Why did you capture a
soul that constantly tries to flee from you? Why did you purify a soul
so foul?

I shudder when I think of the horrors that were in store for me, if
I had continued on the path which I was treading. But even now I feel
that hell is the only proper place for me. O God, I want to hide from
you, because I feel too filthy and ugly to appear in your presence. Yet
whenever I try to escape from you, I find that you are still with me,
because your presence is everywhere. Weeping brings me no peace
or comfort, and repentance seems to bring no sense of forgiveness.
Dear God, punish me as I deserve, so that I may be free of this burden
of sin.

2. NAKED LOVE

Lord, I make you a present of myself. I do not know what to do with myself. So let me make this exchange: I will place myself entirely in your hands, if you will cover my ugliness with your beauty, and tame my unruliness with your love. Put out the flames of false passion in my heart, since these flames destroy all that is true within me. Make me always busy in your service.

Lord, I want no special signs from you, nor am I looking for intense emotions in response to your love. I would rather be free of all emotion, than to run the danger of falling victim once again to false passion. Let my love for you be naked, without any emotional clothing.

3. SUFFERING AND JOY

Lord, let me welcome all the pain and suffering that comes to me, for pain and suffering are sent by you. Ever since you enlightened me, thirty-six years ago, I have sought to suffer, both spiritually and physically. And yet because I have desired suffering, all suffering has seemed sweet and pleasant, knowing that you are its source. Now that I am near to doubt, and my whole body is in agony from head to toe, I find myself wondering if I can endure this final encounter with pain. I know that you rule over my pain, and will bring relief when I am ready to be received into your heavenly kingdom. So even in the midst of this agony, I cannot really say that I am suffering. You make all things bearable, filling my heart with inexpressible joy.

Catherine of Siena
*c.*1347–1380

From the age of twelve, when she vowed virginity to Christ, she claimed to be in direct communication with him, relying solely on his words for guidance.

*As an adult, she gathered round herself a "family"
of friends and disciples, who were inspired by her
teaching and wise counsel. Her most famous work,
The Dialogue, is a prolonged, and at times quite
intimate, conversation between God and herself.
God plays the greater role, but her replies are
charged with both emotional and intellectual power.*

1.   GOD'S MERCY

Merciful Lord, it does not surprise me that you forget completely
the sins of those who repent. I am not surprised that you remain
faithful to those who hate and revile you. The mercy which pours
forth from you fills the whole world.

It was by your mercy that we were created, and by your mercy
that you redeemed us by sending your Son. Your mercy is the light
in which sinners find you and good people come back to you. Your
mercy is everywhere, even in the depths of hell where you offer to
forgive the tortured souls. Your justice is constantly tempered with
mercy, so you refuse to punish us as we deserve. O mad lover! It
was not enough for you to take on our humanity; you had to die
for us as well.

2.   THE FIRE OF LOVE

Your light, dear God, surpasses all other light, because all light
comes from you. Your fire surpasses all fire, because your fire alone
burns without destroying. The flames of your fire reach into the
soul, consuming the sin and selfishness that lie there. But far from
damaging the soul, your fire sets it ablaze with love.

What moved you to enlighten me with your truth? The fire of
your love was the reason. You loved me so much that you could
not bear to see me confused and perplexed. Can I ever repay the
burning love which you have given me? No, because I have nothing
of my own to give. Yet you assure me that the love which you put
into my soul is repayment enough. You desire only the joy of seeing
me receiving your gift. What more perfect Father could there be!

3. TWO QUESTIONS

Eternal Father, let me ask you two questions on matters which perplex me.

Sometimes people come to me, asking for advice as to how they should serve you. Then later, when I pray for these people, some seem bathed in your glorious light, while others are shrouded in spiritual darkness. Should I judge the ones bathed in light as being sincere in their desire to serve you, and the others shrouded in darkness as self-centred hypocrites? Or should I rather urge all to turn to you in repentance for their sins, and then judge those whose penance is greater as the best servant? That is my first question.

The second question I wish to ask is: how can I discern whether a spiritual visitation to the soul is from you or not? Perhaps the test is whether the visitation has left the soul glad and joyful. And yet you do not only bring happiness to the soul, but sometimes inflict suffering.

4. SEA, LIGHT, FIRE

Eternal Trinity, you are like a deep sea, in which the more I seek, the more I find; and the more I find, the more eagerly I seek. You fill the soul, yet never fully satisfy it; the soul continues to hunger and thirst for you, desiring you, longing to see you who are the source of all light.

In your light, eternal Trinity, I have seen into the deep ocean of your love, and have rejoiced in the beauty of your creation. Then looking at myself in you, I have recognized that you have made me in your image. This is the most precious gift which I receive from you in your power and in your wisdom.

Eternal Trinity, you are the creator and I the creature. I have come to know you because you have created me anew in your Son Jesus Christ. You are in love with me out of your love for him. You have given yourself to me. What more could I ask?

You are a fire, ever burning and never consumed. You consume in your heart all the self-love within my soul, taking away all coldness. You are a light, ever shining and never fading. You drive away all the darkness within my heart, enabling me to see your glorious truth.

You are goodness beyond all goodness, beauty beyond all beauty, wisdom beyond all wisdom.

You are the garment that covers all nakedness. You are the food that satisfies all hunger.

5. GOD'S IMAGE AND LIKENESS

Eternal Father, you said, "Let us make humankind to our own image and likeness". Thus you were willing to share with us your own greatness. You gave us the intellect to share your truth. You gave us the wisdom to share your goodness. And you gave us the free will to love that which is true and just.

Why did you so dignify us? It was because you looked upon us, and fell in love with us. It was love which first prompted you to create us; and it was love which caused you to share with us your truth and goodness.

Yet your heart must break when you see us turn against you. You must weep when you see us abusing our intellect in pursuit of that which is false. You must cry with pain when we distort our wisdom in order to justify evil.

But you never desert us. Out of the same love that caused you to create us, you have now sent your only Son to save us. He is your perfect image and likeness, and so through him we can be restored to your image and likeness.

6. MAD LOVER

Dear Lord, it seems that you are so madly in love with your creatures that you could not live without us. So you created us; and then, when we turned away from you, you redeemed us. Yet you are God, and so have no need of us. Your greatness is made no greater by our creation; your power is made no stronger by our redemption. You have no duty to care for us, no debt to re-pay us. It is love, and love alone, which moves you.

Jean-Pierre de Caussade
1675–1751

A Jesuit priest, he was much in demand throughout France to conduct retreats. His talks were preserved, and two centuries after his death were published under the title Self-Abandonment to Divine Providence. *It is now ranked amongst the greatest spiritual classics. He taught that God is present in every event and object, great and small, and that our task is perpetually to submit ourselves to God's providential will.*

1. GOD SPEAKING THROUGH EVENTS

You speak, Lord, to all men in general through general events. Revolutions are simply the tides of your Providence, which stir up storms and tempests in people's minds. You speak to men in particular through particular events, as they occur moment by moment. But instead of hearing your voice, instead of respecting events as signals of your loving guidance, people see nothing else but blind chance and human decision. They find objections to everything you say. They wish to add to or subtract from your Word. They wish to change and reform it.

Teach me, dear Lord, to read clearly this book of life. I wish to be like a simple child, accepting your word regardless of whether I understand your purposes. It is enough for me that you speak.

2. SELF-ABANDONMENT

O Unknown Love! We are inclined to think that your marvels are over, and that all we can do is to copy the ancient Scriptures and quote your words from the past. We fail to see that your inexhaustible action is the source of new thoughts, new sufferings, new actions, new leaders, new prophets, new apostles, new saints, who have no need to copy each other's lives and writings, but live in perpetual self-abandonment to your operations. We hear perpetually of the "early centuries" and the "times of the saints". What a way to talk! Are not all times and all events the successive results of your grace, pouring itself forth on all instants of time, filling them and sanctifying them? Your divine action will continue until the world ends to shed its glory on those souls who abandon themselves to your providence without reserve.

3. THE PASSING MOMENT

Lord, may your kingdom come into my heart to sanctify me, nourish me and purify me. How insignificant is the passing moment to the eye without faith! But how important each moment is to the eye enlightened by faith! How can we deem insignificant anything which has been caused by you? Every moment and every event is guided by you, and so contains your infinite greatness.

So, Lord, I glorify you in everything that happens to me. In whatever manner you make me live and die, I am content. Events please me for their own sake, regardless of their consequences, because your action lies behind them. Everything is heaven to me, because all my moments manifest your love.

4. CONTINUOUS REVELATION

I shall not count the hours or the ways of your approach, dear Lord; you will always be welcome. The mystery of your action in the world has been revealed to me. I no longer move except within your infinite bosom. I lie in the midst of the torrent of your grace, flowing unceasingly all around me. No longer will I seek you in the narrow covers of a book, or in some saint's life, or in some philosophical idea.

Yes, Lord, I want to live as your child, honouring your goodness and wisdom by embracing every event as your gift of love. I wish to depend on your bounty, which can never fail. Through faith in

you, everything becomes bread to nourish me, soap to cleanse me
and fire to purify me.

5.   REFUSING DIVINE FAVOURS

Lord, must it always be that so many people remain ignorant of
your providence? Must you, as it were, shower your favours on
their heads, while they refuse to accept your infinite generosity?
We would think a person absurdly foolish if he refused to breathe
the open air, or to drink the water which he needs. Yet why may
that same person not find you in the air, the water and everything
else around him?

Must I resign myself to possessing so great a treasure from you,
while I watch other souls die of spiritual poverty? Must I see them
dry up like desert plants, while your living waters are all around
them?

Celtic Prayers
c.450–c.700

---

*After the fall of the Roman Empire, an indigenous
form of Christianity developed in the British Isles,
which was regarded by Rome with great suspicion.
It celebrated the divine spirit in all living creatures
and plants, as well as in the human soul. Its heroes
were hermits who lived in the forest, befriending
the animals and birds, and "pilgrims" who travelled into remote regions to spread the gospel. Few of
the prayers which survive have definite authorship,
although* A Pilgrim's Plea *is often attributed to
Brendan, who sailed across the Atlantic in a coracle;*
A Hermit's Desire *is attributed to Kevin, an Irish
hermit famed for his love of nature; and the*

*Evening Hymn is ascribed to Patrick, the apostle
of Ireland.*

1.   A PILGRIM'S PLEA

Shall I abandon, O King of mysteries, the soft comforts of home?
Shall I turn my back on my native land, and my face towards the
sea?

Shall I put myself wholly at your mercy, without silver, without
a horse, without fame and honour? Shall I throw myself wholly on
you, without sword and shield, without food and drink, without a
bed to lie on?

Shall I say farewell to my beautiful land, placing myself under
your yoke? Shall I pour out my heart to you, confessing my manifold sins and begging forgiveness, tears streaming down my cheeks?

Shall I leave the prints of my knees on the sandy beach, a record
of my final prayer in my native land? Shall I then suffer every kind
of wound that the sea can inflict?

Shall I take my tiny coracle across the wide sparkling ocean? O
King of the glorious heaven, shall I go of my own choice upon the
sea?

O Christ, will you help me on the wild waves?

2.   A HERMIT'S DESIRE

I wish, ancient and eternal King, to live in a hidden hut in the
wilderness.

A narrow blue stream beside it, and a clear pool for washing away
my sins by the grace of the Holy Spirit.

A beautiful wood all around, where birds of every kind of voice
can grow up and find shelter.

Facing southwards to catch the sun, with fertile soil around it
suitable for every kind of plant.

And virtuous young men to join me, humble and eager to serve
you. Twelve young men – three fours, four threes, two sixes, six
pairs – willing to do every kind of work.

A lovely church, with a white linen cloth over the altar, a home
for you from heaven.

A Bible surrounded by four candles, one for each of the gospels.

A special hut in which to gather for meals, talking cheerfully as we eat, without sarcasm, without boasting, without any evil words.

Hens laying eggs for us to eat, leeks growing near the stream, salmon and trout to catch, and bees providing honey.

Enough food and clothing given by you, and enough time to sit and pray to you.

3.   A SCHOLAR'S WISH

God help my thoughts! They stray from me, setting off on the wildest journeys.

When I am in church, they run off like naughty children, quarrelling, making trouble.

When I read the Bible, they fly to a distant city, filled with beautiful women.

My thoughts can cross an ocean with a single leap; they can fly from earth to heaven, and back again, in a single second.

They come to me for a fleeting moment, and then away they flee. No chains, no locks can hold them back; no threats of punishment can restrain them, no hiss of a lash can frighten them.

They slip from my grasp like tails of eels; they swoop hither and thither like swallows in flight.

Dear, chaste Christ, who can see into every heart and read every mind, take hold of my thoughts. Bring my thoughts back to me, and clasp me to yourself.

4.   IN THE EVENING

O Christ, Son of the living God,
May your holy angels guard our sleep.
May they watch us as we rest
And hover around our beds.

Let them reveal to us in our dreams
Visions of your glorious truth,
O High Prince of the universe,
O High Priest of the mysteries.

May no dreams disturb our rest
And no nightmares darken our dreams.
May no fears or worries delay
Our willing, prompt repose.

May the virtue of our daily work
Hallow our nightly prayers.
May our sleep be deep and soft,
So our work be fresh and hard.

5.   THE TREE OF LIFE

O, King of the Tree of Life,
The blossoms on the branches are your people,
The singing birds are your angels,
The whispering breeze is your Spirit.

O, King of the Tree of Life,
May the blossoms bring forth the sweetest fruit,
May the birds sing out the highest praise
May your Spirit cover all with his gentle breath.

6.   A MILLION MIRACLES

O Son of God, perform a miracle for me: change my heart. You,
whose crimson blood redeems mankind, whiten my heart.

It is you who makes the sun bright and the ice sparkle; you who
makes the rivers flow and the salmon leap.

Your skilled hand makes the nut tree blossom, and the corn turn
golden; your spirit composes the songs of the birds and the buzz
of the bees.

Your creation is a million wondrous miracles, beautiful to behold.
I ask of you just one more miracle: beautify my soul.

7.   LORD OF MY HEART

Lord, of my heart, give me vision to inspire me, that, working or resting, I may always think of you.

Lord of my heart, give me light to guide me, that, at home or abroad, I may always walk in your way.

Lord of my heart, give me wisdom to direct me, that, thinking or acting, I may always discern right from wrong.

Lord of my heart, give me courage to strengthen me, that, amongst friends or enemies, I may always proclaim your justice.

Lord of my heart, give me trust to console me, that, hungry or well-fed, I may always rely on your mercy.

Lord of my heart, save me from empty praise, that I may always boast of you.

Lord of my heart, save me from worldly wealth, that I may always look to the riches of heaven.

Lord of my heart, save me from military prowess, that I may always seek your protection.

Lord of my heart, save me from vain knowledge, that I may always study your word.

Lord of my heart, save me from unnatural pleasures, that I may always find joy in your wonderful creation.

Heart of my own heart, whatever may befall me, rule over my thoughts and feelings, my words and action.

8.   FOR A LONG LIFE

Wait for me, King of heaven, until I am pure, fit to live in your house.

Wait for me, Mary's Son, until I am old, wise from the passing of years.

When a young boy is carried off before his years of playing are over, no one knows what greatness he has missed; only in adulthood comes the full bloom of our gifts.

A calf should not be killed before it is full-grown, nor a pig slaughtered when it is still sucking at the sow's breast.

A bough should not be cut until it has flowered, nor a field harvested until the grain is full.

The sun should not set at midday, nor rise at midnight.

Keep my soul here on earth, for it is like soft, unformed clay, not ready to be received by you.

Yet even if you cut me off in my youth, I shall not complain, but continue to worship you.

9. FINAL REFLECTIONS

I give you thanks, my King, for the care you have lavished upon me.

I have for six months been lying on my bed, my body racked by disease; I am a prisoner, held in chains by my illness.

My strength is gone, from my head to my feet I can barely move; my weakness is like fetters holding me down.

I am like a blind man unable to see the world around me; for six months I have seen only the walls of my hut.

You have nailed me to my cross; this sickness is my crucifixion.

And so I give you thanks, my King, for bringing me joyfully to judgement.

Tomorrow I shall die, and see you face to face; tomorrow your lash on my body shall cease, and I shall be at peace.

If now my body is shrouded by clouds of darkness, my soul basks in warm light; if now my eyes are filled with bitter tears, my soul can taste the sweetest honey.

I am like a mouse, caught in a trap and shaken in the claws of a cat; tomorrow I shall be as free as the wind.

My present pains are as nothing compared to the enormity of my sin; your mercy is infinite and eternal.

François Chagneau

A lay member of Boquen Abbey in France, he has written a number of prayers for his Community, to be used either by individuals alone, or in group worship. His prayers have a striking honesty and intensity.

1.

IN MY SOLITUDE

I am alone
On the road I travel,
On the road you take me,
Drawing me on with a force
That exceeds all human demands.

I am alone
And I feel this solitude
Like a deeply open wound
In the depths of my being.
All those who surround me
Are only shadowy figures,
Vanishing furtively
At the sound of my appeal.
They flee and disappear
When I try to approach them.
And the time is coming
When I will settle into this solitude
And it will be my lone companion.

I do not know from where
This solitude comes to me.
Does it come from you?
Is it the only road
Where I will discover you
And find at last your truth?
Or does it come from other men
Who refuse to give me love
And thus drive me deeper down
Into a life of cold indifference?
Or does it come from me
Repulsing other human beings
As I try to draw them to me?

I walk, O Lord, in solitude
And the silence resounds in my ears
More loudly than the shouts of men.
I walk, O Lord, in solitude,
Plunging deeper into it
As I journey on to you,
My Lord and God.

2.   WHO ARE YOU, MY GOD?

Who are you, God that I call mine,
My God?
Who are you, God and Son of my God,
You whom I call Christ?

On what horizon beyond the sea,
In what recess of the earth
Is your name inscribed?
In what unknown being
Shall I find you on my way –
You whom I glimpse perhaps
In the motion of a thought
and the uplift of my spirit?

You I have never seen,
Yet in you I believe and hope,
I who do not know your name.

You slip between my fingers
Like the grains of sunlit sand.
You fade away and dissolve
Like snow in the gathering darkness.
When the sun begins to set
And all things fade into the peace of night,
Perhaps then we find your kingdom
As darkness cries out for your light.

At the rising of mankind
You surely did pass on
Life into my numbness
Which I constantly regain.
My whole life seeks for you
And my eye looks for you.

Who are you, God,
You that I believe to be my God,
Christ whom I believe to be Lord,
God of love in whom I hope?

Richard Challoner
1691–1781

The son of a Protestant father and Catholic mother, he trained as a Catholic priest at Douai where he remained as a professor. Then in 1730 he went to work in London where, despite the suspicion in which the Catholic Church was held, he gained a high reputation as a spiritual director. In 1741 he was consecrated bishop, and eventually became head of the Catholic Church in England. His overriding aim was to deepen the spiritual life of both priests and laity, and to this end he published numerous books and pamphlets. His most popular work was The Garden of the Soul, *a collection of prayers and spiritual instructions based on the teachings of Francis of Sales. It included a long prayer which brings together the beliefs, emotions, and hopes of the Christian.*

1.   I BELIEVE, I ADORE, I ASPIRE

O my God, I believe in thee, do thou strengthen my faith. All my
hopes are in thee, do thou secure them. I love thee with my whole
heart, teach me to love thee daily more and more. I am sorry that
I have offended thee, do thou increase my sorrow.

I adore thee as my first beginning. I aspire after thee as my last
end. I give thee thanks as my constant benefactor. I call upon thee
as my sovereign protector.

Vouchsafe, O my God, to conduct me by thy wisdom, to restrain
me by thy justice, to comfort me by thy mercy, to defend me by
thy power.

To thee I desire to consecrate all my thoughts, words, actions,
and sufferings; that henceforward I may think of thee, speak of
thee, and willingly refer all my actions to thy greater glory; and
suffer willingly whatever thou shalt appoint.

Lord, I desire that in all things thy will may be done, because it
is thy will, and in the manner that thou willest.

I beg of thee to enlighten my understanding, to enflame my will,
to purify my body, and to sanctify my soul.

Give me strength, O my God, to expiate my offences, to overcome my temptations, to subdue my passions, and to acquire the
virtues proper for my state.

Fill my heart with tender affection for thy goodness, a hatred for
my faults, a love for my neighbour, and a contempt of the world.

Let me always remember to be submissive to my superiors, considerate to my inferiors, faithful to my friends, and charitable to my
enemies.

Assist me to overcome sensuality by mortification, avarice by
generosity, anger by meekness, and tepidity by devotion.

O my God, make me prudent in my undertakings, courageous in
dangers, patient in afflictions, and humble in prosperity.

Grant, that I may be ever attentive at my prayers, temperate at
my meals, diligent in my employments, and constant in my resolutions. Let my conscience be ever upright and pure, my exterior
modest, and my conversation edifying.

Assist me, that I may continually labour to overcome nature, to correspond with thy grace, to keep thy commandments, and to work out my salvation.

Discover to me, O my God, the nothingness of this world, the greatness of heaven, the shortness of time, and the length of eternity.

Grant, that I may prepare for death, that I may fear thy judgements, that I may escape hell, and in the end obtain heaven.

Rex Chapman

While serving as Anglican chaplain at Aberdeen University, he wrote a series of prayers in which the teachings of Jesus were applied directly to our present condition. These include short prayers on each of the Beatitudes.

1.   BLESSED ARE THE POOR IN SPIRIT

Bring me to see that what I have is there to be shared.
Bring me to see that what I have is not the last word in life.
Bring me to see that ultimately my security, my peace of mind depends not on my talents, not on my achievements, not on the status that goes with these, but on knowing that all that I have gains its meaning from you.
To know this, Lord, is to know both poverty and riches.

2.   BLESSED ARE THE SORROWFUL

My regrets, Lord, are many;
Regrets that what I am is less than it might be;
Regrets too, sometimes, that the easy peace, the easy security, the apathy that engulfs so much of what I am is at its heart unsatisfying;
Regrets from which you alone can take the sting.
You alone can enable us to live with ourselves for the future.

3.   BLESSED ARE THE GENTLE IN SPIRIT

Give me that gentleness of spirit defined by your life:
The spirit that strives for the truth,
   that endures with patience,
   that holds its peace when reproached,
   that holds self back for the sake of another,
   that uses constructively the emotions that well up inside.

4.   BLESSED ARE THOSE WHO HUNGER
           AND THIRST FOR RIGHTEOUSNESS

Shake me out of my indifference.
Shake me out of my satisfaction with partial righteousness.
Shake me until I see the need for right to prevail wherever life
   exists.

5.   BLESSED ARE THE MERCIFUL

Give me the insight, Lord, to feel as others feel.
Give me the imagination to stand in another's shoes.
Your mercy is great because you know in Jesus what it is to be a
   man.
Help me to share in this mercy.

6.   BLESSED ARE THE PURE IN HEART

Strengthen my personality.
Enlighten my inner search.
Prevent the self-centredness of excessive scrupulousness.
Point me back to life.

7.   BLESSED ARE THE PEACEMAKERS

Strengthen me, Lord, to face the task, the crucifying task, of being
   a reconciler amongst guilt and fear, anxiety and anger.
Bring me, Lord, further to the point where I can accept life with

all its problems and pains with gladness and exultation,
Not because of future perks in a future heaven,
But because I know that to be fully a man, to be fully human, I can
do no other.

Clement of Alexandria
c.150–c.215

*A distinguished scholar, well-versed in both Greek
philosophy and in the Bible, he ran a school in
Alexandria for well-educated, pagan young men
who wished to learn about Christianity. He spoke
of Christ as the "divine-tutor"; and his enthusiastic
Hymn to Christ served as the school song.*

1.

TO THE DIVINE TUTOR

Be kind to your little children, Lord. Be a gentle teacher, patient
with our weakness and stupidity. And give us the strength and
discernment to do what you tell us, and so grow in your likeness.

May we all live in the peace that comes from you. May we journey
towards your city, sailing through the waters of sin untouched by
the waves, borne serenely along by the Holy Spirit. Night and day
may we give you praise and thanks, because you have shown us that
all things belong to you, and all blessings are gifts from you. To
you, the essence of wisdom, the foundation of truth, be glory for
evermore.

2.

HYMN TO CHRIST

You who bridles untamed colts,
Who gives flight to birds,
Who steers ships along their course,
Tame our wild hearts,

Lift our souls to you,
Steer us towards the safe harbour of your love.

King of the saints,
Invincible Lord of the Father,
Prince of wisdom,
Source of joy,
Saviour of our race,
Cultivator of all life,
Guardian of our desires.
Whose sure hand guides us to heaven.

Fisher of men,
You cast out the sweet bait of your gospel,
You draw us out of the waters of sin,
Shepherd of men,
You call us with your sweet, gentle voice,
You invite us into your eternal sheepfold.

Fountain of mercy,
Light of truth,
Faith without limits,
Love without end,
Exemplar of virtue,
Proclaimer of justice,
Leader of men,
Your footprints show the way to heaven.

Mother of your people,
Your celestial breasts give pure spiritual milk.
You slake the thirst of all who have faith.
Bridegroom of your people,
Your celestial beauty inspires us to sing your praises,
You lift our voices with hymns of everlasting praise.

Clement of Rome
died c.96

Probably the third bishop of Rome after St Peter.
His Prayer for All Needs *is the oldest Christian*
prayer known outside Scripture. It follows closely
the Eighteen Blessings, *recited daily by the Jews,*
and was probably used as a guide for people leading
public worship. His Epistle to the Corinthians
also includes two passages directed to God, praying
for open eyes and pure hearts.

1.   FOR ALL NEEDS

We have confidence in you.
You were the creator of all that we see.
And you have opened our inward eyes
To give us knowledge of you,
Who alone are the Most High, in the highest heaven.
The Holy One, holiest amongst the holy.

You curb the schemes of the cunning
Frustrate the designs of the wicked,
Raise up the meek and humble,
And bring down the mighty and arrogant.
You give riches and poverty, life and death,
According to your own mysterious plan.
You are the Lord of all flesh;
You watch over all that we do;
You protect us from danger;
You lift us from despair.
And through Jesus Christ, your dear child,
You give us truth, holiness and honour.

You have shown by what you have made and done
How the world has been planned from eternity.
The earth is your creation, Lord,
Reflecting your skill and your sovereignty.
You are loyal to all who trust you,
Merciful to all who confess their sins to you,
Compassionate to all whose hearts are turned to you.
Cleanse us with the cleanest of your truth,
Guide us in the steps of your way,
That we may always do what is just and right.
Let us see your face, sovereign Master,
And we shall peacefully pursue what is good.
Keep us from sin by your mighty arm,
And we shall quietly seek to please you.

Give concord and peace to us all.
Grant us health in body and in soul.
Make our rulers wise and righteous,
That their laws may conform to your laws.
You alone have the means to do this
And much more than this, beyond our asking.
Glory and majesty be yours,
Now at this moment,
In every generation,
Age after age.

2.   OPEN OUR EYES

Open the eyes of our hearts to know you, who are the highest of
the high, the holiest of the holy. You bring down the haughtiness
of the proud, and thwart the schemes of the dishonest. You raise
up the lowly and cast down the lofty. Riches and poverty, death
and life, are in your hand. You alone can discern every spirit, looking into the depths of every soul. You protect those in danger, give
hope to those in despair, and guide every creature on earth. By your
power the nations of the earth can flourish and increase.
    And from all mankind you have chosen us to know and love you

through the knowledge and love of your Son, Jesus Christ. By him you have taught us your truth, and lifted us up to share in your holiness.

Grant us, Lord, we beseech you, your grace. Pity the poor, encourage those who are sad, enlighten those whose spirits are in darkness, heal the sick, guide the confused, feed the hungry, release those who are unjustly imprisoned, support the weak, comfort the faint-hearted. Let all the nations of the world know that you are God, that Jesus Christ is your child, and that we are your people.

3.   MAKE US CLEAN

You, Lord, brought into being the everlasting fabric of the universe; you wove the tapestry of life. From one generation to another you are constant and righteous in your laws, wise and prudent in your actions. To look round is to see your goodness; to trust you is to know your generosity; to confess to you is to receive your forgiveness.

Make us clean with the strong soap of your truth. Make us whole with the powerful medicine of your grace. Show us the light of your smile. Protect us with your mighty arm. Save us from all wrong-doing by your outstretched arm. Deliver us from all those that hate us without cause. And to us and all mankind grant peace and concord.

To you, who alone can grant to us those and all good things, we offer up our praise through Jesus Christ, the high priest and guardian of our souls.

Columbanus
*c.*543–*c.*615

A native of Ireland, he sailed to Gaul where he established two monasteries in heathen areas, in order to evangelize the local people. He then moved to Bobbio in northern Italy, where his monastery

became a centre of learning. He composed one of
the earliest books of private prayer.

1.   THE FOUNTAIN OF LIFE

I beseech you, merciful God, to allow me to drink from the stream
which flows from your fountain of life. May I taste the sweet beauty
of its waters, which spring from the very depths of your truth. O
Lord, you are that fountain from which I desire with all my heart
to drink. Give me, Lord Jesus, this water, that it may quench the
burning spiritual thirst within my soul, and purify me from all sin.

I know, King of glory, that I am asking from you a great gift.
But you give to your faithful people without counting the cost, and
you promise even greater things in the future. Indeed, nothing is
greater than yourself, and you have given yourself to mankind on
the cross. Therefore, in praying for the waters of life, I am praying
that you, the source of those waters, will give yourself to me. You
are my light, my salvation, my food, my drink, my God.

2.   THE LIGHT OF LIFE

Lord, I pray that you may be a lamp for me in the darkness. Touch
my soul and kindle a fire within it, that it may burn brightly and
give light to my life. Thus my body may truly become your temple,
lit by your perpetual flame burning on the altar of my heart. And
may the light within me shine on my brethren that it may drive away
the darkness of ignorance and sin from them also. Thus together let
us be lights to the world, manifesting the bright beauty of your
gospel to all around us.

3.   KNOWING, DESIRING, LOVING

I beg you, most loving Saviour, to reveal yourself to us, that knowing you we may desire you, that desiring you we may love you, that
loving you we may ever hold you in our thoughts.

John Cosin
1594–1672

His Collection of Private Devotions, *compiled for the use of Queen Henrietta Maria's maids of honour, enjoyed wide popularity amongst those who wanted a formal discipline of personal prayer. In addition to the pattern of daily worship, based closely on the traditional monastic offices, he offered a series of prayers to be learned by heart and said, as the individual feels appropriate, through the day.*

1. GRANT ME A PURE INTENTION

Grant me, gracious Lord, a pure intention of my heart, and a steadfast regard to thy glory in all my actions. Possess my mind continually with thy presence, and ravish it with thy love, that my only delight may be, to be embraced in the arms of thy protection.

2. BE THOU A LIGHT

Be thou a light unto mine eyes, music to mine ears, sweetness to my taste, and a full contentment to my heart. Be thou my sunshine in the day, my food at the table, my repose in the night, my clothing in nakedness, and my succour in all necessities.

3. I GIVE THEE MYSELF

Lord Jesu, I give thee my body, my soul, my substance, my fame, my friends, my liberty and my life: dispose of me, and of all that is mine, as it seemeth best to thee, and to the glory of thy blessed name.

4.   I AM NOT MINE, BUT THINE

I am not now mine, but thine. Therefore claim me as thy right,
keep me as thy charge, and love me as thy child. Fight for me when
I am assaulted, heal me when I am wounded, and revive me when
I am destroyed.

5.   GIVE ME VIRTUE

My Lord and my God, I beseech thee to give me patience in
troubles, humility in comforts, constancy in temptations, and victory against all my ghostly enemies. Grant me sorrow for my sins,
thankfulness for thy benefits, fear of thy judgements, love of thy
mercies, and mindfulness of thy presence for evermore.

6.   BE MERCIFUL UNTO ME

Give me modesty in my countenance, gravity in my behaviour,
deliberation in my speech, holiness in my thoughts, and righteousness in all my actions. Let thy mercy cleanse me from my sins, and
let thy grace bring forth in me the fruits of everlasting life.

7.   LET ME TRUST IN THEE

Lord, let me be obedient without arguing, humble without feigning,
patient without grudging, pure without corruption, merry without
lightness, sad without mistrust, sober without dullness, true without
doubleness, fearing thee without desperation, and trusting in thee
without presumption.

8.   LET ME BE JOYFUL

Let me be joyful for nothing but that which pleaseth thee; nor
sorrowful for any thing, but that which doth displease thee. Let my
labour be my delight, which is for thee; and let all rest weary me,
which is not in thee.

9. GIVE ME A WAKING SPIRIT

Give me a waking spirit, and a diligent soul, that I may seek to know thy will, and when I know it truly, may perform it faithfully, to the honour and glory of thy ever blessed name.

William Cowper
1731–1800

Throughout his life he suffered regular attacks of manic depression. Yet far from destroying his faith, his mental illness gave him a profound understanding of God's work within the individual soul. He poured his insights into his poetry, much of which is addressed to God.

1. SELF-ACQUAINTANCE

Dear Lord! accept a sinful heart,
    Which of itself complains,
And mourns, with much and frequent smart,
    The evil it contains.

There fiery seeds of anger lurk,
    Which often hurt my frame;
And wait but for the tempter's work
    To fan them to a flame.

Legality holds out a bribe
    To purchase life from thee;
And discontent would fain prescribe
    How thou shalt deal with me.

While unbelief withstands thy grace,
    And puts thy mercy by,

Presumption, with a brow of brass,
   Says, "Give me, or I die!".

How eager are my thoughts to roam
   In quest of what they love!
But ah! when duty calls them home,
   How heavily they move!

O, cleanse me in a Saviour's blood,
   Transform me by thy power,
And make me thy belov'd abode,
   And let me roam no more.

2.   GOD OUR RIGHTEOUSNESS

My God, how perfect are thy ways!
   But mine polluted are;
Sin twines itself about my praise,
   And slides into my pray'r.

When I would speak what thou hast done
   To save me from my sin,
I cannot make thy mercies known
   But self-applause creeps in.

Divine desire, that holy flame
   Thy grace creates in me,
Alas! impatience is its name
   When it returns to thee.

This heart, a fountain of vile thoughts,
   How does it overflow,
While self upon the surface floats
   Still bubbling from below!

Let others in the gaudy dress
   Of fancied merit shine;

The Lord shall be my righteousness;
    The Lord for ever mine.

3.   RETIREMENT

Far from the world, O Lord, I flee,
    From strife and tumult far;
From scenes, where Satan wages still
    His most successful war.

The calm retreat, the silent shade,
    With pray'r and praise agree;
And seem by thy sweet bounty made,
    For those who follow thee.

There if thy Spirit touch the soul,
    And grace her mean abode;
Oh with what peace, and joy, and love.
    She communes with her God!

There like the nightingale she pours
    Her solitary lays;
Nor asks a witness of her song,
    Nor thirsts for human praise.

Author and Guardian of my life,
    Sweet source of light divine;
And (all harmonious names in one)
    My Saviour; thou art mine!

What thanks I owe thee, and what love
    A boundless, endless store;
Shall echo thro' the realms above,
    When times shall be no more.

4.   LOOKING UPWARDS IN A STORM

God of my life, to thee I call,
Afflicted at thy feet I fall;

When the great water-floods prevail,
Leave not my trembling heart to fail!

Friend of the friendless, and the faint!
Where should I lodge my deep complaint?
Where but with thee, whose open door
Invites the helpless and the poor!

Did ever mourner plead with thee,
And thou refuse that mourner's plea?
Does not the word still fix'd remain,
That none shall seek thy face in vain?

That were a grief I could not bear,
Didst thou not hear and answer prayer;
But a pray'r-hearing, answ'ring God,
Supports me under ev'ry load.

Fair is the lot that's cast for me!
I have an advocate with thee;
They whom the world caresses most,
Have no such privilege to boast.

Poor tho' I am, despis'd, forgot,
Yet God, my God, forgets me not;
And he is safe and must succeed,
For whom the Lord vouchsafes to plead.

Thomas Cranmer
1489–1556

---

*As Archbishop of Canterbury under Henry VIII
and Edward VI, he was the main architect of the
English Reformation, and also the chief compiler of*

the Book of Common Prayer. *Under the Catholic Queen Mary, however, he was tried for heresy,
and condemned to be burnt at the stake. His courageous demeanour at his death, when he offered a
final prayer out loud, left a deep impression on the
huge crowd.*

1.   BEFORE HIS DEATH AT THE STAKE

O Father of heaven; O Son of God, Redeemer of the world; O
Holy Ghost, proceeding from them both; three Persons, and one
God; have mercy upon me, most wretched caitiff and miserable
sinner. I have offended both heaven and earth, more grievously
than any tongue can express. Whither then may I go, or whither
should I flee for succour? To heaven I may be ashamed to lift up
mine eyes, and in earth I find no refuge or succour. What shall I
then do? Shall I despair? God forbid. O good God, thou art merciful, and refusest none that cometh unto thee for succour. To thee,
therefore, do I run; to thee do I humble myself; saying, O Lord
God, my sins be great, but yet have mercy upon me for thy great
mercy. O God the Son, this great mystery was not wrought (that
God became man) for few or small offences; nor thou didst not
give thy Son unto death, O God the Father, for our little and small
sins only, but for all the greatest sins of the world, so that the sinner
return unto thee with a penitent heart, as I do here at this present.
Wherefore have mercy upon me, O Lord, whose property is always
to have mercy; for although my sins be great, yet thy mercy is
greater. And I crave nothing, O Lord, for mine own merits, but for
thy name's sake, that it may be glorified thereby.

Richard Crashaw
1613–1649

The son of a Puritan preacher, he came under High Church influence, and finally joined the Roman Catholic Church. His poetry is profoundly influenced by the passionate mysticism of Teresa of Àvila.

1.   THY SWEET GRACE

Lord, when the sense of thy sweet grace
Sends up my soul to seek thy face,
Thy blessed eyes breed such desire,
I die in love's delicious fire.
O love, I am thy sacrifice.
Be still triumphant, blessed eyes.
Still shine on me, fair suns! that I
Still may behold, though still I die.

Though still I die, I live again;
Still longing so to be still slain,
So gainful is such loss of breath,
I die even in desire of death.
Still live in me this loving strife
Of living death and dying life,
For while thou sweetly slayest me
Dead to myself, I live in thee.

2.   O THESE WAKEFUL WOUNDS

O these wakeful wounds of thine!
    Are they mouths? or are they eyes?

Be they mouths, or be they eyes
    Each bleeding part some one supplies.

Lo! a mouth, whose full-bloom'd lips
    At too dear a rate are roses.
Lo! a bloodshot eye! that weeps
    And many a cruel tear discloses.

O thou that on this foot hast laid
    Many a kiss, and many a tear,
Now thou shalt have all repaid,
    Whatsoe'er thy charges were.

This foot hath got a mouth and lips,
    To pay the sweet sum of thy kisses:
To pay thy tears, an eye that weeps
    Instead of tears such gems as this is.

The difference only this appears,
    (Nor can the change offend)
The debt is paid in ruby tears,
    Which thou in pearls did'st lend.

3.

JESU MASTER

Jesu Master, just and true!
Our good, and faithful shepherd too!
O by thyself vouchsafe to keep,
As with thyself thou feed'st thy sheep.

O let that love which thus makes thee
Mix with our low mortality,
Lift our lean souls, and set us up
Convictors of thine own full cup,
Coheirs of saints, that so all may
Drink the same wine; and the same way,
Nor change the pasture but the place
To feed of thee in thine own face.

Cyprian of Carthage
died 258

*Born into a rich pagan family, he was at the height
of a brilliant political career when he underwent a
conversion to Christianity. He was elected bishop of
Carthage two years later, and composed prayers to
improve public worship in his diocese. He lived during a series of horrific persecutions, and died as a
martyr.*

1.   FOR ALL NEEDS

We pray to you, Lord, with honest hearts, in tune with one another,
entreating you with sighs and tears, as befits our humble position –
placed, as we are, between the spiritually weak who have no concern
for you, and the saints who stand firm and upright before you.

We pray that you may soon come to us, leading us from darkness
to light, oppression to freedom, misery to joy, conflict to peace.
May you drive away the storms and tempest of our lives, and bring
gentle calm.

We pray that you will care for us, as a father cares for his children.

2.   FOR PEACE

O God, we know that the enemies of your Church are constantly
seeking to provoke you into acts of cruelty, in order to blacken your
honour. We beg and beseech that you will tame their wild hearts.
May their rage subside and bring peace to their souls. May their
minds, clouded by the darkness which their sins produce, repent
and turn towards the bright light of your forgiveness. Now they
thirst for our blood because we are your loyal followers; may they
instead thirst for our love and our prayers.

3. FOR PERSEVERANCE

We believe and trust, Lord, that at the time of terrible persecution, you will hear and answer our prayers with the utmost urgency. We pray with all our hearts that you will give us courage to remain true to the gospel, and proclaim your name right up till the moment of death. Then may we emerge from the snares of this world with our souls unscathed, and rise from the darkness of the world into your glorious light. As we have been linked together by love and peace, and together we have endured persecution, may we rejoice together in the kingdom of heaven.

The Didache
2nd century

It is probably Syrian in origin, and contains the earliest eucharistic prayers which still survive.

1. AT THE CONSECRATION

We give you thanks, Father,
for the holy vine of your servant, David,
which you have made known to us
through Jesus, your child.

Glory to you throughout the ages.

We give you thanks, Father,
for the life and knowledge you have sent us,
through Jesus, your child.

Glory to you throughout the ages.

As the ingredients of this bread,
once scattered over the mountains,
were gathered together and made one,
so may your church gather people
from the ends of the earth,
to become one in your kingdom.

2.   AFTER RECEIVING THE BREAD AND WINE

We give you thanks, holy Father,
for your holy name,
which you planted in our hearts;
and for the knowledge, faith and immortality
which you sent us through Jesus Christ, your child.

Glory to you throughout the ages.

You created everything, sovereign Lord,
for the glory of your name.
You gave food and drink to men
for their enjoyment,
and as a cause for thanksgiving.
And to us you have given
spiritual food and spiritual drink,
bestowing on us the promise of eternal life.
Above all we thank you
for the power of your love.

Glory to you throughout the ages.

Deliver your Church, Lord, from all evil
and teach it to love you perfectly.
You have made it holy.
Build it up from the four winds
And gather it into the kingdom
for which you have destined it.

Power and glory to you throughout the ages.

Dimma

7th century

Apart from the fact that he lived in the seventh century, nothing is known of this Irish monk. But his prayers were incorporated into many early Irish liturgies.

1.

FOR A SICK BROTHER

O Lord, holy Father, creator of the universe, author of its laws, you can bring the dead back to life, and heal those who are sick. We pray for our sick brother that he may feel your hand upon him, renewing his body and refreshing his soul. Show to him the affection in which you hold all your creatures.

2.

FOR A SINFUL BROTHER

O God, you do not wish any sinner to die, but want all people to turn from their sins and live. We pray for our sinful brother, forgiving all his wrong-doing and turning his heart towards you. By his own merit he deserves only punishment, but in your mercy we pray that you will bestow upon him eternal life.

3.

FOR A BROTHER IN DESPAIR

O God, you rule over your creation with tenderness, offering fresh hope in the midst of the most terrible misery. We pray for our brother whose soul is blackened by despair, infusing him with the pure light of your love. As he curses the day he was born and yearns for oblivion, reveal to him the miracle of new birth which shall prepare him for the joys of heaven.

Dinka

The major Nilotic people of southern Sudan, the Dinka are now predominantly Christian. But, far from abandoning their ancient beliefs and prayers, they have incorporated them into their new faith, since, like the ancient Hebrew people, they had always believed in a single God who rules the universe.

1.

A DAILY CHANT

Lord, you are here,
Lord, you are there.
You are wherever we go.
Lord, you guide us,
Lord, you protect us.
You are wherever we go.
Lord, we need you,
Lord, we trust you,
You are wherever we go.
Lord, we love you,
Lord we praise you,
You are wherever we go.

2.

FOR RAIN

Give life to the grass
By sending us rain.
Give life to our earth
By sending us rain.

Give life to our crops
By sending us rain.
Give life to our children
By sending us rain.

3.

FOR MERCY

Lord, you have turned your back on us.
Our words and deeds have made you angry.
So our cattle die of hunger
And our children die of disease.

We are frightened that we shall all die.
We know that you rule over life and death.
Show us what we must do to please you.
Take away your anger, and have mercy.

4.

IN THE EVENING

Now that the sun has set,
I sit and rest, and think of you.
Give my weary body peace.
Let my legs and arms stop aching,
Let my nose stop sneezing,
Let my head stop thinking.
Let me sleep in your arms.

5.

DYING WORDS

There are men who hate me;
Let me love them.
There are men I have wronged;
Let them forgive me.

John Donne
1572–1631

*In his early years he imagined himself indifferent
to religion, and he pursued an unsuccessful career
in politics and journalism. But through the influence of his wife he gradually turned to the Christian
faith, and in 1615 was ordained an Anglican
clergyman. Six years later he became Dean of
St Paul's. His prayers are scattered through his
Sermons and Devotions, written in his more
tranquil later years. Today he is most famous for his
poetry, much of which dates from his more troubled
middle years; some of his poems are also prayers.*

1.   A CONFESSION

Forgive me O Lord, O Lord forgive me my sins, the sins of my
youth, and my present sins, the sin that my parents cast upon me,
original sin, and the sins that I cast upon my children, in an ill
example; actual sins, sins which are manifest to all the world, and
sins which I have so laboured to hide from the world, as that now
they are hid from mine own conscience, and mine own memory.
Forgive me my crying sins, and my whispering sins, sins of unchari-
table hate, and sins of unchaste love, sins against thee and against
thy power O almighty Father, against thy wisdom, O glorious Son,
against thy goodness, O blessed Spirit of God; and sins against him
and him, against superiors and equals, and inferiors; and sins against
me and me, against mine own soul, and against my body, which I
have loved better than my soul. Forgive me O Lord, O Lord in the
merits of thy Christ and my Jesus, thine Anointed, and my Saviour.
Forgive me my sins, all my sins, and I will put Christ to no more

cost, nor thee to more trouble, for any reprobation or malediction that lay upon me, otherwise than as a sinner.

2.   A PLEA FOR MERCY

O Lord, I most humbly acknowledge and confess that I have understood sin, by understanding thy laws and judgements; but have gone against thy known and revealed will. Thou hast set up many candlesticks, and kindled many lamps in me; but I have either blown them out, or carried them to guide me in forbidden ways. Thou hast given me a desire of knowledge, and some means to it, and some possession of it; and I have arm'd myself with thy weapons against thee. Yet, O God, have mercy upon me, for thine own sake have mercy upon me. Let not sin and me be able to exceed thee, nor to defraud thee, nor to frustrate thy purposes. But let me, in spite of me, be of so much use to thy glory, that by thy mercy to my sin, other sinners may see how much sin thou canst pardon.

3.   A CIRCLE AND A LINE

O eternal and most gracious God, who, considered in thyself, art a circle, first and last, and altogether; but, considered in thy working upon us, art a direct line, and leadest us from our beginning, through all our ways, to our end, enable me by thy grace to look forward to mine end, and to look backward too, to the considerations of thy mercies afforded me from the beginning; that so by that practice of considering thy mercy, in my beginning in this world, when thou plantedst me in the Christian Church, and thy mercy in the beginning in the other world, when thou writest me in the book of life, in my election, I may come to a holy consideration of thy mercy in the beginning of all my actions here.

4.   THOU HAST MADE ME

Thou hast made me, and shall thy work decay?
Repair me now, for now mine end doth haste,
I run to death, and death meets me as fast,
And all my pleasures are like yesterday;

I dare not move my dim eyes any way,
Despair behind, and death before doth cast
Such terror, and my feebled flesh doth waste
By sin in it, which it t'wards hell doth weigh;
Only thou'rt above, and when towards thee
By thy leave I can look, I rise again;
But our old subtle foe so tempteth me
That not one hour my self I can sustain;
Thy grace may wing me to prevent his art,
And thou like Adamant draw mine iron heart.

5.   BATTER MY HEART

Batter my heart, three person'd God; for, you
As yet but knock, breathe, shine, and seek to mend;
That I may rise, and stand, o'erthrow me, and bend
Your force, to break, blow, burn and make me new.
I, like an usurped town, to another due,
Labour to admit you, but O, to no end,
Reason your viceroy in me, me should defend,
But is captiv'd, and proves weak or untrue.
Yet dearly I love you, and would be loved fain,
But am betroth'd unto your enemy:
Divorce me, untie, or break that knot again,
Take me to you, imprison me, for I
Except you enthrall me, never shall be free,
Nor ever chaste, except you ravish me.

Edmund of Abingdon
c.1180–1240

---

*As Archbishop of Canterbury he strived to protect
the Church in England from the greed of both king
and pope. Earlier, while he taught at Oxford, he*

*wrote a devotional treatise containing two simple
prayers which came to be widely used.*

1.   FOR ALL TIMES

Lord Jesus Christ, into your hands and into the hands of your holy
angels I offer this day (or this night). To you I entrust my soul and
my body, my father and my mother, my brothers and my sisters,
my friends and my neighbours, and all Christian people. Keep us
this day (or this night) free from all sinful and wicked desires, and
save us from sudden death in which we have no time to prepare
ourselves. Enlighten our hearts with your Holy Spirit, that we may
always obey your commands. And never separate us from the joy
and comfort of your love.

2.   YOU AND US

Lord, since you exist, we exist. Since you are beautiful, we are
beautiful. Since you are good, we are good. By our existence we
honour you. By our beauty we glorify you. By our goodness we
love you.

Lord, through your power all things were made. Through your
wisdom all things are governed. Through your grace all things are
sustained. Give us power to serve you, wisdom to discern your laws,
and grace to obey those at all times.

Queen Elizabeth I
1533–1603

She composed her Book of Devotions, *now kept
in the British Museum, purely for her own use.
Her prayers reveal a self-critical, even vulnerable,
side of her character which she kept hidden from*

*those around her; and they also show both the
burden and the joy of her high office.*

1.   A MONARCH'S THANKSGIVING AND CONFESSION

O most glorious King, and Creator of the whole world, to whom all things be subject, both in heaven and earth, and all best princes most gladly obey, hear the most humble voice of thy handmaid, in this only happy, to be so accepted. How exceeding is thy goodness, and how great mine offences. Of nothing hast thou made me not a worm, but a creature according to thine own image, heaping all the blessings upon me that men on earth hold most happy. Drawing my blood from kings and my bringing up in virtue; giving me that more is, even in my youth, knowledge of thy truth, and in times of most danger, most gracious deliverance; pulling me from the prison to the palace; and placing me a sovereign princess over thy people of England. And above all this, making me (though a weak woman) yet thy instrument, to set forth the glorious gospel of thy dear Son Christ Jesus. Thus in these last and worst days of the world, when wars and seditions with grievous persecutions have vexed almost all kings and countries, round about me, my reign hath been peaceable, and my realm a receptacle to thy afflicted church. The love of my people hath appeared firm, and the devices of mine enemies frustrate. Now for these and other of thy benefits, O Lord of all goodness, what have I rendered to thee? Forgetfulness, unthankfulness and great disobedience. I should have magnified thee, I have neglected thee. I should have prayed unto thee, I have forgotten thee. I should have served thee, I have sinned against thee. This is my case. Then where is my hope? If thou Lord wilt be extreme to mark what is done amiss, who may abide it? But thou art gracious and merciful, long suffering and of great goodness, not delighting in the death of a sinner. Thou seest whereof I came, of corrupt seed; what I am, a most frail substance; where I live in the world full of wickedness; where delights be snares, where dangers be imminent, where sin reigneth, and death abideth. This is my state. Now where is my comfort? In the depth of my misery I know no help, O Lord, but the height of thy mercy, who hast sent thine only Son into the world to save sinners. This God of my life and life of my soul, the

King of all comfort, is my only refuge. For his sake therefore, to whom thou hast given all power, and wilt deny no petition, hear my prayers. Turn thy face from my sins, O Lord, and thine eyes to thy handiwork. Create a clean heart, and renew a right spirit within me. Order my steps in thy word, that no wickedness have dominion over me, make me obedient to thy will, and delight in thy law. Grant me grace to live godly and to govern justly: that so living to please thee, and reigning to serve thee, I may ever glorify thee, the Father of all goodness and mercy.

2.   A MONARCH'S SELF-OFFERING

O Lord God, Father everlasting, which reignest over the kingdoms of men, and givest them of thy pleasure; which of thy great mercy hast chosen me thy servant and handmaid to feed thy people and thine inheritance: so teach me, I humbly beseech thee, thy word, and so strengthen me with thy grace, that I may feed thy people with a faithful and a true heart; and rule them prudently with power. O Lord, thou hast set me on high, my flesh is frail and weak. If I therefore at any time forget thee, touch my heart, O Lord, that I may again remember thee. If I swell against thee, pluck me down in my own conceit, that thou mayest raise me in thy sight. Grant me, O Lord, a listening ear to hear thee and a hungry soul to long after thy word. Endue me with thy heavenly spirit. Give me thy spirit of wisdom, that I may understand thee. Give me thy spirit of truth, that I may know thee; thy feeling spirit that I may fear thee; thy spirit of grace that I may love thee; thy spirit of zeal that I may hunger and thirst after thee; thy persevering spirit that I may live and dwell and reign with thee. I acknowledge, O my King, that without thee my throne is unstable, my seat unsure, my kingdom tottering, my life uncertain. I see all things in this life subject to mutability, nothing to continue at one stay, but fear and trembling, hunger and thirst, cold and heat, weakness and faintness, sorrow and sickness, doth evermore oppress mankind. I hear how oft times untimely death doth carry away the mightiest and greatest personages. I have learned out of thy holy word that horrible judgement is nigh unto them which walk not after thy will, and the mighty swerving from thy law shall be mightily tormented. Therefore since all things in this world, both heaven and earth, shall pass and perish, and thy word alone endureth for ever, engraft, O most gracious Lord Christ, this thy word of grace and life so in my heart, that from henceforth I neither follow after feigned comforts, in worldly power, neither distract my mind to transitory pleasures, nor occupy my thoughts in vain delights, but that carefully seeking thee where thou showest thyself in thy word, I may surely find thee to my comfort, and everlastingly enjoy thee to my salvation. Create therefore in me, O Lord, a new heart, and so renew my spirit within me that thy law may be my study; thy truth my delight; thy Church my care; thy people my crown; thy righteousness my pleasure; thy service my government; thy fear my honour; thy grace my strength; thy favour my life; thy gospel my kingdom; and thy salvation my bliss and my glory. So shall this my kingdom through thee be established with peace; so shall thy church be edified with power; so shall thy gospel be published with zeal; so shall my reign be continued with prosperity; so shall my life be prolonged with happiness; and so shall myself at thy good pleasure be translated into immortality.

Ephrem the Syrian
c.306–373

Although most of his life was devoted to biblical exegeses, his hymns addressed to Christ show a quirky originality which was held in both admiration and opposition by his contemporaries. His Christmas Hymn *is one of the earliest Christmas devotions, since the Church had only just begun to celebrate that festival. And his* Hymn of Mary *was his prayerful response to the controversies already raging about Jesus' mother.*

1.   A CHRISTMAS HYMN

The feast day of your birth resembles you, Lord.
Because it brings joy to all humanity.
Old people and infants alike enjoy your day.
Your day is celebrated from generation to generation.
Kings and emperors may pass away,
And the festivals to commemorate them soon lapse.
But your festival will be remembered till the end of time.
Your day is a means and a pledge of peace.
At your birth heaven and earth were reconciled,
Since you came from heaven to earth on that day
You forgave our sins and wiped away our guilt.
You gave us so many gifts on your birthday:
A treasure chest of spiritual medicines for the sick;
Spiritual light for those that are blind;
The cup of salvation for the thirsty;
The bread of life for the hungry.
In the winter when trees are bare,
You give us the most succulent spiritual fruit.
In the frost when the earth is barren,
You bring new hope to our souls.
In December when seeds are hidden in the soil,
The staff of life springs forth from the virgin womb.

2.   A HYMN OF MARY

O Lord, how should we address your mother?
If we call her "virgin", a child stands up,
If we call her "married", a woman stands up,
Yet she was both a virgin, and she was married.

O Lord, what is Mary to you?
Certainly she, and she alone, is your mother.
Yet she is also your sister and your friend.
And, together with your whole Church, she is your lover.
She is all things to you.

She was betrothed to you before you came.
Then she conceived you when the Spirit brought you.
She became your mother when you were born.
And she became your first disciple when you preached.

She conceived you without sexual union,
And she produced milk in her breasts for you to drink.
Her breasts were a sign of your ministry,
Bringing spiritual milk to parched, thirsty souls.

You entered her, and became a servant.
You, whose Word was the agent of all creation,
Fell silent in her womb.
By this means your voice could be heard by all humanity.

You entered her, and became weak and vulnerable.
You, who is the nourisher of all creation,
Became hungry and thirsty within her.
In this way all humanity could receive the bread of life.

You, the King of Kings became lowly within her.
You, the source of all wealth, became poor within her.
You, the mightiest of all warriors, became powerless within
    her.
You, who clothe even the birds, became naked within her.

Thus you can lift up the lowly,
You can feed the poor,
Give strength to the powerless,
And clothe the naked.

Erasmus
1469–1536

The most renowned scholar of his age, he opposed both the corruption of the Catholic Church and the self-righteous zeal of many Protestant reformers. He urged the Protestants not to break with Rome, but his anti-papist satire caused the Pope to ban his works. In his prayers his sharp intellect gives way to a soft, faithful heart.

1.
TO THE FATHER

Most loving Father, may we who seek to dwell in your house be governed wholly by your laws. In adversity and in prosperity, in life and in death, may you reveal to us your gracious will, and then give us strength in body and in heart to obey your commands. We pray that you will make us perfect, because only that which is perfect truly reflects your glory. And through the Holy Scriptures you have shown us the way of perfection.

2.
TO THE SON

Most gracious Son, may your teaching dispel the darkness of ignorance in our mind, and may your commands be beacons of light showing us the path to peace. And as we walk on that path, may we find your footprints on the ground, that we may place our own feet where you have trodden. We believe that you will strengthen our limbs when they grow weary, and raise our spirits when they become heavy, because nothing gives you greater pleasure than watching us follow the way of salvation. We pray that you will always be our friend and our guide, and so bring us to your Father's heavenly kingdom.

3.   TO THE HOLY SPIRIT

Adorable Spirit, may the rushing wind of your mercy blow away all trace of sin within us, and may your unquenchable fire purify our souls. We believe that you comfort those who mourn, uplift those who are depressed, calm those who are angry, guide those who are confused, console those who are lonely, reconcile those who are estranged, and bring joy to all who confess Jesus Christ as Lord. We pray that you will live in our simple and humble hearts, and so make us truly temples of your glorious love.

4.   AT DAYBREAK

Lord Jesus Christ, you are the sun that always rises, but never sets. You are the source of all life, creating and sustaining every living thing. You are the source of all food, material and spiritual, nourishing us in both body and soul. You are the light that dispels the clouds of error and doubt, and goes before me every hour of the day, guiding my thoughts and my actions. May I walk in your light, be nourished by your food, be sustained by your mercy, and be warmed by your love.

5.   AT NIGHT

Lord Jesus Christ, you are the gentle moon and joyful stars, that watch over the darkest night. You are the source of all peace, reconciling the whole universe to the Father. You are the source of all rest, calming troubled hearts, and bringing sleep to weary bodies. You are the sweetness that fills our minds with quiet joy, and can turn the worst nightmares into dreams of heaven. May I dream of your sweetness, rest in your arms, be at one with your Father, and be comforted in the knowledge that you always watch over me.

6.   IN SERIOUS ILLNESS

Lord Jesus Christ, you are the only source of health for the living,
and you promise eternal life to the dying. I entrust myself to your
holy will. If you wish me to stay longer in this world, I pray that
you will heal me of my present sickness. If you wish me to leave
this world, I readily lay aside this mortal body, in the sure hope of
receiving an immortal body which shall enjoy everlasting health. I
ask only that you relieve me of pain, that whether I live or I die, I
may rest peaceful and contented.

The Exeter Book
c.950

Some time around the middle of the tenth century
a collection of religious poems was made. This book
found its way into the hands of Leofric, the bishop
of Exeter, about a century later, and he presented
it to his cathedral. It has survived, and offers a
unique insight into the Anglo-Saxon religious
spirit. It contains two meditations addressed to
Christ, one undoubtedly related to Advent, and the
other probably connected with Lent. The authorship
is unknown.

1.   ADVENT DESIRE

O King of the nations, you are the headstone of the glorious hall
of creation. You are the firm mortar which holds the building
together. Throughout the earth people marvel at your works. But
now the building is being reduced to a ruin by greed and fear.
Reveal yourself to mankind, show yourself as the ruler of the world,
demonstrate the power of your love.

O just and faithful King, you can unlock the prison-house of sin, and let us out into the glorious freedom of love. Now we sit in darkness, grieving over the wrongs we have committed. We long for the sun, we yearn for the warmth and brightness of your truth. Open the gate of this prison, and lead us to your kingdom, which is our true home.

Come now, high king of heaven. Come to us in flesh and bone. Bring life to us who are weary with misery. Bring peace to us who are overcome with weeping, whose cheeks are covered with bitter salt tears. Seek us out, who are lost in the darkness of depression. Do not forget us, but show mercy on us. Impart to us your everlasting joy, so that we, who are fashioned by your hands, may praise your glory.

2.   LENTEN CONTRITION

Give me, O Lord, patience and sense of purpose in each of the things which you send to beset me. You know the many wicked deeds which burden my heart. But out of compassion you set aside all blame, and receive me as your own. Please protect me through the dangers and confusion of my transient life on earth, ensuring that in all things I strive for eternal life in heaven. I know that I am very slow to make amends for my sins, despite the many favours you grant me. Fix my trust, my timid hopes, upon yourself, so that I may stand on a secure foundation. Lift up my thoughts with your wisdom. Take me out of this world as soon as I am fit to be received into the next.

Stand by me, Lord, and hold me upright when the gales of sin blow round me. And when the dark stormy night of wickedness closes in on me, guide my steps. My soul is already battered by the temptations to which I have submitted. My spirit is crushed by the weight of past misdeeds. My mind is stained by the memory of the evil in which I have participated. Throughout my life you have been unfailingly generous to me, although I have deserved only punishment.

The trees around me flourish and spread their branches. But I am hemmed in by the guilt which surrounds me, and I wither because of the poison of sin within me. Ah Lord, you are the only remedy. I accept that while I remain on earth I must endure hardship, and must be spiritually destitute. I may enjoy the affection of friends, and the hospitality of strangers, but these are only brief flashes of light in the darkness. Let my suffering bring me true contrition, that I may receive your forgiveness, and so be made fit for the everlasting joy of heaven.

Fenelon
c.1651–1715

In an age which emphasized human rationality, he taught that our relationship with God must be based on pure spiritual love, without any concern for personal reward. And such love, he believed, depends entirely on God's grace, received in the inner quietness of the soul. Three prayers, contained in letters written to people under his spiritual direction, express beautifully his mystical understanding.

1.   SELF-QUESTIONING

My God, have I sought to frustrate your work in the world? Have I used my wealth, health, influence, intellect, authority, knowledge and status to your dishonour? Have I tried to destroy the seeds of your love which you water with your own blood? Have I found delight in the malice and wickedness that dragged you to the cross? Have I sold myself to the Devil, in order to promote my own glory?

What folly! There is no reward in the Devil except endless misery. I have excused my stupidity by saying that others have treated me so badly that I am merely giving back what I have received. But you came, in your son Jesus Christ, not to be served, but to serve. So I must seek to serve others in whatever situation you put me, without regard to cost or reward. In this way I can glorify you on earth; and I can hope one day to be glorified with you in heaven.

2.   THE BLESSING OF SUFFERING

O my God, you alone can perceive the depths of our weakness;
and you alone can heal us. Turn our eyes continually to you, our
all-powerful Father, and to your Son, our example in courageous
suffering. He was nailed to the cross, so we might learn that suffering can be turned into a blessing. We long for physical comfort
and bodily pleasure; so when we gaze on your Son, his body wracked
with pain, we shudder at such a terrifying sight. Yet when we see
him rise again in glory, we know that the nails which fixed him to
the cross were also used to fashion the gate of eternal life.

   Help us never again to fear suffering, but only to fear sin. Give
us the courage to embrace such suffering as you send us, in the sure
and certain knowledge of your eternal bliss.

3.   A COMPLAINT TO GOD

My God, if I dared to grumble, the only thing of which I would
complain is that you have not sent enough good spiritual guides
into your Church. There are so many who can put on an outward
display of godliness, but inwardly have little real knowledge or
holiness. There are so many who have read innumerable books on
theology, but have no real understanding of your ways. I thank you
that you hid the mysteries of your truth from such people, who are
so great in their own eyes. Instead you chose to reveal yourself to
those who count themselves as nothing. Yet those who have true
holiness and true understanding are often so reluctant to serve as
spiritual directors, saying that they are not worthy to offer guidance
to others. Put into their hearts the courage and the confidence to
share with others the grace which they have received.

Nicholas Ferrar
1593–1637

*He founded the Little Gidding Community, where
families and single people followed a simple rule of
prayer, manual work and service to the needy. He
was a close friend of the poet George Herbert.*

1.   THANKSGIVING FOR COMMUNITY LIFE

Wonderful hath been thy goodness towards us: while the wise have
been disappointed in their counsels, while those full of friends have
been left desolate, while the men whose hands were mighty have
found nothing, while the strong on every side have fallen, we, O
Lord, have been by thy power raised up, by thine arm have we been
strengthened, guided by thy counsels, and relieved by the favour of
thy mercies. And that we might know that it was thy doing, by
those ways and means which we thought not of, thou hast brought
us into a wealthy place, and to these many comforts which we now
enjoy. And although we have not any way deserved thy favours, yet
is thy patience extended towards us. We must needs acknowledge,
O Lord, that the liberality of thy hand is extended even beyond the
largeness of our own hearts. And yet, O Lord, all this is nothing in
comparison of that which we may farther enjoy. By how much
the things of heaven do surpass those of the earth, by how much
everlasting happiness is more worth than the transitory and feeble
pleasures of this life, by so much more surpassing are those graces
and favours with which thou hast furnished us for the knowledge
of thy heavenly will, and for the practices of those duties, of which
our conversation in this world is capable.

Thou hast given to us a freedom from all other affairs, that we
may without distraction attend thy service. That holy gospel which
came down from heaven, which things the angels desire to look

into, is by thy goodness, continually open to our view; the sweet music thereof is continually sounding in our ears; heavenly songs are by thy mercy put into our mouths, and our tongues and lips made daily instruments of pouring forth thy praise. This, Lord, is the work, and this the pleasure of the angels in heaven; and dost thou vouchsafe to make us partakers of so high an happiness? The knowledge of thee, and of thy Son is everlasting life. Thy service is perfect freedom: how happy then are we, that thou dost constantly retain us in the daily exercise thereof!

2.   FOR GEORGE HERBERT, DURING HIS FINAL ILLNESS

O most mighty God, and merciful Father, we most humbly beseech thee, if it be thy good pleasure, to continue to us that singular benefit which thou hast given us in the friendship of thy servant, our dear brother, who now lieth on the bed of sickness. Let him abide with us yet awhile, for the furtherance of our faith. We have indeed deserved by our ingratitude, not only the loss of him, but whatever other opportunities thou hast given us for the attainment of our salvation. We do not deserve to be heard in our supplications; but thy mercies are above all thy works. In consideration whereof we prostrate ourselves in all humble earnestness, beseeching thee, if so it may seem good to thy Divine Majesty, that thou wilt hear us in this, who hast heard us in all the rest, and that thou wilt bring him back again from the gates of death; that thou wilt yet a while spare him, that he may live to thy honour and our comfort. Lord, thou hast willed that our delights should be in the saints on earth, and in such as excel in virtue: how then should we not be afflicted, and mourn when thou takest them away from us! Thou hast made him a great help, and furtherance of the best things amongst us; how then can we but esteem the loss of him, a chastisement from thy displeasure! O Lord, we beseech thee that it may not be so: we beseech thee, if it be thy good pleasure, restore unto us our dear brother, by restoring to him his health.

3.   AFTER A MAJOR DECISION

I thank thee, O blessed Lord God, for of thee cometh this mind; it is not of myself, but from the inspiration of thy blessed Spirit.

Charles de Foucauld
1858–1916

A member of the French aristocracy, he served as a cavalry officer in Africa, giving him a passion for the Sahara. After his conversion to Christianity, he tried the monastic life, but eventually went to live as a hermit in Algeria amongst the desert tribesmen. His spiritual writings take the form of passionate outpourings, in which he bares his soul to God. He came to be revered by the desert people, but was eventually murdered by a tribesman who resented his influence.

1.   CONVERSION

O Lord, guide my thoughts and my words. It is not that I lack subjects for meditation. On the contrary, I am crushed with the weight of them. How many are your mercies God – mercies yesterday and today, and at every moment of my life, from before my birth, from before time itself began! I am plunged deep in mercies; I drown in them; they cover me, wrapping me round on every side.

Lord Jesus, we should all sing of your mercies – we, who were all created for everlasting glory and redeemed by your blood. But if we all have cause to sing your praises, how much more cause have I? From childhood I have been surrounded by so many graces. My saintly mother taught me to know you, to love you, and, as soon as I could speak, to pray to you.

Despite so many blessings I drifted away from you for many years. I withdrew further and further from you, and my life became a death in your eyes. I enjoyed numerous worldly pleasures, and thought I was alive. But beneath the surface there was deep sadness, disgust, boredom, restlessness. Whenever I was alone a great melancholy came over me.

Yet, how good you are to me. You slowly and patiently destroyed my worldly attachments. You broke down everything that prevented me from living for you. You showed me the futility and falsehood of my life in the world. Then you planted in my heart a tender seedling of love, so gradually my heart turned back to you. You gave me a taste for prayer, a trust in your word, a desire to imitate you.

Now I am overwhelmed by your blessings. O beloved Bridegroom there is nothing that you have not done for me. Now tell me what you want of me, how you expect me to serve you. Create in my thoughts, words and actions that which will give true glory to you.

2.   QUEST FOR PERFECTION

Poverty, humility, penitence – you, dear Jesus, know that I long to practise these virtues to the degree and in the way which you want. But what are that way and degree? Until now I have always thought that I should practise them by imitating you as closely as possible, by making myself follow, as far as I could, the way in which you yourself practised them. Now I fear I might be mistaken. While yours is the best and most perfect way, perhaps you are not calling me to a perfect life, and so will not let me follow you so closely. Indeed, if I look at myself, there is such a gap between my wretchedness and true perfection, that I am certainly unworthy to be counted amongst those close disciples who tread in your footsteps.

And yet you have heaped so many blessings on me that it would seem ungrateful not to strive for perfection. To be content with imperfection would seem like a rejection of your generosity. I find it hard to believe that, in giving yourself so freely to me, you do not want me to give myself wholly to you. My only desire is to be and to do what pleases you. Enlighten my mind that I may always conform to your will.

3.   INSPIRED BY THE LORD'S PRAYER

Our Father

O God, how good you are to allow us to call you "our Father"! Not only do you allow it, you command it. What gratitude, what joy, what love, and above all, what confidence it inspires in me. And since you are so good to me. I should be good to others. You are Father to all people, so I should feel like a loving brother towards everyone, however wicked he may be. Our Father, our Father, teach me to have your name continually on my lips.

Who art in heaven
Why did you choose this qualification rather than any other – such as "righteous Father", or "holy Father"? It was doubtless O God, that my soul might be uplifted from the very beginning of this prayer, high above this poor world, and placed at the outset where it ought to be, in heaven which is its native land. It was also to put me at the outset into a state of joy, remembering that you, O God, love me and care for me for all eternity.

Hallowed be thy name
What is it, O Lord, that I am expressing in these words? I am expressing the whole object of my desires, the whole aim and purpose of my life. I want to hallow your name in all my thoughts, words and actions. And this means that I want to imitate your Son, Jesus, since he hallowed your name in his every thought, word and action.

Thy kingdom come
In these simple words, I am asking that you reveal the fullness of your glory, and that you make all people holy. Your kingdom will come when all people acknowledge you as Master, seeking with all their minds to obey you, with all their hearts to love you, and with all their energies to serve you. So in saying those words, I am committing myself to spread the knowledge of your glory to all mankind.

Thy will be done, on earth as it is in heaven
These words show me to what extent every offence against you, and every sinful act of one person against another, cause you pain and grief. With feelings far deeper and far greater than we could ever understand, you desire all people to be reconciled with you and with one another. You desire earth to be a mirror of heaven.

So when people strive to break that mirror through their sinfulness, your heart breaks. Yet equally, for the same reasons, you experience great joy at even the least act of goodness. And your heart is filled with fatherly pleasure whenever any person turns to you in prayer.

Give us this day our daily bread

You desire me, O Lord, to look to you for my every need. And in looking to you, I know that you will provide me with bread to eat, clothes to wear, and a warm place to rest. But it is not only material bread which you provide; you give also spiritual bread. Whenever I eat the bread of Holy Communion, I am reminded that your Son gave his body to die on the cross, to give me spiritual food for all eternity. And in this phrase, I note that it is not "me" for whom I pray, but "us". You do not want me ever to pray selfishly, but always to pray for other's needs, because only through such mutual charity do I become fit to receive the true bread of eternal life.

Forgive us our trespasses as we forgive

Having spoken to you so intimately as "our Father" – having climbed so high, I now realize how low I really am. I remember how I fail to obey your will or work for your kingdom. And so I say, "Father, forgive me". With my whole soul I see how horrible are my sins to you, how they disgust and insult you, and what a price your Son had to pay to redeem me from them. I realize how much pain I have caused you; and in that realization I feel pain myself, crying with remorse at what I have done. At the same time I recognize that I have no right to ask your forgiveness for my sins, unless I forgive others their sins. And, of course, the sins which others commit against me are as nothing compared with the sins I have committed against you. Thus in truth I am asking that all mankind might be forgiven.

Lead us not into temptation

This is a cry suitable for every hour and every minute of my life – a cry for help. I am so beset by temptation that it is impossible for me to accomplish the smallest good deed unless I call for help continually. Indeed my every prayer is in truth a call for help.

Deliver us from evil

If you were to deliver all people from evil then they would all be saints, glorifying you in their holiness. Thus your purpose and my desire would be wholly fulfilled, that you would reign as King over the whole world. But it is not fit for me to worry about the evil of others, unless I first turn inwards to my own soul. I ask only that your purpose be accomplished in me.

Francis of Assisi
1182–1226

The son of a wealthy merchant, as a young man he served as a soldier, renowned for both bravery and high living. After his conversion at the age of twenty-three he embraced total poverty, in imitation of Jesus. At first he devoted himself to repairing a ruined church in his native town of Assisi. Then in 1208 he set out on foot, to preach the gospel. He was soon joined by others, who were inspired by his gentle love and radiant joy, and they eventually formed themselves into a religious order. His most famous prayer, Brother Sun, Sister Moon *expresses his devotion to all God's creation. His authorship of the prayer for peace is doubtful, but it embodies perfectly the Franciscan spirit.*

1.   PRAYER BEFORE THE CRUCIFIX

Most high, glorious God, enlighten the darkness of my heart. And give me, Lord, a correct faith, a sure hope, a perfect love, that I may carry out your holy and true commands.

2.   ALL GOODNESS

Most powerful, most high, most holy, most supreme Lord, you
alone are good, and all goodness comes from you. May we give you
all praise, all glory, all blessing and all honour. And may we offer
back to you all the good things which you have granted to us.

3.   FOLLOWING IN HIS FOOTSTEPS

Almighty, eternal, just and merciful God, grant us the desire to do
only what pleases you, and the strength to do only what you command. Cleanse our souls, enlighten our minds, and inflame our
hearts with your Holy Spirit, that we may follow in the footsteps
of your beloved Son, Jesus Christ.

4.   BROTHER SUN, SISTER MOON

Most high, omnipotent, righteous Lord, to you be all praise, glory,
honour and blessing. To you alone are they due, and no man is
worthy to mention you.

Praise be to you, my Lord, for all your creatures, above all Brother
Sun, who gives us the light of day. He is beautiful and radiant with
great splendour, and so is like you most high Lord.

Praise be to you, my Lord, for Sister Moon and the stars. In heaven
you fashioned them, clear and precious and beautiful.

Praise be to you, my Lord, for Brother Wind, and for every kind
of weather, cloudy or fair, stormy or serene, by which you cherish
all that you have made.

Praise be to you, my Lord, for Sister Water, which is useful and
humble and precious and pure.

Praise be to you, my Lord, for Brother Fire, by whom you lighten
the night, for he is beautiful and playful and robust and strong.

Praise be to you, my Lord, for our Sister Earth, who sustains and gov-
erns us, and produces varied fruits with coloured flowers and herbs.

Praise be to you, my Lord, for those who forgive sins in your love, and for those who bear sickness and tribulation.

Blessed are those who endure in peace, for by you, most high Lord, they shall be crowned.

Praise be to you, my Lord, for our Sister Bodily Death, from whom no living person can escape. Pity those who die in mortal sin.

Blessed are those who in death are found obedient to your most holy will, for death shall do them no harm.

Praise and bless my Lord, giving him thanks and serving him with great humility.

5.   INSPIRED BY THE LORD'S PRAYER

Our Father.
Our Creator, Redeemer, Comforter and Saviour.

Who art in heaven.
You are with the angels and the saints, bathing them in your light that they may be enlightened by your love, and dwelling within them that they may be filled with your joy. You are the supreme good, the eternal good, from whom comes all goodness, and without whom there is no goodness.

Hallowed be your name.
May our knowledge of you become ever clearer, that we may know the breadth of your blessings, the length of your promises, the height of your majesty, and the depth of your judgements.

Your kingdom come.
Rule in our hearts with your grace, that we may become fit subjects for your kingdom. We desire nothing more than to dwell in your kingdom, where we can watch you on your throne, and enjoy your perfect love.

Your will be done, on earth as it is in heaven.
May we love you with our whole heart by always thinking of you, with our whole soul by always desiring you, with our whole mind by directing all our intentions to you, and with our whole strength

by spending all our energies in your service. And may we love our neighbours as ourselves, drawing them to your love, rejoicing in their good fortunes, and caring for them in their misfortunes.

Give us this day our daily bread.
In memory and understanding and reverence of the love which our Lord Jesus Christ has for us, revealed by his sacrifice for us on the cross, we ask for the perfect bread of his body.

And forgive us our trespasses.
We know that you forgive us, through the suffering and death of your beloved Son.

As we forgive those who trespass against us.
Enable us to forgive perfectly and without reserve any wrong that has been committed against us. And strengthen our hearts truly to love our enemies, praying for them and striving to serve them.

And lead us not into temptation.
Save us not only from obvious and persistent temptations, but also those that are hidden or come suddenly when our guard is lowered.

But deliver us from evil.
Protect us from past evil, protect us against present evil, and free us from future evil.

6.   FOR PEACE

Lord, make me an instrument of your peace.
Where there is hatred, let me sow love.
Where there is injury, let me sow pardon.
Where there is doubt, let me sow faith.
Where there is despair, let me give hope.
Where there is darkness, let me give light.
Where there is sadness, let me give joy.
O divine master, grant that I may
not try to be comforted, but to comfort;
not try to be understood, but to understand;
not try to be loved, but to love.
Because it is in giving that we receive,

in forgiving that we are forgiven,
and in dying that we are born to eternal life.

Francis of Sales
1567–1622

---

*As Bishop of Geneva he was one of the leaders of
the Counter-Reformation in the Roman Catholic
Church. His particular concern was the renewal of
spiritual discipline amongst the laity, for whom he
wrote* An Introduction to the Devout Life. *This
includes a series of meditations on the human condition, as well as prayers which elucidate the basic
aspects of God's relationship with man.*

1.

FIRST MEDITATION: CREATION

O my great and good Creator, how much I owe to you, that in your
mercy you raised me from nothing to make me what I am. What
can I possibly do to bless your name or thank you enough for your
inestimable goodness?

Yet, my Creator, instead of uniting myself to you by loving service, my inordinate desires have made me a rebel. I have cut myself
off from you by preferring sin, dishonouring you as if you were not
my Creator.

O my God, with all my heart I offer you myself, as you have
made me. I dedicate and consecrate myself to you.

2.

SECOND MEDITATION: SIN

What was I thinking about, my God, when not of you? What was
I remembering when I was forgetful of you? Where was my heart
when not set on you? Truth should have been my food and yet I
gorged myself with vanity, a slave to my own desires.

My God and my Saviour, from now on I will think only of you; no more will I think of the things which displease you. My memories will always be of your greatness and of your mercy which you have so tenderly exercised on me. My heart shall find all its joy in you, and you shall be the object of its love. From now on I will detest the vain follies which have occupied my days and all the vain objects of my love.

Accept, O God, these desires and aspirations, and give me your blessing, that I may put them into practice through the grace of your Son, who shed his blood for me on the cross.

3.   THIRD MEDITATION: DEATH

One day my soul must depart from his body. When will it be? In winter or summer? In town or country? During the day or night? Suddenly or with warning? Due to illness or an accident? Shall I have a chance to confess my sins? Shall there be a priest to assist me? I know none of these things. One thing only is certain, that I will die, and sooner than I would like.

Dear God, take me into your arms on that most important day. May all other days be sad, if only that day may be happy. I tremble with fear at the prospect, yet I know that you, and you alone, can save me.

Set my whole heart on your promise of heaven. Guide my feet in your ways, O Lord, that I may walk the straight path towards eternal life. Let me cast off everything that holds me back on my journey there, so that all my strength may be directed towards that goal.

4.   GOD'S PERFECTION

Lord, you lack nothing, and have no need of anything I can give. But if I could imagine that you stood in need of anything, though it were to cost my life, though it were to mean the end of me and of everything in the world, I would still seek to supply it. If it were even remotely possible for you to grow in perfection, dear Lord, I should long for you to do so. It is all I should live for. Yet, for all that, such desires are far from my thoughts, because your utter perfection perfectly satisfies me, and it is beyond the realms of imagination to increase it.

5. MAN'S DESIRE

If only I possessed the grace, good Jesus, to be utterly at one with you! Amidst all the variety of worldly things around me, Lord, the only thing I crave is unity with you. You are all my soul needs. Unite, dear friend of my heart, this unique little soul of mine to your perfect goodness. You are all mine; when shall I be yours? Lord Jesus, my beloved, be the magnet of my heart; clasp, press, unite me for ever to your sacred heart. You have made me for yourself; make me one with you. Absorb this tiny drop of life into the ocean of goodness whence it came.

6. GOD'S PROVIDENCE

I do not eat, Lord, just because I am hungry, nor merely to give me pleasure. No, I eat because, in your providence, you have created me with the need for food.

When I must turn to a friend for help, I recognize that you have created man to help, comfort and encourage each other. And since this is your wish, I will turn to those whose friendship is your gift to me.

When I have good reason to be afraid of something, I recognize that you want me to be afraid, in order that I should take suitable steps to avoid danger. So I shall act on my fear, according to your will. If fear becomes excessive, I can turn to you, knowing that as your child I can nestle in your loving arms.

Thus, Lord, I try to do the right thing. And when I have done all I can, I know that whatever happens is an expression of your will.

7. MAN'S OFFERING

Lord, shall we delay any longer our offering to you of all that we have and all that we are? Shall we keep back any longer the complete gift of our free will, which we cling too so stubbornly? Shall we refuse to stretch out our will on the wood of your cross, to transfix it with the thorns and lance that pierced you? Let our will be swallowed up in the fire of your perfect, loving will! Let our will burn for all eternity as a sacrifice to you.

8.   · DEATH AND LOVE

Love or death! Death and love! Death to all other loves! I live only for your love, Lord Jesus, that I may escape eternal death. I live in your perfect love – you who has freed my soul from sin. I give my all to you. May you live and reign for ever.

Johann Freylinghausen
1670–1739

His Spiritual Songbook *provided the popular music of the German Pietist movement, which urged people to enter a personal relationship with Jesus as their saviour. The words of his hymns are mostly directed to Jesus, and are charged with the passion of a lover for the beloved.*

1.   WHO IS LIKE YOU?

Who is like you,
Jesus, sweet Jesus?

You are the light of those who are spiritually lost.
You are the life of those who are spiritually dead.
You are the liberation of those who are imprisoned by guilt.

You are the glory of those who hate themselves.
You are the guardian of those who are paralysed by fear.
You are the guide of those who are bewildered by falsehood.

You are the peace of those who are in turmoil.
You are the prince of those who yearn to be led.
You are the priest of those who seek the truth.

2.

KING, PROPHET AND PRIEST

Jesus, the mightiest king,
I will kiss your sceptre.
Jesus, the lowliest servant,
I will work by your side.

Jesus, the wisest prophet,
I will hasten to your teachings.
Jesus, the despised fool,
I will be reckless in your service.

Jesus, the great high priest,
I will receive your grace.
Jesus, the common carpenter,
I will stand with the poor.

3.

DRAW ME INTO YOURSELF

Draw me completely into yourself,
So that I might completely melt in your love.

Lay upon me, stamp upon me,
So that my stubborn pride might be destroyed.

Embrace me, kiss me,
So that my spiritual ugliness may turn to beauty.

Lock me into your chamber,
So that I might never stray from your presence.

4.

SEEING, KNOWING AND FEELING

May your Spirit guide my mind,
Which is so often dull and empty.

Let my thoughts always be on you,
And let me see you in all things.

May your Spirit quicken my soul,
Which is so often listless and lethargic.
Let my soul be awake to your presence,
And let me know you in all things.

May your Spirit melt my heart,
Which is so often cold and indifferent.
Let my heart be warmed by your love,
And let me feel you in all things.

5.   YEARNING FOR DEATH

Praise to you, O God,
That I have completed another step
Towards eternity.
With the movement of time
My heart moves closer to you,
And I long to reach your presence.

I count the hours, the days, the years
Until you take me to heaven.
Time seems never-ending.
I yearn for that which is mortal
To be swallowed up in you,
That I may become immortal.

O let that time come quickly.
Let me reach you before I tire,
Before my heart grows cold,
And my desire for you vanishes.
I am a bride ready for her groom,
A flower ready to be picked.

But I must leave the time
Totally to your choice.

The hour, the day and the year
Must be according to your will.
You above can know when I am truly ready
To be received into your presence.
O Jesus, my soul has already
Flown up to you.
Though my body remains on earth
Your Spirit has blown my spirit to heaven.
Let me forget the hours, the days, the years.
In truth I am already immortal.

6.   THE NIGHT IS HERE

The night is here.
Be near to me, dear Jesus.
Be a bright candle shining in the dark,
Driving the sin from my heart.

The day will come.
Hasten the dawn, dear Jesus.
Hasten the time when the sun of righteousness
Shines into the depths of my heart.

The moon casts her gentle rays.
Guide me, dear Jesus.
Guide my steps through this gloomy path
That I may arrive safely in heaven.

The stars glisten in the sky.
Teach me, dear Jesus,
Teach me to discern the truth amidst falsehood,
That even now I may see signs of your glory.

7.   ON GOING TO BED

As my head rests on my pillow
Let my soul rest in your mercy.

As my limbs relax on my mattress,
Let my soul relax in your peace.

As my body finds warmth beneath the blankets,
Let my soul find warmth in your love.

As my mind is filled with dreams,
Let my soul be filled with visions of heaven.

Fulbert of Chartres
c.970–1028

---

*The son of a peasant family in northern France, he
rose to become bishop of Chartres, renowned for his
witty and brilliant sermons, and for his mastery of
philosophical argument. Though outwardly he often
appeared proud and haughty, in his prayers he
remained acutely conscious of his lowly origins and
of the transience of worldly success.*

1.   LET ME BE FREE

Jesus Christ, the beginning and the end, the resurrection and the
life, the perfect man who gave his life for sinners, I worship you, I
adore you, I sing aloud your name. I am one of those whom you
saved, whom you set free, when you died on the cross. You redeemed me from the slavery of sin. And yet I cannot escape the
over-powering sense that I am still a wretched sinner, that my every
action is worthless or evil. I am like the dry sand of a desert thirsting
for water. I am like a criminal languishing in prison. Good people
try to help me, and I pray that you will reward them; but their
goodness does nothing to assuage my sense of wickedness. Patient
people try to teach me your ways; but I am so stubborn that I

cannot learn. Humble people seek to serve me; but in my pride I cannot truly appreciate their services. Lift the burden of wickedness; break down my stubbornness; root out my pride. Let me receive your life-giving love. Let me be free.

2. ## A PLEA FOR A SIGN

I come to you, dear Jesus, in my confusion, for I do not know what I should do, nor do I know how to be at peace. It was rash of me to have accepted a bishopric, for I fear I do my flock more harm than good. So I feel I should give up my position in favour of someone superior to me. And yet I remember that it was without the advantage of high birth or wealth that I rose to this great office. Thus I wonder if, in choosing someone of such humble origins and dire poverty, the Church was making your choice. Dear Lord, I will not resign my office as bishop without some sign from you, despite my many sins. Give me a sign.

3. ## GOD'S CARE

How brief is our span of life compared with the time since you created the universe. How tiny we are compared with the enormity of your universe. How trivial are our concerns compared with the complexity of your universe. How stupid we are compared with the genius of your creation. Yet during every minute and every second of our lives you are present, within and around us. You give your whole and undivided attention to each and every one of us. Our concerns are your concerns. And you are infinitely patient with our stupidity. I thank you with all my heart – knowing that my thanks are worthless compared with your greatness.

Dominic Gaisford

A monk of Worth Abbey, he spent seven years at their daughter house in Peru, before returning to Worth in 1988 as abbot. In this long conversation with God, he speaks with gratitude of his experience of regular daily prayer, and of his conviction that all can share the peace which prayer brings.

1.   I COME TO YOU IN PRAYER

Lord, you know I come to you in prayer in all sorts of moods and shapes. So often I come to you in duty bound and because I am dutiful and cold, I find you academic and cold; Lord, you know that our conversation then is a sort of skirmish, circling around the things that are troubling or irritating or weighing me down. It's all a heavy effort of will and I get bored by you – as you probably are with me. It's like talking to a member of my community who bores me and I feel I ought to talk because he and I have this radical link of belonging to each other. But the heart of me, my inner longings and interests, aren't really met or satisfied, so I leave feeling empty and yet satisfied in that I have done my duty. It's funny, Lord, but so often my prayer is like that.

How I want to be on fire with you and yet I am not. Why? Do I lack faith in you, Lord, as a real living person? I think I do. Am I so steeped in the mess of selfishness that I really have no time for you when you don't seem to give me what I want? I think this is part of the answer. I sometimes wonder – no, fear, but I don't like admitting this very often – that the root cause of my dull, frigid, dutiful praying is the nasty fact that I'm not good at loving, that I have a small heart. I love myself, yes, but can I love you, or indeed anyone, with that reckless absorbing passion that is so giddily wonderful? This reflection makes me curl up, Lord, when what I long for – I think I do truly long for it and it's not just make-believe – is to love you passionately, to hold your feet like Mary Magdalene in the garden and just look at you, saying, "Rabbi". Lord, you know that this is what I want but I haven't got this love in me to give you.

Lord, I think that what I really want from you in prayer is a huge pulsating heart to love you and other people, to live for you and others, be enraptured in you. But I don't seem to have it. I'm not being mock modest, Lord; my heart is small and fickle and you know it. I know this because there are so many things I want that aren't you, and if I don't have them my prayer is no satisfaction and my moods are governed not by you and prayer but by the emptiness I feel.

I think I used to be worried that you didn't seem to answer prayers, for myself, for friends, for all sorts of things large and small, but this doesn't really worry me now. I am often saddened, Lord, that you don't give good health or happiness or faith to the people I'm praying for, but this doesn't make me doubt you. It just makes me realize I don't comprehend you, I don't comprehend *how* you love others, or me, that you are a stupendous mystery; but I do believe that the only thing you have and can give is love, though I don't understand very often how you give it. You are mysterious.

But I think, Lord – no, I know it – that what you have given me over the years in prayer is a peace that is a yearning. In my inner heart, I am not bored by you at all, and you have helped me to understand, though I do it badly and fitfully as you know too well, how to love you, how to love others, how to work and how to accept myself. You sometimes suffuse all those jealousies and pettinesses, cruelties and lazinesses, that are part of the fibre of my being, with your peace, and I feel you are healing me and helping me to grow into your likeness. I thank you, Lord, that you have transformed and do transform my life. This is a lovely experience. My yearning is to have you do this totally now, though this all too often gets covered up and submerged in daily affairs. But it's there, and I can feel it growing in pain and am frustrated when it's not growing.

I think, Lord, that what you give me and everyone in prayer is a new vision, or a new dimension. The people I am fond of and love, the things I like doing, the places I like, are in some intangible way different, added to, increased by you. You don't possess or own anyone or anything in an obsessive, grasping, desperately clutching way, and this tender compassion is what you are slowly giving me in prayer, and it's wonderful. The people and places and activities (like golf!) which I love and like become different in you. The threats, menaces, pangs of loss and absence somehow don't matter when lapped around in your peace and your yearning, even though they hurt. But they hurt in a new way, the way you give us when you say, "Let not your hearts be troubled". And this is a wonderful revelation and I thank you for it.

Lord, I may be being heretical or untheological, but I don't mind and you know what I mean, when I say that your abiding presence – yes, that's it, Lord, prayer is your abiding presence made real – somehow takes the sting out of my sins. They matter but they also don't matter, because of you.

What I long for is for others, for everyone, to persevere in praying, in letting you yearn and groan and doubt and rejoice in their prayer. I want you to come alive in others so that they can taste and see you and have another vision and dimension in their living. In all the sorrow and bitterness and heaviness of heart I see in people, I yearn for them to find you in prayer. You don't make the pain or the problems less, but you make them different, you transform them. And this, Lord, is your peace. Please give it.

I don't know where all this outpouring has taken me, it's so full of "I", but I think it's shown me that prayer means that you come alive in the heart of everyone who prays. Your Spirit begins to take over and it's through you living, struggling to breathe in me, yearning, that I am coming to realize, in odd moments, that it is in prayer that we live and move and have our being.

Gemma Galgani
1878–1903

*During her short life she suffered persistent bouts of
illness. But through prayer she acquired a profound
spiritual tranquillity which remained undisturbed
even by the most severe physical pain. The joyful
simplicity of her writings, and her desire to share
with others the peace she had received, brought her
great popularity in her native Italy.*

1.   SWEET FIRE, SWEET FLAMES

Great God, how I love you; O, how I love you!
I feel myself burning; you are the fire that burns me.
O pain, O infinitely happy pain of love!
O sweet fire! O sweet flames!

You, O sweet Lord, have set my heart ablaze.
Your fire destroys my sinful self, reducing it to ashes.
Stop, stop! I cannot pull myself away from such fire.
No, let me stay! Let the fire consume me.

Come, Lord Jesus! My heart is now open to you.
All the sin that encrusted my heart is reduced to ashes.
Let your holy body take the place of my sinful body.
Let your Holy Spirit infuse my spirit.

2.   WALKING, HEARING, WATCHING, DYING, RISING

In my prayers, dear Jesus, I am with you wholly.
If I meditate on the cross, I suffer with you.

If I meditate on the resurrection, I rise with you.
So daily I die and rise.

If I walk with you along the hot dusty roads,
I become hot, sweaty, tired, as you surely did.
If I hear you preach, my ears tingle with excitement,
And my heart is pierced by the sharpness of your words.
If I watch you heal people, I can feel your touch,
So my own body trembles at your power.

Let me walk with you during every minute of my life,
Let me constantly be inspired by your words,
Let me daily be renewed by your power,
That I may die to sin and rise to perfect righteousness.

3.   MAY ALL SINNERS BE SAVED WITH ME

You know, O Lord, how ready I am to sacrifice everything
    to you.
I will bear every sort of pain for you.
I will give every drop of my blood to please your heart,
And to hinder the wicked schemes of sinners against you.

O Lord, do not abandon those poor sinners.
When you think of sinners, think also of me.
I want you to save them all, as you save me.
Let us all be saved together.

I want to pour out my blood on every place
Where people have slandered your good name.
I want my blood to mingle with yours, dear Jesus,
That all sinners may be saved with me, by you.

The Gelasian Sacramentary
c. 500

This is the oldest official prayer book of the Western Church. Parts of it were probably composed by Gelasius, who became pope in 492, but it also contains prayers from Gaul and Britain. Its most striking feature is its compilation of collects for the major festivals, many of which were adapted for use in later prayer books, including the Book of Common Prayer.

1.   THE PROMISE OF ADVENT

Stir up our hearts, we beseech you, to prepare ourselves to receive your Son. When he comes and knocks, may he find us not sleeping in sin, but awake to righteousness, ceaselessly rejoicing in his love. May our hearts and minds be so purified, that we may be ready to receive his promise of eternal life.

2.   THE MIRACLE OF CHRISTMAS

We marvel at the miracle, Lord, which you wrought when Jesus was born. She that gave him birth was a virgin, and he that was born was your child.

No wonder the heavens sang, the angels rejoiced, the wise men were transformed, the king was seized with fear, and the tiny children were crowned with the glory of martyrdom. He came to be our spiritual food, yet his mother fed him. He was the bread that came from heaven, yet he was laid in the manger like fodder.

Then the ox recognized its master and the ass its master. Then the Jews recognized their messiah and the Gentiles their saviour.

3. LENT

We beseech you, O Lord, that as our bodies grow weaker for lack of food during the season of fasting, so our souls may grow stronger. May we learn to fight more valiantly against evil, and strive more earnestly for righteousness. Thus, through abstaining from the fruits of the earth, may we bear more abundantly the fruits of your spirit.

4. PASSION-TIDE

O God, we pray that the burden of sin which we carry on our souls may be dissolved for ever in the blood of our Lord Jesus Christ. And, free from this deadly weight, may our souls rise with him to eternal life.

5. THE MIRACLE OF EASTER

The moment we have longed for has come; the night of our desires is here. What greater occupation could there be than for us to proclaim the power of your resurrection! This was the night when you shattered the gates of hell, and you took up the victory banner of heaven. This was the night when you set us among the stars.

When your mother Mary gave birth to you, she was overwhelmed with joy at your beauty. Now we are overwhelmed with joy at your power. The blood which flowed from your side has washed away our sins. Your body rising from the tomb has promised us eternal life. Eternal are the blessings which in your love you have poured upon us.

6. ASCENSION

O God, we give thanks that your Son Jesus Christ, who has shared our earthly life, has now ascended to prepare our heavenly life. Grant that, through coming to know him by faith on earth, we may come to know him by sight in heaven.

7. PENTECOST

We beseech you, O Lord, to ignite our souls with love, faith and hope by the fire of your Holy Spirit. And may the wind of your Spirit so inspire our minds, that we may proclaim your gospel to others in words which they can understand.

Paul Geres

This is a nom de plume of a French priest, who is in charge of a parish in an industrial city. These prayers are taken from Prayers for Impossible Days.

1. WHEN LIFE HAS BECOME ROUTINE

Lord, when I woke up this morning, I said to myself that this would be a day just like every other day. And it was.

I took the same tube train as every morning, I read the same comments in the paper on an international situation which never changes.

I went up the same staircase as usual, and on my desk I found the same piles of papers to go through – papers which have been exactly the same for almost ten years.

The porter was the same and so was the supervisor. They looked just as they usually do; they had that blank expression which says that nothing new is going to happen today.

For lunch I had the same old thing to eat. It was Monday. I went back to my desk until five o'clock. And then I just came home, knowing full well that tomorrow it will start all over again.

God, I'm tired of it all.

I had hoped for something completely different. I had dreamed that some day I would lead an active and exciting life. That was a dream. Yet it can be painful to wake up from a dream.

I'll never be anything but what I am. I know that some people would be happy in my situation. True. But that doesn't help my fatigue and boredom.

Lord, let me talk to you tonight about my fatigue, about my desire to get away from here. To whom can I speak about this, if not to you?

Nobody understands. They say, "What is he complaining about?". And perhaps they are right. It's only normal that you do your job.

Therefore I shall talk about it only with you.

Don't change anything. My life doesn't have to change. I must change.

Lord, help me to think less about myself. Help me to see that there are other people besides myself for whom today is just like every other day.

2.   WHEN YOU WORRY ABOUT MONEY

Lord, I have just balanced my cheque book. And now I must turn to you to find calm and peace. And dignity as well. This dignity which has been eroded for twenty years because of the awful worry about "making ends meet".

This peace which I'm deprived of for fear of not getting through another month. This calm which I lose when my small income disappears and I never have a penny left.

What I fear, Lord, is not really poverty. I'll survive one way or another.

What I'm afraid of is degradation. Afraid of no longer thinking of anything but money, just because I don't have any. Afraid of always making easy comparisons with others who earn more. And this a hundred times a day, in front of shop windows and at the counters of department stores.

Lord, I'm also afraid of jealousy. Afraid of saying, with a scornful grin, "Some people are just lucky . . .". Afraid of hatred also. And to top it all off, Lord, I've discovered that I'm getting greedy.

That's why I'm talking to you, Lord. To ask you for the grace to let me keep my dignity.

3.   FOR A SINNER WHO THOUGHT HE HAD CHANGED

Lord, nothing is going right tonight. I didn't think I was capable of this. I thought I had got rid of it. But, no!

This time I really feel like letting go of everything. If this is what it all comes to, I would rather give up at once. For you know, Lord, that I have tried.

What hurts me deep down is that I must give up the habit of thinking so highly of myself.

Lord, I must admit that the thing that bothers me most is my wounded pride.

Lord, I know it isn't good. But I would rather admit it to you directly, without beating about the bush. My regret isn't pure. I do regret my sin.

But what I regret most is myself. The self I thought had changed. The self that I was beginning to feel proud of – like Seneca, I believe it was, who visited his soul every evening and took pleasure in finding it in order.

Forgive me, Lord, for having loved myself more than you. For having put myself before you.

Teach me to bear my sin and not just drag it behind me. Help me to accept with courage that in your eye I am a sinner, and help me not to sulk about it like a little child.

Give me your forgiveness. For my sin. But also ... for my wounded pride.

Lord, I thank you for having made me realize that I am like all other men.

Kahlil Gibran
1883–1931

Born near Mount Lebanon, he became one of the most famous religious poets of the twentieth century. His most popular work, The Prophet, *has been translated into over twenty languages. His imagination spread far beyond the confines of any particular religious tradition. But in* Jesus, the Son of Man *he puts himself at the feet of Jesus, listening to his words and speaking to him.*

1.
MASTER LOVER

Master, Master Lover,
The Princess awaits your coming in her fragrant chamber,
And the married unmarried woman in her cage;
The harlot who seeks bread in the streets of her shame,
And the nun in her cloister who has no husband;
The childless woman too at her window,
Where frost designs the forest on the pane,
She finds you in that symmetry,
And she would mother you, and be comforted.

2.
MASTER POET

Master, Master Poet,
Master of our silent desires,
The heart of the world quivers with the throbbing of your
    heart,
But it burns not with your song.
The world sits listening to your voice in tranquil delight,
But it rises not from its seat

To scale the ridges of your hills.
Man would dream your dream, but he would not wake to
  your dawn,
Which is his greater dream.
He would see with your vision,
But he would not drag his heavy feet to your throne;
Yet many have been enthroned in your name
And mitred with your power,
And have turned your golden visit
Into crowns for their head and sceptres for their hand.

3.   MASTER OF LIGHT

Master, Master of Light,
Whose eye dwells in the seeking fingers of the blind,
You are still despised and mocked,
A man too weak and infirm to be God,
A God too much man to call forth adoration.
Their mass and their hymn,
Their sacrament and their rosary, are for their imprisoned
  self.
You are their yet distant self, their far-off cry, and their
  passion.

4.   MASTER SKY-HEART

But Master, Sky-heart, Knight of our fairer dream,
You do still tread this day;
Nor bows nor spears shall stay your steps;
You walk through all our arrows.
You smile down upon us,
And though you are the youngest of us all
You father us all.

Gilbert of Hoyland
Died c.1170

*Abbot of the Cistercian monastery of Swineshead
in Lincolnshire, he wrote a series of treatises, epistles
and sermons inspired by St Bernard of Clairvaux.
Most of his work seems turgid to the modern reader,
but occasionally when he turns to address God there
is a vivid freshness to his words.*

1.   COME TO US

When, good Lord, will you manifest yourself to us in bright sunshine? Yes, we are slow to understand and slow to see. But we are
quick to believe; and we believe that if you chose to reveal yourself
to us, you could do so this very day.

Dear Lord, please appear to us, at dawn or at dusk or at the
height of day. Come to our table at mealtimes, that we may share
our meals with you. Come to our bed, that we may share our rest
with you. Come to us at our prayers, that we may rejoice and be
glad.

2.   RIVER AND SKY

Move our hearts with the calm, smooth flow of your grace. Let the
river of your love run through our souls. May my soul be carried
by the current of your love, towards the wide, infinite ocean of
heaven.

Stretch out my heart with your strength, as you stretch out the
sky above the earth. Smooth out any wrinkles of hatred or resentment. Enlarge my soul that it may know more fully your truth.

3.   GREY CLOUDS

When we see dark grey clouds forming in the sky, we fear a mighty
storm. In the same way when we see the darkness of our sin, we
fear the storm of your wrath. But just as in truth rain brings new life
to the earth, so you rain down mercy on our sinful souls, bringing
forgiveness and peace. Be to us always like a mighty storm, raining
down upon us the abundant waters of your mercy.

Elizabeth Goudge
1900–1984

---

*The daughter of an Anglican clergyman, she made
her name as a popular novelist, displaying in her
books both deep compassion for human suffering,
and unshakeable faith in the power of good over
evil. This same compassion and faith is expressed
in her* Diary of Prayer.

1.   TEACH US TO LOVE

Lord, we thank thee for all the love that has been given to us, for
the love of family and friends, and above all for your love poured
out upon us every moment of our lives in steadfast glory. Forgive
our unworthiness. Forgive the many times we have disapppointed
those who love us, have failed them, wearied them, saddened them.
Failing them we have failed you, and hurting them we have
wounded our Saviour who for love's sake died for us. Lord, have
mercy on us, and forgive. You do not fail those who love you. You
do not change nor vary. Teach us your own constancy in love, your
humility, selflessness and generosity. Look in pity on our small and
tarnished loving, protect, foster and strengthen it, that it may be
less unworthy to be offered to you and to your children. O Light
of the world, teach us how to love.

2.   TEACH US TO PRAY

O Saviour of the world, teach us how to pray for those who are lost in desolations of darkness without the knowledge of the mercy that is yourself. We remember the innocent victims of war and all the agony they suffer, those who are sunk in the wretchedness of sin and can find no deliverance, those in despair, those beset by temptation, those who are greatly afraid, those who have been overwhelmed by torment of mind or body. Save us from the cowardice that would turn away from the thought of these things, from the indifference that would pass them by. Give us penitence for the evil in ourselves which has added to the darkness of the world, and if there be any small thing we can do to lighten any misery, show us what it is and help us to do it. Teach us how to pray with the compassion which is not afraid to suffer with those who suffer and, if need be, to enter into darkness with them.

O Everlasting Mercy, who once in time came from the height of heaven down to the depth of our need, come again in power to forgive us and renew us and set us on fire, that through the labours and prayers of broken-hearted sinners your mercy may banish the darkness and bring new life upon the earth.

Gregory of Nazianzus
329–389

An anxious and melancholic man, he pioneered a more personal, intimate style of prayer. Until his time prayers had tended to be formal and scriptural, composed for public worship. He, however, wrote prayers for private use, through which the individual can express his deepest feelings to God.

1.   ## WHAT NAME SHALL I CALL YOU?

O transcendent, almighty God,
What words can sing your praises?
No tongue can describe you.
No mind can probe your mystery.
Yet all speech springs from you,
And all thought stems from you.
All creation proclaims you,
All creatures revere you.
Every gust of wind breathes a prayer to you,
Every rustling tree sings a hymn to you.
All things are upheld by you.
And they move according to your harmonious design.
The whole world longs for you,
And all people desire you.
Yet you have set yourself apart,
You are far beyond our grasp.
You are the purpose of all that exists,
But you do not let us understand you.
Lord, I want to speak to you.
By what name shall I call you?

2.   ## AT DAWN

I rise and pledge myself, Lord,
That this day I shall do no evil deed,
But offer every moment as a sacrifice to you.
I blush when I remember my sinfulness,
I shudder to recall how I have betrayed you.
Yet you know that now I want only to serve you.
Make me this day your devoted slave.

3.   ## AT NIGHT

Lord Jesus, you are light from eternal lights.
You have dissolved all spiritual darkness

And my soul is filled with your brightness.
Your light makes all things beautiful.

You lit the skies with the sun and the moon.
You ordered night and day to follow each other
    peaceably.
And so you made the sun and the moon friends.
May I be friends with all whom I meet.

At night you give rest to our bodies.
By day you spur us on to work.
May I work with diligence and devotion,
That at night my conscience is at peace.

As I lay down on my bed at night,
May your fingers draw down my eyelids.
Lay your hand of blessing on my head
That righteous sleep may descend upon me.

4.   IN SICKNESS

Christ, give me strength; your servant is not well.
The tongue that praised you is made silent,
Struck dumb by the pain of sickness.
I cannot bear not to sing your praises.
O, make me well again, make me whole,
That I may again proclaim your greatness.
Do not forsake me, I beseech you.
Let me return now to your service.

5.   IN DEPRESSION

The breath of life, O Lord, seems spent.
My body is tense, my mind filled with anxiety,
Yet I have no zest, no energy.
I am helpless to allay my fears
I am incapable of relaxing my limbs.
Dark thoughts constantly invade my head,
And I have no power to resist them.

Was ever an oak tree buffeted by wind,
As the gales of melancholy now buffet my soul?
Was ever a ship tossed by the waves,
As my soul is now tossed by misery?
Did ever the foundation of a house crumble,
As my own life now crumbles to dust?

Friends no longer want to visit me.
You have driven away my spiritual brethren.
I am now an outcast from your church.
No longer the flowers want to bloom for me.
No longer the trees come into leaf for me.
No longer the birds sing at my window.

My fellow Christians condemn me as an idle sinner.
Lord, raise up my soul, revive my body.

6. BEFORE READING SCRIPTURE

Lord, as I read the psalms let me hear you singing. As I read your
words, let me hear you speaking. As I reflect on each page, let me
see your image. And as I seek to put your precepts into practice,
let my heart be filled with joy.

Lady Jane Grey
1537–1554

*A young woman who was both brilliant and devout,
she was declared queen at the age of sixteen, in
an attempt to prevent her Roman Catholic cousin,
Mary, from ascending the throne. She was a reluctant monarch, and after nine days was deposed by
Mary's allies and committed to the Tower of*

*London, where she was beheaded. Shortly before her
death she composed a prayer in which her intense
emotions are expressed with great dignity and com-
posure.*

1.   CONSIDER MY MISERY

O merciful God, consider my misery, best known unto thee; and
be thou now unto me a strong tower of defence, I humbly require
thee. Suffer me not to be tempted above my power, but either be
thou a deliverer unto me out of this great misery, or else give me
grace patiently to bear thy heavy hand and sharp correction. It was
thy right hand that delivered the people of Israel out of the hands
of Pharaoh, which for the space of four hundred years did oppress
them, and keep them in bondage; let it therefore likewise seem
good to thy fatherly goodness, to deliver me, sorrowful wretch, for
whom thy Son Christ shed his precious blood on the cross, out of
this miserable captivity and bondage, wherein I am now. How long
wilt thou be absent? For ever? O Lord, hast thou forgotten to be
gracious, and hast thou shut up thy loving kindness in displeasure?
Wilt thou be no more entreated? Is thy mercy clear gone for ever,
and thy promise come utterly to an end for evermore? Why dost
thou make so long tarrying? Shall I despair of thy mercy? O God,
far be that from me; I am thy workmanship, created in Christ Jesus.
Give me grace therefore to tarry thy leisure, and patiently to bear
thy works, assuredly knowing, that as thou canst, so thou wilt deliver
me, when it shall please thee, nothing doubting or mistrusting thy
goodness towards me; for thou knowest better what is good for me
than I do. Therefore do with me in all things what thou wilt, and
plague me what way thou wilt. Only, in the meantime, arm me, I
beseech thee, with thy armour, that I may stand fast, my loins being
girded about with verity, having on the breast-plate of righteousness, and shod with the shoes prepared by the gospel of peace;
above all things, taking to me the shield of faith, wherewith I may
be able to quench all the fiery darts of the wicked; and taking the
helmet of salvation, and the sword of thy spirit, which is thy most
holy word; praying always, with all manner of prayer and suppli-
cation, that I may refer myself wholly to thy will, abiding thy plea-

sure, and comforting myself in those troubles that it shall please thee to send me; seeing such troubles be profitable for me, and seeing I am assuredly persuaded that it cannot but be well all thou doest.

Guigo the Carthusian
d.1188

As superior of the Carthusian religious order, he saw his main task as encouraging mystical prayer amongst his monks. He saw prayer not as a withdrawal from the material world, but rather as a means through which material objects become windows onto God. Thus his writings and prayers are filled with metaphors, bringing together the material and spiritual realms.

1.   A GRAPE, A WELL, A SPARK, A SEED

Lord, how much juice you can squeeze from a single grape.
How much water you can draw from a single well.
How great a fire you can kindle from a tiny spark.
How great a tree you can grow from a tiny seed.
My soul is so dry that by itself it cannot pray;
Yet you can squeeze from it the juice of a thousand prayers.
My soul is so parched that by itself it cannot love;
Yet you can draw from it boundless love for you and for my
    neighbour.
My soul is so cold that by itself it has no joy;
Yet you can light the fire of heavenly joy within me.
My soul is so feeble that by itself it has no faith;
Yet by your power my faith grows to a great height.
Thank you for prayer, for love, for joy, for faith;
Let me always be prayerful, loving, joyful, faithful.

2. A DROP OF HEAVENLY RAIN

Lord you are invisible, except to the pure of heart.
I seek to understand true purity of heart
By reading the Scriptures and by meditating.
Lord, I have read your words and meditated on your person
For more years that I can remember.
I long to see you face to face.
It is the sight of you, Lord, that I have sought.
Over the years the fire of desire to see you
Has grown hotter and hotter.
As I have meditated, my soul has received greater light.
And the Scriptures excite my soul more than ever.
Lord, I do not dare to call you
To reveal yourself now or soon.
But give me a sign, a pledge
To ensure me that one day I will be rewarded.
Give me a single drop of heavenly rain
To assuage my spiritual thirst.

Joseph Hall
1574–1656

Although a distinguished bishop and a royalist, he was Puritan in both his beliefs and his austere pattern of life; thus he was distrusted by both sides in the English Civil War, and ended his days in lonely penury. Early in his career, while still an obscure country parson, he wrote The Art of Divine Meditation *in which he taught that true Puritans had much to learn from the monastic and mystic approach to spirituality. His own prayers, while unmistakably Puritan, could equally have been written by a medieval mystic.*

1.   A HEARTY WISH OF THE SOUL

O Lord, that I could wait and long for thy salvation! O that I could
mind the things above, that as I am a stranger in deed, so I could
be also in affection! O that mine eyes, like the eyes of the first
martyr, could by the light of faith see but a glimpse of heaven! O
that my heart could be rapt up thither in desire! How should I
trample upon these poor vanities of the earth! How willingly should
I endure all sorrows, all torments! How scornfully should I pass by
all pleasures! How should I be in travail of my dissolution! O, when
shall that blessed day come when, all this wretched worldliness
removed, I shall solace myself in my God?

2.   THE SOUL'S DESIRE FOR LIBERTY

Thus I desire, O Lord, to be aright affected towards thee and thy
glory. I desire to come to thee, but alas, how weakly, how heart-
lessly! Thou knowest that I can neither come to thee nor desire to
come but from thee. It is nature that holds me from thee; this
treacherous nature favours itself, loveth the world, hateth to think
of a dissolution, and chooseth rather to dwell in this dungeon with
continual sorrow and complaint than to endure a parting although
to liberty and joy. Alas, Lord, it is my misery that I love my pain.
How long shall these vanities thus beset me? It is thou only that
canst turn away mine eyes from regarding these follies and my heart
from affecting them. Thou only, who as thou shalt one day receive
my soul in heaven, so now beforehand canst fix my soul upon
heaven and thee.

3.   THE SOUL'S DESIRE FOR LIGHT

O, let me not always be thus dull and brutish; let not these scales
of earthly affection always dim and blind mine eyes. O, thou that
layedst clay upon the blind man's eyes, take away this clay from
mine eyes, wherewith (alas) they are so daubed up that they cannot
see heaven. Illuminate them from above, and in thy light let me see
light. O, thou that hast prepared a place for my soul, prepare my
soul for that place; prepare it with holiness, prepare it with desire.

And even while it sojourneth on earth, let it dwell in heaven with thee, beholding ever the beauty of thy face, the glory of thy saints and of itself.

4.   A PLEDGE TO WALK WITH GOD

I see man walketh in a vain shadow and disquieteth himself in vain; they are pitiful pleasures he enjoyeth while he forgetteth thee. I am as vain, make me more wise. O, let me see heaven and I know I shall never envy nor follow them. My times are in thine hands; I am no better than my fathers, a stranger on earth. As I speak of them, so the next, yea, this generation shall speak of me as one that was. My life is a bubble, a smoke, a shadow, a thought; I know it hath no abiding in this thoroughfare. O, suffer me not so mad as while I pass on the way I should forget the end. It is that other life that I must trust to. With thee it is that I shall continue.

5.   A MEDITATION ON DEATH

Yea, O my Lord, it is thou that must raise up this faint and drooping heart of mine. Thou only canst rid me of this weak and cowardly distrust. Thou that sendest for my soul canst prepare it for thyself; thou only canst make thy messenger welcome to me. O that I could but see thy face through death! O that I could see death not as it was but as thou hast made it! O that I could heartily pledge thee, my Saviour, in this cup, that so I might drink new wine with thee in thy Father's kingdom!

But alas, O my God, nature is strong and weak in me at once. I cannot wish to welcome death as it is worthy; when I look for most courage, I find strongest temptations. I see and confess that when I am myself, thou hast no such coward as I. Let me alone and I shall shame that name of thine which I have professed. Every secure worldling shall laugh at my feebleness. O God, were thy martyrs thus nailed to their stakes? Might they not have been loosed from their racks but chose to die in those torments? Let it be no shame for thy servant to take up that complaint which thou mad'st of thy better attendants, "the spirit is willing but the flesh is weak".

O thou God of spirits that has coupled these two together, unite them in a desire of their dissolution. Weaken this flesh to receive and encourage this spirit either to desire or to contemn death. And now as I grow nearer to my home, let me increase in the sense of my joys. I am thine, save me, O Lord.

Dag Hammarskjöld
1905–1961

When he was serving as Secretary-General of the United Nations, he gave the impression of being an agnostic humanist. So it was a great surprise, when, after his death in a plane crash, there was found in his apartment the manuscript of Markings, recording his "negotiations with myself – and with God." He was deeply influenced by the Christian mystics, and the prayers which pepper his book have the naked honesty of someone truly confronting his Maker.

1.   1954

Let me finish what I have been permitted to begin.
Let me give all without any assurance of increase.
The pride of the cup is in the drink, its humility in the serving.
What, then do its defects matter?

Thou who hast created us free, Who seest all that happens – yet art confident of victory.
Thou who at this time art the one among us who suffereth the uttermost loneliness,
Thou – who art also in me,
May I bear thy burden, when my hour comes,
May I –

Thou who art over us,
Thou who art one of us,
Thou who art –
Also within us,
May all see thee – in me also,
May I prepare the way for thee,
May I thank thee for all that shall fall to my lot,
May I also not forget the needs of others,
Keep me in thy love
As thou wouldest that all should be kept in mine.
May everything in this my being be directed to thy
    glory
And may I never despair.
For I am under thy hand,
And in thee in all power and goodness.

Give me a pure heart – that I may see thee,
A humble heart – that I may hear thee,
A heart of love – that I may serve thee,
A heart of faith – that I may abide in thee.

Righteous in thine eyes,
With thy courage,
Within thy peace.

2.   1955

Before thee in humility, with thee in faith, in thee in peace.

3.   1956

Before thee, Father,
    In righteousness and humility,
With thee, Brother,
    In faith and courage,
In thee, Spirit,
    In stillness.

Thine – for thy will is my destiny,
Dedicated – for my destiny is to be used and used up according to
thy will.

For thy holy life is our way, and your adorable patience the road
by which we must approach thee.

4.   1957

In thy wind – in thy light –
    How insignificant is everything else, how small are we – and how
happy in that which alone is great.

5.   1958

So shall the world be created each morning anew, forgiven – in
thee, by thee.

Didst thou give me this inescapable loneliness so that it would be
easier for me to give thee all?

                   Lord – thine the day,
                   And I the day's.

6.   1961

                   Have mercy
                   Upon us.
                   Have mercy
                   Upon our efforts,
                   That we
                   Before thee,
                   In love and in faith,
                   Righteousness and humility,
                   May follow thee,
                   With self-denial, steadfastness and courage,

And meet thee
In the silence.

Give us
A pure heart
That we may see thee,
A humble heart
That we may hear thee,
A heart of love
That we may serve thee,
A heart of faith
That we may love thee,

Thou
Whom I do not know
But whose I am.

Thou
Whom I do not comprehend
But who hast dedicated me
To my fate.
Thou –

Bernard Häring
1912–

A leading Roman Catholic theologian from the Black Forest region of Germany, he was advisor to Pope Paul during the Second Vatican Council. Beneath the rigorous logic of his theological writings lies the conviction that truth ultimately can only be known through a warm personal relationship with God.

1. HUMILITY

My dear Lord and Saviour, I come to you burdened and oppressed by many worries and slavish work, by an unbearable yoke, which I have imposed on myself because of my lack of humility. It is a burden which I have deserved, but it is also the heavy yoke of a sinful world, of collective pride and arrogance. We are tied together in this lamentable condition. I groan and sigh, realizing my plight in this double slavery of mine and of the world. What a relief if I listen to your invitation, "Come to me all whose load is heavy"! Yes, now I dare to come.

The more I meditate on the crushing burdens you have carried in your humility, accepting even the most atrocious humiliation from proud and arrogant human beings, the more I am filled with grateful wonder. In your divine glory and your human humility you are totally Other, so different from the close-mindedness and high-handedness of man. You are the wholly Other, the only true God, so unlike man-made gods. You have come into the valley of tears where misery is constantly multiplied by humankind's ridiculous pride. You come with the astonishing remedy, the humility of the Son of God, of the Redeemer, who has freely made himself "one-of-us" in all things except sin: the totally holy and humble One.

You come to us whose vanity and pride are odious. You come on the royal road of humility, showing us that this is the way to you and to the heart of the Father, the way to the hearts of our fellow men and the way of salvation.

Humble heart of our Divine Master, I entrust myself to your school. I want to learn from you, day by day, the royal way of humility. It is our own love that teaches us.

Lord, transform our hearts, make them mirror images of your own heart. Make them fountains of healing for many. Lord, make us humble.

2. ZEAL

Lord, I yearn to decide firmly and forever to love you with all my heart, and I am ashamed that in the past I have often offended you by inconsistency and half-heartedness. Looking at your loving heart

I begin to realize the greatness of this injustice. I see it as injustice to your love and majesty. If I love you with only half my heart, I have not yet really acknowledged you as my God. I see also now that it is a terrible injustice to humankind, which is so much in need of credible witnesses, people who show by their lives what it is to adore God.

O faithful heart of Jesus, change us, enlighten and strengthen us in this time of separation. Help all Christians to join together in strong faith and faithful love, so that the world may believe and find the truth of life, the trust that an infinitely merciful God is concerned with fatherly love for all his creatures. O Lord, free the godless from their misery and emptiness.

Beloved Saviour, it is terrible to see that in spite of the alarming signs of the times so many Christians are apathetic and lazy. Awaken us all, fill us with new zeal and enthusiasm and show us the most effective ways to proclaim faith in you and in the heavenly Father.

3.   VICTORY

O Divine Heart filled with love, you have won my heart. You have widened it, enlivened and enriched it with your most powerful gift, your gracious and attractive love. To you I entrust myself.

The world wants to entice me with dreams of success, achievements and other vain victories. Help me to be vigilant in the fight against these seductions. Grant me wisdom, so that I may have only one thing in mind: the victory of your love in my heart, in my conduct and in the world around me.

It is good that painfully I had to experience my weakness, for now nothing remains for me but to put all my trust in you. If I realize and fully acknowledge that I can do nothing in the realm of saving love but long for it with all my heart and pray for it, then I may not doubt that I shall be admitted to the triumphal procession of those who eternally celebrate with you the victory of your love in us.

My Saviour, humankind needs love; everyone's heart is made for abiding love. We need witnesses of your saving love whose hearts have become fountains of its "living water". Lord, help us to become ever more "light to the world", increase in us faith in your love and trust in its final victory.

George Herbert
1593–1633

After a brief and flamboyant political career which ended when the king turned against him, he became a country parson. His religious poems date from the period immediately after his political fall, and they describe with the most vivid imagery both his joy and his anguish. Two of his poems, The Elixir *and* The Call, *which are addressed to God, have frequently been set to music as hymns.*

1.
THE ELIXIR

Teach me, my God and King,
In all things thee to see,
And what I do in any thing,
To do it as for thee.

Not rudely, as a beast,
To run into an action;
But still to make thee prepossest
And give it his perfection.

A man that looks on glass,
On it may stay his eye;
Or if he pleaseth, through it pass,
And then the heav'n espy.

All may of thee partake:
Nothing can be so mean,

Which with this tincture (for thy sake)
Will not grow bright and clean.

A servant with this clause
Makes drudgery divine:
Who sweeps a room as for thy laws,
Makes that and th' action fine.

This is the famous stone
That turneth all to gold:
For that which God doth touch and own
Cannot for less be told.

2.

THE CALL

Come, my Way, my Truth, my Life:
Such a Way, as gives us breath:
Such a Truth, as ends all strife:
And such a Life, as killeth death.

Come, my Light, my Feast, my Strength:
Such a Light, as shows a feast:
Such a Feast, as mends in length:
Such a Strength, as makes his guest.

Come, my Joy, my Love, my Heart:
Such a Joy, as none can move:
Such a Love, as none can part:
Such a Heart, as joys in love.

3.

BITTER-SWEET

Ah my dear angry Lord,
Since thou dost love, yet strike;
Cast down, yet help afford;
Sure I will do the like.
I will complain, yet praise;
I will bewail, approve;

And all my sour-sweet days
I will lament, and love.

4.   DISCIPLINE

Throw away thy rod,
Throw away thy wrath;
          O my God,
Take the gentle path.

For my heart's desire
Unto thine is bent;
          I aspire
To a full consent.

Not a word or look
I affect to own,
          But by book,
And thy book alone.

Though I fail, I weep;
Though I halt in pace,
          Yet I creep
To the throne of grace.

Then let wrath remove;
Love will do the deed;
          For with love
Stony hearts will bleed.

Love is swift of foot;
Love's a man of war,
          And can shoot,
And can hit from far.

Who can 'scape his bow?
That which wrought on thee,
          Brought thee low,
Needs must work on me.

Throw away thy rod;
Though man frailties hath,
Thou art God.
Throw away thy wrath.

Hilary of Poitiers
c.310–367

Brought up as a pagan, he came to Christianity through reading the Scriptures. And although he was married, the Christians in Poitiers chose him as their bishop. The need for faith arose, he believed, not from sin but from ignorance; and through constant prayer in which the individual conducts a continuous conversation with God, true knowledge, based on divine love, is achieved.

1.   DRAWN TO FAITH

The poverty and imperfection of my language do not so undermine my thoughts about you that I am reduced to silence. Your Word is translated, by your Holy Spirit, into my words in which I can proclaim your truth. Your Wisdom is brought down to the level of my mind, that I may offer guidance to others. Your Virtue is expressed in the small good deeds that you enable me to perform.

When I see your sea surging so wonderfully, and I reflect that I cannot understand the origin of water or its measured movements, I am drawn to faith – because only you could have created the sea and its waves. When I see all the trees and flowers in the earth, and I reflect that I cannot understand how they grow and multiply, I am drawn to faith – because only you could have created the trees and flowers. When I look at myself, and I reflect that I cannot understand how my mind and body work, I am drawn to faith –

because only you could have created mankind. Ignorance of myself does not prevent me from knowing and worshipping: on the contrary, ignorance of the mysteries of myself and of all things around me tells me that I depend wholly on you to create and sustain all life.

2.   HOISTING MY SAILS

The chief service I owe you, O God, is that every thought and word of mine should speak of you. The power of speech which you have bestowed on me can give me no greater pleasure than to serve you by preaching your gospel.

But in saying this, I am merely expressing what I want to do. If I am actually to use this gift, I must ask you for your help – ask you to fill the sails I have hoisted for you with the wind of your Holy Spirit, inspiring my mind and my voice. I know that I am often heavy with stupor, so that I am too lazy to speak of you. And I do not spend sufficient time studying your Scriptures, to ensure that my words conform to your Word. Give me the energy and the courage to share the spirit of the apostles, that like them I may truly be an ambassador of your grace.

3.   SATURATED IN HIS LOVE

Although I am dust and ashes, Lord, I am tied to you by bonds of love. Therefore I feel I can speak freely to you. Before I came to know you, I was nothing. I did not know the meaning of life, and I had no understanding of myself. I have no doubt that you had a purpose in causing me to be born; yet you had no need of me, and on my own I was of no use to you.

But then you decided that I should hear the words of your Son, Jesus Christ. And that as I heard his words, you enabled his love to penetrate my heart. Now I am completely saturated in his love and faith, and there is no remedy. Now, Lord, I cannot change my attitude to my faith; I can only die for it.

Hildegard of Bingen
1098–1179

*Born into a noble family, she received supernatural
visions even as a child. At the age of eighteen she
became a nun, and rose to become abbess of
Rupertsberg, near Bingen, on the Rhine. Her most
famous work,* Scivias, *is a series of visions, which
include denunciations of the world and prophecies
of disaster. In her response to these visions, she
acknowledges to God her own spiritual ugliness and
despair, begging him for virtue and joy. She also
wrote songs in which she expresses herself to God in
far happier and lighter tones. She herself set them
to music, and they gained wide popularity.*

1.   WHO WILL HELP ME?

Where am I? How did I get here? Whom can I ask to comfort me?
How will I break these chains of sin that enslave me? Whose eye
can bear to look at these ugly spiritual wounds that disfigure me?
Whose hands will anoint me with oil that I may be healed? Who
will help me unless it is you, O God?

Whenever I think of the glorious freedom which you promise,
my slavery to sin seems even more oppressive. Whenever I think
of the beauty of your Son, my spiritual ugliness seems even more
terrible. Whenever I think of the joyful music of your love, my soul
sinks into despair.

Dear God, what will become of me?

2.

THE FLAMING DOVE

I beg you, O God, to reveal to me the mystery of your love. Let
your love be to me a new dawn at the end of a long night of gloom.
Let your love be to me a new plan, showing the way of spiritual
slavery. And let that plan be so simple that I can understand and
follow it. Your love is like a white dove with orange flames bursting
from its wings. The dove brings the promise of peace to my
troubled soul, and the flames promise joy to my miserable heart.

3.

THE FLAMING DRAGON

Most strong God, who is able to fight against you? I want you to
help me fight against the flaming dragon of sin within me, that eats
away my very soul. I want to have the strongest sword in my hand,
fashioned by you, with the sharpest blade that will cut through the
dragon's scales. And when I have slayed the dragon within myself,
I want to offer a safe refuge for all who, like me, are frail and
vulnerable. I will give them a sword to slay their own dragons, so
that together we may live in joy and peace.

4.

THE POISONOUS THORNS

How rigid and inflexible I am! I can overcome my own stubbornness
only with the greatest difficulty. And yet when I beg you for help,
you seem to do nothing. Are you ignoring me on purpose? Are you
waiting for me to take the thorns of sin from my flesh before you
will assist me? Yes, I know I must dig out these thorns before they
poison and destroy me completely. But I cannot do it without you.

5.

LILIES AND ROSES

Dear God, I want you to plant every virtue in my heart, as if you
were planting roses and lilies of every colour in a field. And I want
you to water those flowers with your Holy Spirit. If any thorns or
thistles of vice sprout amongst the flowers, I want you to root out
those weeds. And I want you to prune and cut back those flowers,

regardless of the pain I will suffer, that they may grow more strongly. Finally I want seeds from those flowers to blow into other souls, that they too may share the beauty which you alone can give.

6.   THE SPIRIT AND THE LAMB

Beautiful God, strip from me this ugly, dirty coat of sin, and put on me the bright, pure garment of Spirit.

Brave God, drive from me the growling wolves of corruption that threaten to attack me, and bring to my side your gentle Lamb who can always protect me.

7.   LIMBS OF CHRIST

O eternal God,
Turn us into the arms and hands,
The legs and feet
Of your beloved Son, Jesus.
You gave birth to him in heaven
Before the creation of the earth.
You gave birth to us on earth,
To become his living body.
Make us worthy to be his limbs,
And so worthy to share
In his eternal bliss.

8.   THE LOVE THAT GIVES LOVE

Jesus Christ, the love that gives love,
You are higher than the highest star;
You are deeper than the deepest sea;
You cherish us as your own family;
You embrace us as your own spouse;
You rule over us as your own subjects;
You welcome us as your dearest friend.
Let all the world worship you.

9.   THE LIFE THAT GIVES LIFE

Holy Spirit, the life that gives life.
You are the cause of all movement;
You are the breath of all creatures;
You are the salve that purifies our souls;
You are the ointment that heals our wounds;
You are the fire that warms our hearts;
You are the light that guides our feet.
Let all the world praise you.

Hippolytus
c.190–c.236

---

*His eucharistic prayers, composed in the third-
century, have profoundly influenced twentieth-
century liturgical writers. Both the new Roman
Catholic Mass and the new Anglican Communion
Service are based on the* Apostolic Tradition, *as
his liturgy came to be called. His hymn for Easter
was widely used throughout the western church. He
served as a priest in Rome, but was deported during
a persecution to Sardinia where he died.*

1.   AT THE CONSECRATION

We give you thanks, O God, through your dear child, Jesus Christ,
who in these last days you sent to save us and instruct us. He is
your word, inseparable from you; you made all things through him,
and you were well pleased with him.

You sent him from heaven to a virgin's womb. He lay in that
womb and took flesh, and you were presented with a Son, born of
the Holy Spirit and of a virgin. He did what you wanted him to do.
When he suffered, he stretched out his hands to free those who

believed in you from suffering. When he died he destroyed death, breaking the chains of the Devil which held us and crushing hell beneath his feet. When he rose again he gave light to the righteous, revealing his new covenant with mankind.

Thus, calling to mind his death and resurrection, we offer you bread and wine, thanking you for enabling us to stand before you and serve you. We ask you to send down your Holy Spirit on the offering which we make to you, uniting all who receive Holy Communion in the bond of your truth.

2.   BEFORE RECEIVING THE BREAD AND WINE

Almighty God, Father of our Lord Jesus Christ, we beg you that when we receive this sacred mystery it may bring us blessing. May Christ's body and blood not bring condemnation upon us, but rather ennoble all who receive it.

Eternal God, to whom that which is invisible is as clear as that which is visible: before you your people bow their heads, submitting to you their hard hearts and unruly bodies. Send down blessings from your glorious dwelling on these men and women, lending to their prayers a ready ear. Hold them upright with your strong hand, controlling all their evil passions. Preserve their bodies and souls, filling them with faith in your gospel and awe at your majesty.

3.   EASTER, OUR MARRIAGE CEREMONY

You have protected us, Jesus, from endless disaster.
You spread your hands over us like wings.
You poured your blood over the earth,
Because you loved us.
The anger which we deserved you turned away from us
And restored us to friendship with God.

The heavens may have your spirit, paradise your soul,
But the earth has your blood.
We celebrate the coming of your Spirit always:
The Spirit leads the mystic dance throughout the year.
But Easter comes and goes.

Power came from heaven to raise you from death,
So that we and all creatures could see you.
All living things gather round you at Easter.
There is joy, honour, celebration, delight.

The darkness of death is driven away.
Life is restored everywhere.
The gates of heaven are thrown open.
In you, risen Jesus, God has shown us himself,
So we can rise to him as gods.
The gates of hell are shattered.
In you, risen Jesus, those already dead rise to life,
Affirming the good news of eternal life.
Now your promise has been fulfilled.
Now the earth is singing and dancing
Easter is our marriage ceremony.
At Easter, dear Jesus, you make us your brides.
Sealing the union with your Spirit.
The great marriage hall is full of guests,
All dressed for the wedding.
No one is rejected for want of a wedding dress.
We come to you as spiritual virgins,
Our lamps are fresh and bright, with ample oil,
The light within our souls will never go out.
The fire of grace burns in us all.

We pray you, our sovereign Christ,
Stretch out your strong hands over your whole church
And over all your faithful people.
Defend, protect, and preserve them,
Fight and do battle for them,
Subdue the invisible powers that oppose them.
Raise now the sign of victory over us
And grant that we may sing the song of triumph.
May you rule for ever and ever.

Henry Scott Holland
1847–1918

A canon at St Paul's Cathedral and later a pro-
fessor of divinity at Oxford, he sought in his writ-
ings and sermons to apply socialist political ideas
to a Christian morality. Yet beneath his radical
thinking was a troubled soul that sought peace and
comfort in a personal relationship with Christ.

1.   IN THEE I PUT MY TRUST

Not only in the high places of thy revelation do I find thy tokens!
Not only at the close of my long pilgrimage do I throw myself upon
thy heart, or fall before thy feet! Not only there, but from afar I
greet thee; from the lowest levels of my rational soul! In thy name,
even there, I move forward! By faith in thee, from the first hour, I
set out! Upon thee did I cast myself when first my thought stirred
itself into life! Thine arms, even then, were under me! In thee did
I put my trust!

2.   LAY HOLD OF US

O Jesu, in whom we all may be made desirable! O Lord, redeemer
and saviour, prince of all holiness and peace! We have sinned, we
have done amiss, we have fallen, we have gone astray, we are not
worthy so much as to gather up the crumbs under the table of God!
Enter thou, therefore, into our souls. Possess our spirits with thy
spirit, our body with thy body, our blood with thy blood. Feed us
with thyself, who art perfect righteousness. Lay hold of us by thy
grace, who art the truth and the life. Uplift us, mould us, transform
us by thy own power into thyself, into the image of the holy and
the eternal. We will shrink from no suffering, we will endure all,

in the energy of thy broken body and outpoured blood, if only we may be drawn upward into the likeness of thyself, into the joy of thy holiness! Fill us with sorrow, if so only thou canst fill us with thyself: for only by abiding in thee, only by eating thy flesh and drinking thy blood, only by fastening on the grace of thy perfect, holy, and sufficient oblation, can we hope to pass from death into life, and to be raised up at the last day from the lowliness of the grave to the holiness of heaven!

3.
TEACH US TO REPENT

O Lord Jesus, thou, whom we, by our sins, have robbed of that good gift of joy, which might have been thine! Thou, whom we have forbidden to partake of flesh and blood, except at the bitter cost of that agony and blood-sweat! O holy, merciful, all-forgiving redeemer, teach us more worthily to repent of the terror and horror of our fall, by the memory of that innocent gladness with which we should have gone with thee to the altar of God, to offer there, no sorrow-stricken, death-stained, sin-worn sacrifice, but the un-shrinking homage of a spotless heart!

Michael Hollings
1921–

A Catholic priest in London, his spiritual writings combine acute political and social awareness with traditional Catholic spirituality. Many of his prayers are composed with Etta Gullick.

1.
TORTURE

I don't understand how people do the horrible things to each other which I read about in the newspapers. I find it hard to believe that they can torture each other the way they seem to, because they have different political views or different religious beliefs. But eye-witnesses tell me it really happens.

Lord, I cry to you to help those who inflict such injuries. Take hatred from their hearts; give them understanding of the evil they do.

Strengthen the persecuted; give them courage and a firm belief in you.

Give me and all who try to serve you the desire to serve the suffering and fill us with the love which will defeat the power of evil in the world.

2. RACISM

I read the other day, Lord, about some lion cubs. They were different from others because they were white.

I think their parents accepted them – did other tawny yellow lions look down on them or persecute them, Lord?

If so, then I hate this animal instinct; but, if not, why do we who are intelligent human animals – homosapiens – fear, hate, dislike and despise other humans who are coloured differently from us? Help us to be colour-blind, Lord.

3. POLITICIANS

Lord, I know I should pray for our rulers, and statesmen and women, but they seem hopeless and beyond praying for. Yet I know quite well we have to pray for those who despitefully use us, and you never thought people were so bad as to be impossible to save. But didn't you have your doubts about the Pharisees? Probably you prayed about them a lot but the Bible doesn't tell us how.

Teach us how to pray for politicians, and give me faith to keep on praying in the hopes that you will give them wisdom and eyes to see beyond their own party to the wider world, and encourage them to work for the good of all mankind.

Gerard Manley Hopkins
1844–1889

He became a Roman Catholic in 1866, and joined the Jesuits two years later. His poetry found no favour amongst his superiors, and he destroyed much of what he wrote. But when the surviving poems were published after his death, their emotional intensity and their verbal brilliance won a wide audience. While all his poetry has a spiritual basis, he composed a number of poetic prayers which have by his standards an innocent simplicity.

1.
LET ME BE TO THEE

Let me be to thee as the circling bird,
Or bat with tender and air-crisping wings
That shapes in half-light his departing rings,
From both of whom a changeless note is heard.
I have found my music in a common word,
Trying each pleasurable throat that sings
And every praisèd sequence of sweet strings,
And know infallibly which I preferred.

The authentic cadence was discovered late
Which ends those only strains that I approve,
And other science all gone out of date
And minor sweetness scarce made mention of:
I have found the dominant of my range and state –
Love, O my God, to call thee Love and Love.

2.   O GOD, I LOVE THEE

O God, I love thee, I love thee –
Not out of hope of heaven for me
Nor fearing not to love and be
     In the everlasting burning.
Thou, thou, my Jesus, after me
     Didst reach thine arms out dying,
For my sake sufferedst nails and lance,
Mocked and marrèd countenance,
     Sorrows passing number,
     Sweat and care and cumber,
Yea and death, and this for me,
     And thou couldst see me sinning:
Then I, why should not I love thee,
Jesu so much in love with me?
Not for heaven's sake; not to be
Out of hell by loving thee;
Not for any gains I see;
But just the way that thou didst me
I do love and I will love thee:
What must I love thee, Lord, for then? –
For being my king and God. Amen.

3.   THOU ART INDEED JUST, LORD

Thou art indeed just, Lord, if I contend
With thee; but, sir, so what I plead is just.
Why do sinners' ways prosper? And why must
Disappointment all I endeavour end?

Wert thou my enemy, O thou my friend,
How wouldst thou worse, I wonder, than thou dost
Defeat, thwart me? Oh, the sots and thralls of lust
Do in spare hours more thrive than I that spend,

Sir, life upon thy cause. See, banks and brakes
Now, leavèd how thick! lacèd they are again
With fretty chervil, look, and fresh wind shakes

Them; birds build – but not I build; no, but strain,
Time's eunuch, and not breed one work that wakes.
Mine, O thou lord of life, send my roots rain.

4.   MOONLESS DARKNESS

Moonless darkness stands between.
Past, the Past, no more be seen!
But the Bethlehem-star may lead me
To the sight of him who freed me
From the self that I have been.
Make me pure, Lord: thou art holy;
Make me meek, Lord: thou wert lowly;
Now beginning, and alway:
Now begin, on Christmas day.

Ignatius of Loyola
c.1491–1556

---

*Born into an aristocratic family in the Basque
region of Spain, he began his career as a soldier.
But after a severe wound in 1521 he decided to
devote his life to Christ. During his long convales-
cence he began writing* The Spiritual Exercises,
*based on his own experiences. It consists of a series
of meditations, designed to lead souls to overcome
their passions and fight as spiritual soldiers for
Christ. In 1538 he and six companions formed the
Society of Jesus – which came to be known as the
Jesuits – putting themselves at the Pope's service.*

*The Spiritual Exercises formed the basis of Jesuit
training, enabling men to go to the remotest corners
of the globe as missionaries. Within* The Spiritual
Exercises *are three short prayers which embody
the Jesuit spirit.*

1.   SELF OFFERING

Lord of all things, I offer myself to you. I offer not only my labour,
but also my affections and emotions. I am willing to defy my own
sensitivities and desires in your service, with your grace and favour.
I make this offering in the presence of your infinite Goodness, and
of your glorious Mother, and of all the holy men and women in
your heavenly court. I wish to imitate you in bearing all injuries
and insults, and in enduring material and spiritual poverty, in order
to serve and praise you. I beg you to receive my offering, and to
show me how to imitate you.

2.   TAKE AND RECEIVE

Take, Lord, and receive all my freedom, my memory, my intelli-
gence and my will – all that I have and possess. You, Lord, have
given those things to me. I now give them back to you, Lord. All
belongs to you. Dispose of these gifts according to your will. I ask
only for your love and your grace, for they are enough for me.

3.   TEACH ME

Dearest Lord, teach me to be generous. Teach me to serve you as
you deserve; to give and not to count the cost; to fight and not to
heed the wounds; to toil and not to seek for rest; to labour and not
to seek reward, save that of knowing that I do your will.

Jacopone da Todi
c.1230–1306

Until the age of forty-seven he worked as a lawyer in Umbria. But when his wife died he adopted the life of a beggar, in imitation of St Francis of Assisi, wandering from place to place singing hymns which he himself composed. Ten years later he became a Franciscan lay brother, but soon broke away from the main order to form a separate community in which Francis' rule was followed with the utmost strictness. For a period the Pope imprisoned him for his outspoken opposition to papal corruption. But he continued to write hymns of passionate devotion to Christ.

1.　　SUFFERING THROUGH CHRIST

Why do you wound me, Lord, with your cruel charity?
Why do you bind me with the ropes of your love?
My heart trembles, and my soul cracks and breaks,
Why do you cast me into the furnace of suffering?
Like wax melting under heat, I feel I am melting into death.

Before I knew the nature of your love, O Christ,
Before I suspected your cruelty, O Lord,
I begged you to pour your grace upon me,
Confident that it would bring gentle peace,
That my soul would soar to a great height,
Leaving pain far behind.

Yet the torment which I now experience
Is far harsher than I could have imagined.

The searing heat which rends my heart
Makes the hottest summer's day seem like cold winter.
Your love is beyond image or description.
If death offered an escape, I would gladly die.

For your love, O Lord, I have renounced all.
Indeed I would have traded the world for you.
I would have exchanged all creation to know you.
Yet now you drive me out of my senses.
You are dragging me down to the lowest depths,
Where there is only misery,
And you have made me powerless to resist.
I have sold myself entirely to you.
Stones will turn to liquid before you let me go.
Iron will turn to butter before you release me.
If only, Lord, I could be separated from your love.
Yet not even a blazing fire could prise us apart.

1.   ECSTASY THROUGH CHRIST

Lord, you take me beyond the reach of suffering.
You have taken me to a sphere beyond death itself.
I look down on all creation and bask in its peace.
Dear Christ, how did you bring me to this wonderful place?
You embraced me, and carried me here in your arms.
Your beauty swept my heart and soul upwards,
Taking me out of myself and out of my natural senses.

Once I felt I was melting under the heat of anguish.
Once all hope of happiness had left me.
Now I melt under the heat of your warm joy,
And my present bliss excludes even the memory of past
    misery.

You have stripped me of my former self, O Christ,
And you have dressed me in your holy self.
My soul wears the garment of your eternal glory.
My body wears the indelible mark of your blessing.
I am drowning in ecstasy.

I am a new creature, Lord, reborn in you.
Your grace rises up and rushes through my veins.
You re-fashion my heart, as a sculptor fashions a statue,
Shaping it in the perfect image of love.

Once you drove me mad with suffering.
Now you madden me with joy.

Philip Jebb

*A monk at Downside, where he eventually became
Head Master of the school, he experienced as a
novice a severe breakdown. During this time he
found relief in composing prayers in which he
struggles to relate his faith to his suffering.*

1.   LORD, I CONFESS

Lord, I confess that you are good, and that to you all gentleness
and love belong. And when there comes upon me the great pain of
my heart and head, it is to you that I must look, and the look must
be one of love, not reproach. If any should be reproachful it is you,
who have stretched out your hands all the day and I would not.

O Lord, my God, I stand upright when I should bow and kneel:
how else can I learn but through the humbling discipline of pain –
and that (at first) the least of pains, which is in the body.

Let me not forget that pain is our work, and is the token which
has the power of being honoured in much gold. You have said that
those you love you chastise. Can it be that you love me? That
cannot be – and yet, it must be, for yours is the true love, which
stretches forth its hands all the day.

Do you remember when I longed for death, and thought to be,
in one brief hour, with you in Paradise? And do you remember how

that changed, and how I saw that I was standing penniless before your door? And how in fear I prayed for life?

What now? Life is a pain indeed, but it makes for Death. Still am I penniless. But you are rich, and you and I (but how, O God? O, to see that mystery!), you and I are one.

But if you and I are one, then my pain is your pain, and since the pain is your love, why then, it is my love. And if I have your love when I feel your pain then surely have I overcome the world.

Lord, I am a poor fool: teach me the Wisdom which played before the eternal hills. Teach me the Wisdom which is Love divine, and give me the Trust which brings your Peace.

O Lord, show me gratitude, for I am yours.

2.   MY LORD, MY ALL

Dear Lord, my Lord, my all, make me to want, to want to need ever and ever so much more. Was there fatigue? Let the nights become shorter. Hunger and thirst? Let food and drink be withheld. Longing for love and companionship? Let there be rejection and forgetfulness – so be the longing, the desire, the want be increased; the capacity grow beyond limit.

A chance to give? The power to be generous? Yes: and a thousand times more.

I have so little time, so little space.
Take from me, that I may give.
Open wide that wound to let your Spirit in.
I must watch, I must wait, I must need, I must beg.
You live in the darkness. So be it.
Ah, grant me but this: that I stand in want
Till that want is so wide that only you can fill it.
Keep me from safe, warm acquiescence. Give me urgency and the raging spirit.
Take all, that I may be all for you, that all from me may mean all from you, all for you.
May you be my all, in all.
Only your strength, your vision, your command, your wilderness.
Mine to follow after.

I fear, even as I say it, but I confess
I hold,
I affirm.

Jeremiah

7th century BC

---

*Throughout his long ministry he warned the people
of Judah of the catastrophe that would befall them
unless they repented of their idolatry and sin; and
his prophecy was fulfilled when the Babylonian
army destroyed Jerusalem, and took the people into
exile. He was a sensitive man who hated having to
pronounce judgement; and he frequently turned to
God in desperation at his own plight.*

1.   QUESTIONING GOD'S JUSTICE

Lord, if I argued my case with you, you would prove to be right.
Yet I must question you about matters of justice. Why do the
wicked prosper? Why do dishonest men succeed? You plant them,
and they take root; they grow and bear fruit. They always speak
well of you, but they do not really care about you.

But you, Lord, know me; you see what I do, and how I love you.
Drag these evil men away like sheep to the slaughter, and set them
apart until the day of their death.

2.   A DESPERATE PLEA

Lord, have you utterly rejected Judah? Do you hate the people of
Zion? Why have you hurt us so badly we cannot be healed? We
looked for peace, but nothing good happened. We hoped for healing, but terror came instead.

We confess that we have sinned against you, as our forefathers did. Do not spurn us. Do not bring disgrace on Jerusalem, the place of your glorious throne. Do not break the covenant you have made with us. None of the false gods of other nations can send rain, and the sky by itself cannot make showers fall. We put our trust in you, Lord, because you alone can do these things.

3.　　　THE PROPHET'S DILEMMA

Lord, you have deceived me, and I was deceived. You are stronger than I am, and you have overpowered me. Everyone jeers at me, mocking me all day long.

Whenever I speak, I have to cry out "Violence! Destruction!". Lord, I am ridiculed and scorned all the time, because I proclaim your message. But when I say, "I will forget the Lord, and no longer speak in his name" then your message is like a fire burning deep within me. I am weary of trying to contain that fire.

I hear people whispering, "Terror is on every side! Denounce him to the authorities!" Even my close friends are watching for my downfall. "Perhaps he can be tricked," they say, "then we can catch him and get revenge".

But you, Lord, are on my side, strong and mighty, and those who persecute me will fail. They will be disgraced for ever, because they cannot succeed, and their disgrace will never be forgotten.

Almighty Lord, you test me justly. You know what is in their hearts and minds. Let me see you take revenge on my enemies, for I have placed my cause in your hands.

John of the Cross
1542–1591

As a young Carmelite friar he met Teresa of Ávila, and under her influence set about reforming the Carmelite order, seeking to restore the primitive simplicity of the first friars. He founded fifteen new houses throughout Spain for friars who shared his zeal, but met strong opposition amongst those who preferred a more comfortable life. He was imprisoned in Toledo, where he wrote a number of poetic prayers, including The Spiritual Canticle. *These, plus a number of prose works including* The Dark Night of the Soul, *have come to be regarded as amongst the finest mystical works ever written.*

1.   REVEAL YOURSELF

I no longer want just to hear about you, beloved Lord, through messengers. I no longer want to hear doctrines about you, nor to have my emotions stirred by people speaking of you. I yearn for your presence. These messengers simply frustrate and grieve me, because they remind me of how distant I am from you. They reopen wounds in my heart, and they seem to delay your coming to me. From this day onwards please send me no more messengers, no more doctrines, because they cannot satisfy my overwhelming desire for you. I want to give myself completely to you. And I want you to give yourself completely to me. The love which you show in glimpses, reveal to me fully. The love which you convey through messengers, speak it to me directly. I sometimes think you are mocking me by hiding yourself from me. Come to me with the priceless jewel of your love.

2.   TEARING OFF THE MASK

Dear Lord, give me the truths which are veiled by the doctrines and articles of faith, which are masked by the pious words of sermons and books. Let my eyes penetrate the veil, and tear off the mask, that I can see your truth face to face.

3.   I DIE BECAUSE I DO NOT DIE

O Lord, listen to my plea
With each new day comes death.

I can no longer endure the darkness of my life.
I die because I do not die.

For what purpose do I still draw breath?
The only purpose is to delay the pains of death,
But my life is as painful as death.
I die because I do not die.

A fish out of water finds both suffering and relief.
At first he suffers mortal pain,
But then, as the fire of pain fades, death brings relief.
I die because I do not die.

To assuage my pain I gaze on you,
In the form of the holy bread and sacred wine.
But my heart sinks because I cannot see your face.
I die because I do not die.

If I look forward to the joy of heaven,
When I shall at last see you face to face,
My present pain at your absence grieves me more.
I die because I do not die.

Draw me out of death's dark lair.
Make me free to live in your sight.
At present my soul is as dark as night.
I die because I do not die.

I long to be taken from this dark earth,
I long to be released from this dark body.
Then I shall cry out with ecstatic joy.
I live because I live in you.

4. WHY ARE YOU WAITING?

Lord God, my beloved, if you still remember my sins, and so with-
hold the blessing for which I yearn, I beg you either to punish me
as I deserve, or to have mercy on me. If you are waiting for me to

behave well and do good to others, then give me the strength and
the will to act as you want.

Why are you waiting? Why do you delay in pouring out the love
for which I yearn? How can I behave well and love others, if you
do not strengthen and guide me? How can I be worthy of you, if
you do not make me worthy? How can I rise up to you, if you do
not raise me up?

Surely you will not take from me the grace which you gave me
in your dear Son Jesus Christ? Surely the love which he revealed
to all mankind will be granted to me? Why are you waiting?

The earth and the heavens are mine! All the people in the world,
righteous and sinful alike, are mine! The angels, the saints and the
martyrs, are mine! All these are mine because I would offer them
all to you, in exchange for your love.

I give you my life, my all! Why are you waiting to receive it?

5.   FLAME OF THE SPIRIT

O flame of the Holy Spirit, you pierce the very substance of my
soul and cauterize it with your heat. You love me so much, that
you have put into my heart the hope and the knowledge of eternal
life. Earlier my prayers never reached your ears, because my love
was so weak and impure; so, although I yearned for you, and begged
you to warm my cold heart, you could not hear me. But now you
have chosen to come to me, and my love burns with such passion
that I know you hear my every prayer. I pray what you want me to
pray; I desire what you want me to desire; I do what you want me
to do. You have freed me to be your slave.

6.   PLEASURE IN TORMENT

Who but you, Lord, could bring sweetness in the midst of bitterness, pleasure in the midst of torment? How wonderful are the
wounds in my soul, since the deeper the wound, the greater is the
joy of healing!

7.   HAND OF GOD

O Lord of God, you are as generous as you are powerful, as kind as you are rich. How powerfully and richly you pour out your gifts upon me! O soft hand of God, you lay your hand so softly on my soul. Yet if you were to press the world with your hand, all creatures would perish. If you were to look at the world with anger, the whole earth would quake and the mountains crumble to pieces. And yet you treat me so gently, so softly, so lovingly. You have the power of life and death over all creatures. And yet you put aside that power. Instead you allow my soul to be wounded by sin, in order to give me the joy of being healed by your touch. You slay in me that which should be slain; and in this way you save me for your life.

Samuel Johnson
1709–1784

Famous for compiling the first English dictionary, he was a staunch high Anglican who composed sermons for others to preach and prayers for his private use. His personal life was frequently dissolute and chaotic, but through the majestic prose of his prayers he expressed his higher aspirations. He wrote a most moving series of prayers in response to the death of his wife.

1.   COMPILING THE DICTIONARY

O God, who hast hitherto supported me, enable me to proceed in this labour, and in the whole task of my present state; that when I shall render up, at the last day an account of the talent committed to me, I may receive pardon.

2.

STUDYING RELIGION

Almighty God, our heavenly Father, without whose help labour is useless, without whose light search is vain, invigorate my studies and direct my enquiries, that I may, by due diligence and right discernment, establish myself and others in thy holy faith. Take not, O Lord, thy Holy Spirit from me, let not evil thoughts have domination in my mind. Let me not linger in ignorance, but enlighten and support me.

3.

PRACTISING TEMPERANCE

O God, grant that I may practise such temperance in meat, drink, and sleep, and all bodily enjoyments, as may fit me for the duties to which thou shalt call me. And by thy blessing procure me freedom of thought and quietness of mind, that I may so serve thee in this short and frail life, that I may be received by thee at my death to everlasting happiness. Take not, O Lord, thy Holy Spirit from me, deliver me not up to vain fears, but have mercy on me.

4.

HIS WIFE'S DEATH – AFTER A MONTH

O Lord, our heavenly Father, almighty and most merciful God, in whose hands are life and death, who givest and takest away, castest down and raisest up, look with mercy on the affliction of thy unworthy servant, turn away thine anger from me, and speak peace to my troubled soul. Grant me the assistance and comfort of thy Holy Spirit, that I may remember with thankfulness the blessings so long enjoyed by me in the society of my departed wife. Make me so to think on her precepts and example, that I may imitate whatever was in her life acceptable in thy sight, and avoid all by which she offended thee. Forgive me, O merciful Lord, all my sins, and enable me to begin and perfect that reformation which I promised her, and to persevere in that resolution, which she implored thee to continue. And now, O Lord, release me from my sorrow, fill me with just hopes, true faith, and holy consolations, and enable me to do my duty in that state of life to which thou hast been pleased to call me, without disturbance from fruitless grief, or tumultuous imaginations; that in all my thoughts, words, and actions, I may glorify thy Holy Name.

5.   HIS WIFE'S DEATH – AFTER TWO YEARS

Almighty God, vouchsafe to sanctify unto me the reflections and resolutions of this day, let not my sorrow be unprofitable; let not my resolutions be vain. Grant that my grief may produce true repentance, so that I may live to please thee, and when the time shall come that I must die like her whom thou hast taken from me, grant me eternal happiness in thy presence.

Ben Jonson
1573–1637

As a young man he worked as a bricklayer, then as a soldier, and finally as an actor. He killed a fellow actor in a duel, and while in prison for this deed he wrote his first major play. He also became a Roman Catholic though later he returned to Anglicanism. In his day his plays were compared with those of Shakespeare. Amongst his poems are two prayers of repentance.

1.   TO HEAVEN

Good and great God, can I not think of thee
        But it must, straight, my melancholy be?
Is it interpreted in my disease
        That, laden with my sins, I seek for ease?
O be thou witness, that the reins dost know
        And hearts of all, if I be sad for show,
And judge me after, if I dare pretend
        To aught but grace, or aim at other end.

As thou art all, so be thou all to me,
First, midst, and last, converted, one and three;
My faith, my hope, my love; and in this state
My judge, my witness, and my advocate.
Where have I been this while exil'd from thee,
And whither rap'd, now thou but stoop'st to me?
Dwell, dwell here still, O being everywhere,
How can I doubt to find thee ever, here?
I know my state, both full of shame and scorn
Conceiv'd in sin, and unto labour born,
Standing with fear, and must with horror fall,
And destin'd unto judgement, after all.
I feel my griefs too, and there scarce is ground
Upon my flesh t'inflict another wound.
Yet dare I not complain, or wish for death
With holy Paul, lest it be thought the breath
Of discontent; or that these prayers be
For weariness of life, not love of thee.

2.

TO GOD THE FATHER

Hear me, O God!
A broken heart
Is my best part;
Use still thy rod,
That I may prove
Therein, thy Love.

If thou hadst not
Been stern to me,
But left me free,
I had forgot
My self and thee.

For sin's so sweet
As minds ill bent
Rarely repent,

Until they meet
Their punishment.

Who more can crave
Than thou hast done,
That gav'st a Son
To free a slave?
First made of nought,
With all since bought.

Sin, Death, and Hell
His glorious Name
Quite overcame,
Yet I rebel
And slight the same.

But I'll come in
Before my loss,
Me farther toss,
As sure to win
Under his Cross.

Julian of Norwich
c.1332–c.1420

Her Revelations of Divine Love, *recalling a series of fifteen visions she received during a serious illness, ranks today as one of the most popular spiritual works ever written. She is homely and gentle, yet uncompromising in her devotion to God. The book contains only one passage of prayers, in which she tussles over the problem of sin, which constantly disturbed her.*

1.

THE PROBLEM OF SIN

Good Lord, I can see that you are real truth. And I know that we sin grievously every day of our lives, and are most blameworthy. I can never hide from you the truth about myself. Yet I never see you blame us. How is this?

Since you do not seem to blame us, perhaps there is no such thing as sin. Yet surely such thinking is wrong, and I am ignorant of the truth. On the other hand, if we are sinners, terrible blame hangs over us.

Good Lord, how is it that I cannot see the truth about sin? My God and my Creator, you know that I yearn to see all truths about you.

Kalahari Bushmen

By Western standards, they are extremely primitive, depending on hunting wild animals and gathering roots and berries. But as missionaries have found, their traditional religion has much in common with Christianity. In particular they believe in a supernatural creator who listens to and answers prayer.

1.

YOU ARE THE MASTER

Lord, Lord, you are the Lord.
You created all things.
You are the master of the forest.
You are the master of the animals.
You are our master, and we your servants.
You are the master of life and death.
You rule, we obey.

2.

FOR A NEWBORN CHILD

I lift up this newborn child to you.
You brought it to birth, you gave it life.
This child is a fresh bud on an ancient tree,
A new member of an old family.
May this fresh bud blossom.
May this child grow up strong and righteous.

3.

FOR PROTECTION AGAINST SNAKES

When the foot in the night stumbles,
Let the obstacle not rear up and bite.
There are many branches strewn across our path
Which threaten no harm to the clumsy foot.
Protect against those sharp-toothed branches
That spring to life and kill.

4.

ON A JOURNEY

Keep us safe from every ill,
Every mishap, every pain.
Let no men or animals attack us.
Lord, bring us safely home.

Margery Kempe
c.1373–c.1432

---

*She composed the first autobiography in English,
dictated to a priest because she herself was illiterate.
She describes with searing honesty her bouts of madness, her tears and anger and her sexual anxieties.
But through her psychological turmoil emerges a
woman of profound prayer, who would lay every*

joy and every misery before God. After abandoning
her husband, whom she regarded with contempt,
she travelled Europe in search of spiritual enlight-
enment. She was disappointed by the priests and
bishops she met, but learnt to see Christ in ordinary
people. Finally she returned to her native King's
Lynn, where her husband was now an invalid and
she devoted her old age to nursing him. Her prayers
punctuate her book in response to her moods and
circumstances.

1.

A PLEA FOR MERCY

Lord I ask for your mercy. Chastise me for my sins and purge me
of all evil, that I may be saved from everlasting damnation. I am
willing, even happy, to endure any suffering here on earth, that I
may be spared the torments of hell.

2.

GIVE ME STRENGTH

Lord God, you know all things. You know how much I long to be
chaste, that I may give my whole self, body and soul, to you. And
you know how I struggle to abstain from meat and strong drink,
that my mind may be pure for you. I desire never to go against
your will; so whenever I fail to keep your commands, I am overcome
with sorrow. Now, blessed Jesus, make your will known to me at
all times, and give me the strength to obey it.

3.

YOU RAN AFTER ME

Ah, Lord, virgins are now dancing merrily in heaven. Shall I not
do so? I fear not, because I am not a virgin. I wish I had been killed
as soon as I had been taken from the font, so that I would never
have displeased you. Then you would have had my perpetual virginity. Ah, dear God, I have not loved you for all my life, and now I
bitterly regret the time when I ignored you. I ran away from you.
Yet you ran after me, so now, for all my impurity, you have given
me hope.

4.   AT MASS

Lord, make my eyes walls of tears, that when I receive your body tears of devotion may pour down my cheeks. You are my joy, Lord, my bliss and my comfort. You are all the treasure I have in this world. I want no earthly pleasures; I want only you. And so, dearest Lord, let your body which I now receive be your pledge that you will never forsake me, for all eternity.

5.   DURING A SERIOUS ILLNESS

Dear Lord, you suffered so much pain in order to save me and all mankind from sin. Yet I find it hard to bear even this little pain in my body. Lord, because of your great pain, have mercy on my little pain. And if you wish me simply to bear the pain, send me the patience and the courage which I lack. It may seem strange to say it, but I would rather suffer the spiritual pain from the insults people hurl against me, in place of this physical pain. Indeed I enjoy spiritual pain suffered for your sake; and I happily embrace the disrespect of this world, so long as I am obeying your will. But in my feebleness, I cannot endure this present illness. Save me from it.

6.   A CONSTANT PETITION

Ah, blessed Lord, I wish I knew how I might best love you and please you, and that my love were as sweet to you as your love is to me.

7.   A RESPONSE TO PERSECUTORS

Beloved Lord Jesus, do not punish any of those who insult and persecute me. You know well that I desire no vengeance, but I ask mercy and grace for all people – if that be your will. Nevertheless it would be better that you inflict some punishment on them now, rather than you condemn them to eternal punishment after death. Lord, my soul tells me that you are full of love, for you do not wish to condemn anyone. You want all people to be saved. And since you wish all to be saved, I must wish the same. I wept and cried out for many years, begging to be saved. Now I must wish the salvation of others, even if they hate me.

8.   A PLEA FOR THE FAITHLESS

Lord, you say that no man may be drawn to you unless you draw him. Therefore, Lord, I pray that you will draw all people to you, regardless of how sinful they are. I never deserved to be drawn to you, Lord, and yet in your great mercy you drew me. If people around me knew my great wickedness as you do, they would marvel at the great goodness you have shown to me. If you can make such an unworthy creature as me worthy to be your servant, then you can turn the lowest sinner into the highest saint. I beg that you will turn all sinners into saints.

9.   A RESPONSE TO INVOLUNTARY CRYING

Lord, why do you make me cry out loud, when I am in a public place? It causes them to condemn me as mad or stupid, and so they cannot see that I am really your most faithful servant. In particular, I beg you to prevent me from crying during sermons. When I cry listening to holy preaching, I have no choice but to run away; so my cries bar me from hearing your doctrines. And I fear that one day I will be arrested and put in prison, so I will hear no more sermons. If I must cry, please ensure that I only cry in the privacy of my bed-chamber.

10.   A FINAL THANKSGIVING

I thank you, Lord, for all the sins which I have not done, because you restrained me. I thank you for the sorrow I have felt for all the sins I have done. I thank you for all the people I have met, both friends and enemies. And I pray for them all, that they may all be your friends.

Thomas Ken
1637–1711

As a bishop he saw his primary task as teaching ordinary people how to pray. To this end he composed Directions for Prayers, *addressed to "the poor inhabitants within the diocese". It offered a precise method of daily prayer which consists of a series of "ejaculations" to be said at particular moments throughout the day. Since these ejaculations are so short and simple, Ken believed that those who were illiterate should learn them by heart from their priests. Before becoming a bishop Ken served as chaplain at Winchester College where he wrote prayers in the form of hymns including his evening hymn which remains popular.*

1. ## GOING TO BED

I will lay me down in peace, and take my rest; for it is thou, Lord, only, that makest me dwell in safety.

2. ## RISING FROM BED

I laid me down and slept, and rose up again, for thou Lord, sustained me: all love, all glory, be to thee.

3. ## GOING OR COMING

Lord, bless my going out and coming in, from this time forth, for evermore.

4.   MEALS

Lord, grant that whether I eat or drink, or whatever I do, I may do
all to thy glory.

5.   WORK

Prosper thou the works of my hands, O Lord; O, prosper thou my
handiwork.

6.   AT THE MARKET

Lord, give me grace to use this world so as not to abuse it. Lord,
grant that I may never go beyond or defraud my brother in any
matter; for thou art the avenger of all such.

7.   AT ANY TIME

Wherever I am, whatever I do, thou, Lord, seest me: O, keep me
in thy fear all day long.

Lord, give me grace to keep always a conscience void of offence
towards thee and towards men.

Lord, teach me so to number my days, that I may apply my heart
to wisdom.

O, let my mouth be filled with thy praise, that I may sing of thy
glory and honour all the day long.

8.   GLORY TO THEE, MY GOD, THIS NIGHT

            Glory to thee, my God, this night
            For all the blessings of the light;
            Keep me, O keep me, King of kings,
            Beneath thy own almighty wings.

            Forgive me, Lord, for thy dear Son,
            The ill that I this day have done,
            That with the world, myself, and thee
            I, ere I sleep, at peace may be.

Teach me to live, that I may dread
The grave as little as my bed;
Teach me to die, that so I may
Rise glorious at the awful day.

O may my soul on thee repose,
And with sweet sleep mine eyelids close,
Sleep that may me more vigorous make
To serve my God when I awake.

When in the night I sleepless lie,
My soul with heavenly thoughts supply;
Let no ill dreams disturb my rest,
No powers of darkness me molest.

Søren Kierkegaard
1813–1855

---

*Born into a wealthy Lutheran family, he spent
almost all his life in his native Copenhagen. His
philosophical writings, which have come to be
regarded as the origin of modern existentialism,
arose from his own prolonged spiritual crisis, in
which he struggled to make sense of his faith. He
came to regard subjective experience as the only
source of truth. To him Jesus was not an historical
figure, but a contemporary spiritual figure with
whom he could communicate directly.*

1.   CHRIST'S INFINITE PATIENCE

Through your whole life, O Lord Jesus Christ, you suffered that I
might be saved. And yet your suffering is not at an end. For still
you have to bear with me, stumbling as I walk along the path,

and constantly going astray. How often have I become impatient, wanting to give up your way! And how often have you given me the encouragement and helping hand that I need. Every day I increase the burden that you must bear; but just as I am impatient so you are infinitely patient.

2.   COVERING OUR SINS

Your love covers the multitude of my sins. So when I am fully aware of my sin, when before the justice of heaven only wrath is pronounced upon me, then you are the only person to whom I can escape. If I try to cover myself against the guilt of sin and the wrath of heaven, I will be driven to madness and despair. But if I rely on you to cover my sins, I shall find peace and joy. You suffered and died on the cross to shelter us from our guilt, and take upon yourself the wrath that we deserve. Let me rest under you, and may you transform me into your likeness.

3.   CHRIST THE HIDING-PLACE

The birds have their nests and the foxes their holes. But you were homeless, Lord Jesus, with nowhere to rest your head. And yet you were a hiding-place where the sinner could flee. Today you are still such a hiding-place, and I flee to you. I hide myself under your wings, and your wings cover the multitude of my sins.

4.   FROM YOUR HAND

From your hand, O Lord, we receive everything. You stretch your powerful hand, and turn worldly wisdom into holy folly. You open your gentle hand, and offer the gift of inward peace. If sometimes it seems that your arm is shortened, then you increase our faith and trust, so that we may reach out to you. And if sometimes it seems that you withdraw your hand from us, then we know that it is only to conceal the eternal blessing which you have promised – that we may yearn even more fervently for that blessing.

5.   OUR WEAKNESS, YOUR STRENGTH

There is much to drag us back, O Lord: empty pursuits, trivial pleasures, unworthy cares. There is much to frighten us away: pride that makes us reluctant to accept help; cowardice that recoils from sharing your suffering; anguish at the prospect of confessing our sins to you. But you are stronger than all these forces. We call you our redeemer and saviour because you redeem us from our empty, trivial existence, you save us from our foolish fears. This is your work which you have completed and will continue to complete every moment.

6.   SEE YOU AS YOU ARE

O Lord Jesus Christ, I long to live in your presence, to see your human form and to watch you walking on earth. I do not want to see you through the darkened glass of tradition, nor through the eyes of today's values and prejudices. I want to see you as you were, as you are, and as you always will be. I want to see you as an offence to human pride, as a man of humility, walking amongst the lowliest of men, and yet as the saviour and redeemer of the human race.

John Knox
c.1513–1572

After a period living under Calvin's rule in Geneva, he returned to his native Scotland to apply the same Protestant principles there. He became the leader of the Scottish Reformation, inspiring people with both his fiery preaching and his personal holiness. He taught that each activity of the day should begin with prayer in which God's blessing is sought.

1.
ON RISING

Help to amplify and increase thy kingdom, that whatsoever thou sendest, we may be heartily well content with thy good pleasure and will. Let us not lack the thing, O Father, without which we cannot serve thee. But bless thou all the works of our hands that we may have sufficient, and not to be chargeable, but rather helpful unto others. Be merciful, O Lord, to our offences. And seeing our debt is great, which thou hast forgiven us in Jesus Christ, make us to love thee, and our neighbours so much the more. Be thou our Father, our Captain and Defender in all temptations. Hold thou us by thy merciful hand, that we may be delivered from all inconveniences, and end our lives in the sanctifying and honour of thy holy name.

2.
BEFORE DAILY WORK

O Lord, we beseech thee, that thou wouldest strengthen us with thy Holy Spirit, that we may faithfully travel in our state and vocation without fraud or deceit; and that we may endeavour ourselves to follow thy holy ordinance, rather than to seek to satisfy our greedy affections or desire to gain. And if it please thee, O Lord, to prosper our labour, give us a mind also to help them that have need, according to that ability that thou of thy mercy shalt give us. And knowing that all good things come of thee, grant that we may humble ourselves to our neighbours, and not by any means lift ourselves up above them which have not received so liberal a portion, as of thy mercy thou hast given unto us. And if it please thee to try and exercise us by greater poverty and need than our flesh would desire, O Lord, grant us grace to know that thou wilt nourish us continually through thy bountiful liberality, that we be not so tempted, that we fall into distrust.

3.
BEFORE MEALS

O heavenly Father, which art the fountain and full treasure of all goodness, we beseech thee to show thy mercies upon us thy children, and sanctify these gifts which we receive of thy merciful liberality, granting us grace to use them soberly and purely, according to thy blessed will; so that hereby we may acknowledge thee to be the author and giver of all good things; and, above all, that may we remember continually to seek the spiritual food of thy word, wherewith our souls may be nourished.

William Laud
1573–1645

A fervent opponent of the Puritans, he sought to restore the colour and ritual of medieval worship to the Anglican Church. As Archbishop of Canterbury under King Charles I, he used increasingly forceful means to impose his ideas. But during the Civil War the Parliamentary forces imprisoned and executed him. In his prayers he emulated the majestic language of Thomas Cranmer's Book of Common Prayer.

1.   FOR THE UNIVERSAL CHURCH

Gracious Father, we humbly beseech thee for thy universal church. Fill it with all truth, in all truth with all peace. Where it is corrupt, purge it; and where it is in error, direct it; where it is superstitious, rectify it; where anything is amiss, reform it; where it is right, strengthen and confirm it; where it is in want, furnish it; where it is divided and rent asunder, make up the breaches thereof, O thou holy one of Israel.

2.   FOR THE KINGDOM

Lord, bless this kingdom, we beseech thee, that religion and virtue may increase amongst us, that there may be peace within the gates, and plenty within the palaces of it. In peace, we beseech thee, so preserve it, that it corrupt not; in war so defend it, that it suffer not; in plenty, so order it, that it riot not; in want, so pacify and moderate it, that it may patiently and peaceably seek thee, the only full supply both of men and state; that so it may continue a place and a people to do thee service to the end of time.

3.

FOR THE MONARCH

O Lord, grant the king a long life, that his years may be rich with thy blessing; furnish him with wise and safe counsels, and give him a heart of courage and constancy to pursue them. O prepare thy loving mercy and faithfulness for him, that they may preserve him, so will we always sing praises unto thy name.

4.

FOR A RIGHTEOUS MIND

Lord, here we are, do with us as seemeth best in thine own eyes, only give us, we humbly beseech thee, a penitent and patient spirit to expect thee. Lord, make our service acceptable to thee while we live, and our souls ready for thee when we die.

5.

FOR A RIGHTEOUS HEART

Give unto us, O Lord, we humbly beseech thee, a wise, a sober, a patient, an understanding, a devout, a religious, a courageous heart; a soul full of devotion to do thee service, strength against all temptations.

6.

FOR SWEET SLEEP

Lord, when we sleep let us not be made afraid, but let our sleep be sweet, that we may be enabled to serve thee on the morrow.

7.

LIVING, DYING, RESTING, RISING

Grant, O Lord, that we may live in thy fear, die in thy favour, rest in thy peace, rise in thy power, reign in thy glory.

Brother Lawrence
1611–1691

After serving in the French army for eighteen years, he entered the Carmelite monastery in Paris as a lay brother, working for thirty years as the community's cook until blindness forced him to retire. After his death, letters and notes found in his cell were published, along with many of his sayings which his brothers could recall. This short book came to be called The Practice of the Presence of God. *For him prayer consists of finding God through everyday events and in learning to trust his providence, so that the soul becomes constantly aware of God's presence. In his writings there are two short prayers which summarize his spirituality.*

1.

PRAYER BEFORE WORK

My God, you are always close to me. In obedience to you, I must now apply myself to outward things. Yet, as I do so, I pray that you will give me the grace of your presence. And to this end I ask that you will assist my work, receive its fruits as an offering to you, and all the while direct all my affections to you.

2.

A CONSTANT PRAYER

My God, here I am, my heart devoted to you. Fashion me according to your heart.

The Leonine Sacramentary
5th Century

A collection of prayers, rather than a complete liturgy, it probably dates from the fifth-century. While it is unlikely that Pope Leo composed it, many of its expressions and phrases are based on his work, and so he came to be regarded as its inspiration.

1.

IN THE MORNING

O God, who divides the day from the night, separate our deeds from the darkness of sin, and let us continually live in your light, reflecting in all that we do your eternal beauty.

2.

IN THE EVENING

O God, who gives the day for work and the night for sleep, refresh our bodies and our minds through the quiet hours of night, and let our inward eyes be directed towards you, dreaming of your eternal glory.

3.

AT THE HOUR OF DEATH

O God, the saviour of both the living and the dying, I humbly beg you to pardon all my offences, both those committed deliberately and those committed without thought and intention. And when at last you command that my soul should depart from my body, may your holy angels protect my soul from all evil powers, and carry it safely to your heavenly kingdom.

4.   THE SPIRITUAL LAW OF LIFE

You have made for us this law: that the effect of what comes to us
from without should depend on what we are like within.

Thus no external misfortune will overcome us if we restrain the
vices inside us.

No public disgrace will overwhelm us if we resist our own dis-
graceful desires.

No outward disturbance will daunt us if our intentions are
pure.

No enemy can rob us of our peace if our hearts are fixed on
you.

No one can do more harm to us than we do to ourselves; and as
soon as we master ourselves, everything else loses its power to hurt
us.

For this spiritual law, we give you thanks.

5.   AT TIMES OF PERSECUTION

Our weakness, Lord, gives you continual opportunity for displaying
your strength. And opposition to your church gives you continual
opportunity for displaying your power. Thus at times of persecution, when we feel weak in the face of our enemies, sustain our
hearts with your strength, and defeat your enemies by your mighty
power. And may the blood which your faithful people shed today
become the soil in which your church grows and flourishes in the
future.

George MacDonald
1824–1905

After training for the Christian ministry in Aber-deen, he was dismissed from his first post on sus-picion of heresy. He then turned to writing, and won fame with a series of children's books. But in recent years his religious works have won greater attention, especially his Unspoken Sermons, *which present the Christian faith with humour and imagination. The few prayers which these sermons contain are typical of his quirky profundity.*

1.   IMPOSSIBILITIES

I thank thee, Lord, for forgiving me, but I prefer staying in the darkness: forgive me that too. No, that cannot be. The one thing that cannot be forgiven is the sin of choosing to be evil, of refusing deliverance. It is impossible to forgive that. It would be to take part in it.

2.   DEEDS

I would go near thee – but I cannot press
Into thy presence – it helps not to presume.
Thy doors are deeds.

3.   ANSWERS

My prayers, my God, flow from what I am not;
I think thy answers make me what I am.
Like weary waves thought follows upon thought,

But the still depth beneath is all thine own,
And there thou mov'st in paths to us unknown.
Out of strange strife thy peace is strangely wrought;
If the lion in us pray – thou answerest the lamb.

4.   GLIMPSES

In holy things may be unholy greed.
Thou giv'st a glimpse of many a lovely thing
Not to be stored for use in any mind,
But only for the present spiritual need.
The holiest bread, if hoarded, soon will breed
The mammon-moth, the having pride.

5.   OBSTINATE ILLUSION

Have pity on us for the look of things,
When blank denial stares us in the face.
Although the serpent mask has lied before
It fascinates the bird.

6.   PREACHER'S REPENTANCE

O Lord, I have been talking to the people;
Thought's wheels have round me whirled a fiery zone,
And the recoil of my word's airy ripple
My heart heedful has puffed up and blown.
Therefore I cast myself before thee prone:
Lay cool hands on my burning brain and press
From my weak heart the swelling emptiness.

7.   FOR THE PAST

All sights and sounds of day and year,
All groups and forms, each leaf and gem,
Are thine, O God, nor will I fear
To talk to thee of them.

Too great thy heart is to despise,
Whose day girds centuries about;
From things which we name small, thine eyes
See great things looking out.

Therefore the prayerful song I sing
May come to thee in ordered words:
Though lowly born, it needs not cling
In terror to its chords.

I think that nothing made is lost;
That not a moon has ever shone,
That not a cloud my eyes hath crossed
But to my soul is gone.

That all the lost years garnered lie
In this thy casket, my dim soul;
And thou wilt, once the key apply,
And show the shining whole.

But were they dead in me, they live
In thee, whose parable is – Time,
And Worlds, and Forms – all things that give
Me thoughts, and this my rhyme.

Father, in joy our knees we bow:
This earth is not a place of tombs:
We are but in the nursery now;
They in the upper rooms.

For are we not at home in thee,
And all this world a visioned show;
That, knowing what Abroad is, we
What Home is too may know?

George MacLeod
1895–1991

After his experiences in the trenches in the First World War, when he won medals for bravery, he became a pacifist and a socialist. He was ordained minister in the Church of Scotland, serving slum parishes in Edinburgh and Glasgow. In 1938 he founded the Iona Community, based on the island from which St Columba evangelized Scotland. Large numbers were inspired by his religious and social ideals and met each summer on Iona to pray and to discuss how to transform society. His robust prayers, while rooted in the concerns of his time, are universal in their application, since he sees God in all social situations and in all living creatures.

1.   THE WHOLE EARTH SHALL CRY GLORY

Almighty God, Creator:
the morning is yours, rising into fullness.
The summer is yours, dipping into autumn.
Eternity is yours, dipping into time.
The vibrant grasses, the scent of flowers, the lichen on
   the rocks, the tang of sea-weed,
All are yours.
Gladly we live in this garden of your creating.

But creation is not enough.
Always in the beauty, the foreshadowing of decay.
The lambs frolicking careless: so soon to be led off to
   slaughter.
Nature red and scarred as well as lush and green.

In the garden also:
always the thorn.
Creation is not enough.

Almighty God, Redeemer:
the sap of life in our bones and being is yours,
lifting us to ecstasy.
But always in the beauty: the tang of sin, in our
    consciences.
The dry lichen of sins long dead, but seared upon our
    minds.
In the garden that is each of us, always the thorn.

Yet all are yours as we yield them again to you.
Not only our lives that you have given are yours:
but also our sins that you have taken.
Even our livid rebellions and putrid sins:
you have taken them all away
and nailed them to the Cross!
Our redemption is enough: and we are free.

Holy Spirit, Enlivener:
breathe on us, fill us with life anew.
In your new creation, already upon us, breaking
    through, groaning and travailing,
but already breaking through,
breathe on us.

Till that day when night and autumn vanish:
and lambs grown sheep are no more slaughtered:
and even the thorn shall fade
and the whole earth shall cry Glory at the marriage feast
    of the Lamb.
In this new creation, already upon us,
fill us with life anew.

2.   ETERNAL SEEPING THROUGH THE PHYSICAL

We come into thy house, our home
once more to give thanks:
for earth and sea and sky in harmony of colour,
the air of the eternal seeping through the physical,
the everlasting glory dipping into time.
We praise thee.

For nature resplendent:
growing beasts, mergent crops, singing birds,
and all the gayness of the green.
We bless thee.

For swift running tides, resistant waves, thy spirit on
    the waters,
the spirit of the inerrant will,
Striving with the currents that are also thine.
We bless thee.
O Lord: how marvellous are thy works.
In majesty hast thou created them.

As we look on man
we thank thee above all that thou hast been mindful of
    us
in Jesus Christ, our Lord:
that even as man fell from thy creation which was good,
so thou didst send the Proper Man to restore in us thy
    image:
that we find the road to harmony again in him.
We praise thee.
Yes: already vibrant with the everlasting,
we are enriched beyond the noblest works of nature.
That the spirit moves upon the turbulent waters of our
    lives:
we bless thee.
Yes: that thou dost honour each of us
with a flowing tide and also with resistant waves,

and that the waves only engulf when we lose our trust
    in thee:
We give thee manly thanks.
And that even thou who hast set the stars upon their
    courses
hast also set each one of us within the orbit of thy love.
The hairs of our head are numbered.
We give thee humble praise.

3.   THE GLORY IN THE GREY

Almighty God, Creator:
In these last days storm has assailed us.
Greyness has enveloped and mist surrounded
our going out and our coming in.
Now again thy glory clarifies,
thy light lifts up our hearts to thee,
and night falls in peace.
But through mist and storm and sunshine,
the crops have ripened here
and vines of Spain have grown.
Thy constant care in all and everywhere is manifest.

Almighty God, Redeemer:
Even as with our bodies, so also with our souls.
Redeemer, Christ:
Sunshine and storm, mist and greyness
eddy round our inner lives.
But as we trace the pattern, looking back,
we know that both darkness and light have been of thine
    ordaining,
for our own soul's health.
Thy constant care in all, and everywhere,
is manifest.

Almighty God, Sustainer:
Sun behind all suns,
Soul behind all souls,

everlasting reconciler of our whole beings:
Show to us in everything we touch and in everyone we meet
    the continued assurance of thy presence round us:
lest ever we should think thee absent.
In all created things thou art there.
In every friend we have
the sunshine of thy presence is shown forth.
In every enemy that seems to cross our path,
thou art there within the cloud
to challenge us to love.
Show to us the glory in the grey.
Awake for us thy presence in the very storm
till all our joys are seen as thee
and all our trivial tasks emerge as priestly sacraments
in the universal temple of thy love.

Of ourselves we cannot see this. Sure physician give us
    sight.
Of ourselves we cannot act. Patient lover give us love:
till every shower of rain speaks of thy forgiveness:
till every storm assures us that we company with thee:
and every move of light and shadow speaks of grave and
    resurrection:
to assure us that we cannot die:
thou creating, redeeming and sustaining God.

Frederick Macnutt

1873–1949

---

*He began both collecting and composing prayers
while serving as an army chaplain in the First
World War. He continued writing prayers, for both
private and public use, throughout his ministry.
And shortly before his death he put them together*

in a Prayer Manual. *While in form and style he follows the traditional Anglican collect, the substance of his prayers is fresh and sharp.*

1.   FAITH, HOPE, LOVE

Lord, give me faith that tries and tests the things unseen, and assures itself of thee who art the truth, that doubt may not overwhelm, nor darkness cover me; give me hope, that I may follow the light of thy sure promises, and lose not the way nor fall into byways; give me love, that I may give thee myself as thou givest; for thou, O Lord God, art the thing that I long for; and thou art blessedness beyond all thought and heart's desiring.

2.   INWARD PEACE

O Lord Jesus Christ, who didst say that in thee we may have peace, and hast bidden us to be of good cheer, since thou hast overcome the world: give us ears to hear and faith to receive thy word; that in all the tensions and confusion of this present time, with mind serene and steadfast purpose, we may continue to abide in thee.

3.   TRUE KNOWLEDGE

O Lord our God, who dost guide those who seek thee through the vain shows of earth into the knowledge of thy heavenly reality: let thy goodness uphold us and thy right hand lead us, that we may obediently reject the illusions of things temporal and walk without faltering in the light of things eternal.

4.   INWARD UNITY

O Holy Spirit the Comforter, Spirit of Jesus, come thou upon us and dwell within us. Not of ourselves, but of thee is our life. Teach us that we may know; cleanse us and purify us within; strengthen us to persevere, lest we fall away from thee. Come into us, thou who art already there, that by thine arrival again thou mayest enter into thy possession anew. And out of worldly death in which we languish, create in us the life that shall make us as thou art, through inward unity in which we are one with thee.

Mahayana Buddhism
c.7th century

Early Buddhism had no belief in a supreme deity. But as the religion spread northwards, through Tibet and into China, more theistic ideas were added. These included both the notion of God coming down to earth, and the hope of being reborn with God in eternal paradise.

1.   COME TO THIS DUSTY WORLD

Supreme One, you are an obscure mystery to us. You made all things and can purify all things. You are far beyond our understanding. Even to speak to you is to enter an unknown region. Yet your light shines on all creatures, and your wonder illumines their souls. We beg you to leave your bright celestial palace in heaven, and come to this dusty world. Reveal yourself to us. Use your power to extinguish all evil and banish all sickness. Give peace to troubled souls. Reconcile those who are enemies, turning them into friends. Show us how we should live, that we may learn to obey you in all things.

2.   WE DESIRE TO BE REBORN WITH YOU

Light without equal, so pure;
Beauty without peer, so serene;
We desire to be reborn with you.
Power without limits, so strong;
Glory without end, so majestic;
We desire to be reborn with you.

In your kingdom every flower blossoms continuously;
Every tree is always newly in leaf;
We desire to be reborn with you.
Music of sublime charm plays everywhere;
Perfume of sweetest fragrance fills the nostrils;
We desire to be reborn with you.

Thought of you fills our minds;
Love of you fills our hearts;
We desire to be reborn with you.
Desire for you fills our bodies;
Knowledge of you fills our souls;
We desire to be reborn with you.

Peter Marshall
1902–1949

---

*Born in Scotland, he emigrated to the United States
where he trained as a Presbyterian minister. In
1947 he was made chaplain to the United States
Senate, and received national publicity. His prayers
combined the grace of dignity needed for a public
occasion, with a homely simplicity that appealed to
the American spirit.*

1.   OUR SEEKING GOD

Our Father, sometimes thou dost seem so far away, as if thou
art a God in hiding, as if thou art determined to elude all who seek
thee.

Yet we know that thou art far more willing to be found than we
are to seek. Thou hast promised "If with all thy heart ye truly seek
me, ye shall ever surely find me". And hast thou not assured us that
thou art with us always?

Help us now to be as aware of thy nearness as we are of the material things of every day. Help us to recognize thy voice with as much assurance as we recognize the sounds of the world around us.

We would find thee now in the privacy of our hearts, in the quiet of this moment. We would know, our Father, that thou art near us and beside us; that thou dost love us and art interested in all that we do, art concerned about all our affairs.

May we become aware of thy companionship, of him who walks beside us.

At times when we feel forsaken, may we know the presence of the Holy Spirit who brings comfort to all human hearts, when we are willing to surrender ourselves.

May we be convinced that even before we reach up to thee, thou art reaching down to us.

2.   I NEED THEE, LORD

I do need thee. Lord, I need thee now. I know that I can do without many of the things that once I thought were necessities, but without thee I cannot live, and dare not die.

I needed thee when sorrow came, when shadows were thrown across the threshold of my life, and thou didst not fail me then. I needed thee when sickness laid a clammy hand upon my family, and I cried to thee, and thou didst hear. I needed thee when perplexity brought me to a parting of the ways, and I knew not how to turn. Thou didst indicate the better way. And though the sun is shining around me today, I know that I need thee even in the sunshine, and shall still need thee tomorrow.

I give thee my gratitude for that constant sense of need that keeps me close to thy side. Help me to keep my hand in thine and my ears open to the wisdom of thy voice.

Speak to me, that I may hear thee giving me courage for hard times and strength for difficult places; giving me determination for challenging tasks. I ask of thee no easy way, but just thy grace that is sufficient for every need, so that no matter how hard the way, how challenging the hour, how dark the sky, I may be enabled to overcome.

3.   TEACH US TO PRAY

Lord, teach us to pray. Some of us are not skilled in the art of prayer.
As we draw near to thee in thought, our spirits long for thy Spirit,
and reach out for thee, longing to feel thee near. We know not how
to express the deepest emotions that lie hidden in our hearts.

In these moments, we have no polished phrases with which to
impress one another, no finely moulded, delicately turned clauses
to present to thee. Nor would we be confined to conventional
petitions and repeat our prayers like the unwinding of a much-
exposed film. We know, our Father, that we are praying most when
we are saying least. We know that we are closest to thee when we
have left behind the things that have held us captive so long.

We would not be ignorant in prayer and, like children, make want
lists for thee. Rather, we pray that thou wilt give unto us only what
we really need. We would not make our prayers the importuning of
thee, an omnipotent God, to do what we want thee to do. Rather, give
us the vision, the courage, that shall enlarge our horizons and stretch
our faith to the adventure of seeking thy loving will for our lives.

We thank thee that thou art hearing us even now. We thank thee
for the grace of prayer. We thank thee for thyself.

4.   FOR CHILDLIKENESS

Forgive us, Lord, that as we grow to maturity, our faith is blighted
with doubts, withered with worry, tainted with sophistication. We
pray that thou wilt make us like children again in faith – not childish, but childlike in the simplicity of a faith that is willing to trust
thee even though we cannot see what tomorrow will bring.

We ask thee to give to each of us that childlike faith, that simplicity of mind which is willing to lay aside all egotism and conceit,
which recognizes vanity for what it is – an empty show, which
knows that we are incapable of thinking the thoughts of God, which
is willing to be humble again.

Then may we feel once more as do our children who whisper
their love to thee, who trace with chubby little fingers the pictures
of Jesus in a picture book – those pictures that portray thee, Lord
Jesus, with a hurt lamb in thy arms or a child on thy knee. Help

us, even now, to feel again like that, that we may be as loving, as trusting, as innocent, as grateful, as affectionate.

And as we are willing to kneel again as children, then shall we discover for ourselves the glory thou hast revealed, and find the wonder of it gripping our hearts and preparing them for thy peace. So shall we, along with our children, enter into the Kingdom of God, and know it, and feel it, and rejoice in it. In thy name, who didst dare to come to earth as a little child, we pray.

Mechthild of Magdeburg
c.1210–c.1280

At the age of twelve she had an intense religious experience in which she saw herself as Christ's bride; and this sense of being married to Christ remained with her throughout her life. She joined the Béguine community at Magdeburg, where she imposed on herself the most rigorous austerities. After a serious illness she felt moved to write about her spiritual experiences, and produced The Flowing Light of the Godhead. *It is a loose-knit collection of spiritual songs and moral reflections. The songs are mostly poetic prayers, with much erotic imagery.*

1.   YOU ARE MY LOVER

Lord, you are my lover,
The object of my desire,
You are like a stream flowing through my body,
A sun shining on my face.
Let me be your reflection.

2.   LORD, LOVE ME

Lord, love me passionately,
Love me often,
Love me long.
The more passionately you love me, the more beautiful I
    become.
The more often you love me, the purer I become.
The longer you love me, the holier I become.

3.   THE LOWEST OF ALL CREATURES

Lord, because I am the lowest of all creatures,
You have raised me high above them to yourself.
Lord, because I have no earthly treasures,
You have poured upon me heavenly treasure.
Lord, because I am dressed in the grey rags of sin,
You have clothed me in the pure white robe of virtue.
Lord, because I desire the merest hovel for my home,
You have welcomed me to your eternal palace.

4.   GOD'S ABSENCE

Dear absent Lord,
I am bound to you with chains of love.
I am waiting for you to come to me.
The wait is long, cold and blank.
I want you to be near to me.
I want to be embraced by you,
Held in your wonderful arms of love.
I know it is my sinful pride that drove you away,
But in my humility I beg you to return.
I have fallen in love with you.
And the deeper is my fall, the sweeter is my love.

5.   SWEETNESS AND LIGHT

Ah, dear God, dear love,
Hold my soul close to you.

It pains me above all things
To be separated from you.
Do not let my ardour grow cool.
Everything I do seems pointless and worthless
Unless it is done for your sake.
You sweeten our sufferings,
You lighten our burdens,
You console us in our anxieties.
You let us rest in your arms.

6.   GOD'S POWER

Almighty Lord, I rejoice in your power.
I regard it as my own victory
When you conquer my stubborn will.
I offer joyful thanks
When you subdue my wayward heart.
And I look forward to the moment of death
When you will vanquish this mortal body.

7.   SONG WITHOUT NOISE

O sweet and loving God
When I stay asleep too long,
Oblivious to all your many blessings,
Then, please, wake me up,
And sing to me your joyful song.
It is a song without noise or notes.
It is a song of love beyond words,
Of faith beyond the power of human telling.
I can hear it in my soul,
When you awaken me to your presence.

8.   A PEACEFUL DEATH

Lord, Father, I thank you for creating me.
Lord Jesus Christ, I thank you for saving me.
Lord, Holy Spirit, I thank you for purifying me.

Lord, one and undivided Trinity, I pray
That you will remember my faithfulness,
And so grant me a peaceful death,
At which suffering ceases for all eternity,
And I shall abide in your everlasting joy.

9.   I WILL DANCE EVERMORE

I cannot dance, O Lord, unless you lead me.
If it is your will, I can leap with joy.
But you must show me how to dance and sing
By dancing and singing yourself!
With you I will leap towards love,
And from love I will leap to truth,
And from truth I will leap to joy,
And then I shall leap beyond all human senses.
There I will remain
And dance for evermore.

10.   DRINKING THE FINEST WINE

Ah, Lord, I am overwhelmed by your love.
I am overcome by your presence by my side.
My soul has no love of itself,
But you alone can arouse love with it.
I feel I am drinking the finest wine.
And drunk with love I will obey your every command,
Even laying down my life for you.
Now that I have known your presence
All other pleasures are empty.
My only joy is to be with you.

11.   THE BLESSINGS OF DEPRIVATION

Lord, I thank you that in your love you have taken from me all
earthly riches, and that now you clothe and feed me through the
generosity of others.

Lord, I thank you that you have taken from me the sight of my eyes, and that now you serve me with the eyes of others.
Lord, I thank you that you have taken from me the power of my hands, and that now you care for me by the hands of others.
Lord, I pray for them. Reward them in your heavenly love, that they may faithfully serve and please you until death.

12.   THE DOG'S GIFT

Lord, since you have taken from me all earthly favours, I can now see that you have left me with a spiritual gift beyond price, which every dog has by nature. You have made me faithful to you even at times of the greatest distress, bereft of all comforts. This faithfulness I cherish more fervently than all the riches of the world.

Thomas Merton
1915–1968

After an unhappy childhood and a hedonistic period in early adulthood, he became a Roman Catholic, and at the age of twenty-six entered a Trappist monastery in Kentucky. At first his Catholicism was narrow and rigid, but his experiences of monastic spirituality gradually broadened his religious horizons, so that in later years he was in close contact with Buddhist and Hindu monks.

1.   ON BECOMING A MONK

How far have I to go to find you in whom I have already arrived?
    From now, O my God, it is to you alone that I can talk, because nobody else will understand. I cannot bring any other man on this earth into the cloud where I dwell in your light, that is, your darkness, where I am lost and abashed. I cannot explain to any other man

the anguish which is your joy, nor the loss which is the possession of you, nor the distance from all things which is the arrival in you, nor the death which is the birth in you because I do not know anything about it myself and all I know is that I wish it were over – I wish it were begun.

You have contradicted everything. You have left me in no-man's land.

You have got me walking up and down all day under those trees, saying to me over and over again: "Solitude, solitude". And you have turned me around and thrown the whole world in my lap. You have told me, "Leave all things and follow me", and then you have tied half of New York to my foot like a ball and chain. You have got me kneeling behind the pillar with my mind making a noise like a bank. Is that contemplation?

Before I went to make my solemn vows on the Feast of St Joseph, in the thirty-third year of my age, being a cleric in minor orders – before I went to make my solemn vows, this is what it looked like to me. It seemed to me that you were almost asking me to give up all aspirations for solitude and for a contemplative life. You were asking me for obedience to superiors who will, I am morally certain, either make me write or teach philosophy or take charge of a dozen material responsibilities around the monastery, and I may even end up as a retreat master preaching four sermons a day to the seculars who come to the house. And even if I have no special job at all, I will always be on the run from two in the morning to seven at night.

2.   FOR UNITY OF FAITHS

O God, we are one with you. You have made us one with you. You have taught us that if we are open to one another, you dwell in us. Help us to preserve this openness and to fight for it with all our hearts. Help us to realize that there can be no understanding where there is mutual rejection. O God, in accepting one another wholeheartedly, fully, completely, we accept you, and we thank you, and we adore you, and we love you with our whole being, because our being is in your being, our spirit is rooted in your spirit. Fill us then with love, and let us be bound together with love as we go our diverse ways, united in this one spirit which makes you present in the world, and which makes you witness to the ultimate reality that is love. Love has overcome. Love is victorious.

Eric Milner-White
1884–1963

A founder-member of an Anglican religious order of priests, the Oratory of the Good Shepherd, he became Dean of York where he gained a reputation as a composer of hymns and prayers.

1.   SPIRITUAL TROTH

Almighty eternal Father,
thou dost marry justice and mercy in thyself,
God and man in thy Son,
might and peace in thy Spirit.

O! marry in me
the fear of thee and the love of thee,
the knowledge, and the practice, of thy will,
a contrite and a thankful heart,
the present and the eternal all day long.
Thyself, Lord, be the consort of my soul,
wedding immortal grace to mortal birth,
wedding my happiness with thy glory,
wedding my weakness and thy strength,
thy desires and my obedience,
thy Cross and my crown.
O! clothe me with thy wedding garment;
he that is joined to the Lord
is one spirit with him.

My Lord and Master, hear me pledge my troth:
with my body I thee worship,
with mine understanding, with my heart,
with all my worldly goods,
with all thy heavenly gifts,
I thee worship, thee adore.

Those, Lord, whom thou hast joined together
let no man, nothing, put asunder.

2. PILGRIMAGE

Control me, O my God,
gently, pervasively, irresistibly, increasingly;
so that I walk my pilgrim way
steadily and in a sure light;
so that I neither dally nor disobey,
nor slip aside, nor stand still, nor sink down.

Control me, O God,
by the pulse of thy presence,
by thy brightness about me;
by the spur of spiritual longing
after thy holy praise,
after the image of thy Son;
so that I move onward and upward with a song,
and melody in my heart.

Then, O my God, change control into grasp,
lest I ever deny my truest will,
so that I cannot escape or fall away,
and the world pull back the pilgrim
and steal his glory.

O Lord, let thine arm grip me, lift me,
land me safe home.
Bring me to Jerusalem that is thine,
and set me with thy blessed ones
with the princes of thy people;

the way ended, the peace unending,
the perfect and pure for ever imperishable,
and thou all in all.

3.

GOD THE GIVER

O thou that hast given us hands to work:
Grant us to work faithfully as unto thee and not unto
    men.

Thou that hast given us eyes to see:
Turn them away from wrongful desire;
show them thy handiwork, thy providence, thyself.

Thou that hast given us ears to hear:
Speak in them thy Word; thy Word is truth.

Thou that hast given us minds to think:
Grant them to consider and contrive that only
which is pure, lovely and of good report.

Thou that hast given us tongues to speak:
Let them tell of thy salvation from day to day,
and give thanks for a remembrance of thy holiness.

Thou that hast given us hearts to love:
Give us also grace to love thee with all our strength;
and, for thy sake, our neighbour more than ourself.

Thou that hast given us immortal souls:
Bless us and help us to grow more and more
into the image of thy glory,
of thy Son Jesus Christ our Lord.

4.

THE MIRROR

O my Father and God,
let the glory, divine glory, glory inexhaustible, of thy
    being

find reflection, visible and invisible, in mind:
as the sun touches to life and joy the surfaces of land
    and sea
and the moon draws silver patterns across them.
The small dark pool welcomes the likeness of the sky
and, by all that it reflects, as in a glass,
is transformed itself into loveliness.

So make my whole being respond to thy love,
and leap to life with thy light,
and shine more and more with the likeness
of thy Son Christ Jesus my Lord;
in whom, yesterday, today and for ever,
thou art well pleased, and thou art seen.

Mohammed
570–632

---

*The founder of Islam – which means "submission
to the will of God" – he received a series of divine
revelations while meditating on a mountain near
Mecca. He continued to hear such messages for the
following two decades, and they were collected to
form the Koran, Islam's sacred Scripture. It
includes a number of prayers, most of which come
from the mouths of the ancient Hebrew prophets,
Noah, Abraham and Moses.*

1.   PUT COURAGE INTO MY HEART

Lord, put courage into my heart, and take away all that may hinder
me serving you. Free my tongue to proclaim your goodness, that
all may understand me. Give me friends to advise and help me, that
by working together our efforts may bear abundant fruit. And,

above all, let me constantly remember that my actions are worthless unless they are guided by your hand.

2.   SUSTAIN ME WITH YOUR POWER

Lord, may everything that I do start well and finish well. Sustain me with your power. And in your power let me drive away all falsehood, ensuring that truth may always triumph.

3.   IN YOU WE PUT OUR TRUST

Lord, in you we put our trust. To you we turn in times of need. To you we shall go at the moment of death. Do not allow us to be deceived and misled by the designs of those whose hearts are evil. Forgive us for the evil in our own hearts. You alone are mighty; you alone are wise.

4.   WE LISTEN TO YOU AND OBEY YOU

Lord, you do not put a greater burden on a soul than it can bear. You are not angry with us when we make mistakes, but are quick to forgive us and set us right. You do not lead us into moral and spiritual danger without protecting and guiding us, so our souls can emerge unscathed. You do not allow us to be defeated by the deceits of unbelievers, but ensure that ultimately truth will be victorious. Lord, we listen to you, and we obey you.

Thomas More
1478–1535

Under King Henry VIII he held a series of high political offices, eventually becoming Lord Chancellor. But he opposed the King over his divorce of Katherine of Aragon, and remained loyal to the papacy when the King broke with Rome. He was imprisoned in the Tower of London, and after a dramatic trial for treason he was beheaded. He was a reluctant martyr, and his spiritual struggles as he awaited trial and execution are expressed in the final prayers he composed.

1.

A GODLY MEDITATION

Give me grace, good Lord
To count the world as nothing,
To set my mind firmly on you
And not to hang on what people say;
To be content to be alone,
Not to long for worldly company,
Little by little to throw off the world completely
And rid my mind of all its business;
Not to long to hear of any worldly things;
Gladly to be thinking of you,
Pitifully to call for your help,
To depend on your comfort,
Busily to work to love you;
To know my own worthlessness and wretchedness,
To humble and abase myself under your mighty hand,
To lament my past sins,
To suffer adversity patiently, to purge them,
Gladly to bear my purgatory here,
To be joyful for troubles;
To walk the narrow way that leads to life,
To bear the Cross with Christ,
To keep the final hour in mind,
To have always before my eyes my death, which is always
    at hand,
To make death no stranger to me,
To foresee and consider the everlasting fire of hell,
To pray for pardon before the judge comes;
To keep continually in mind the passion that Christ
    suffered for me,

For his benefits unceasingly to give him thanks;
To buy back the time that I have wasted before,
To refrain from futile chatter,
To reject idle frivolity,
To cut out unnecessary entertainments,
To count the loss of worldly possessions,
    friends, liberty and life itself as absolutely
    nothing, for the winning of Christ;
To consider my worst enemies my best friends,
For Joseph's brothers could never have done him
    as much good with their love and favour
    as they did with their malice and hatred.

2.   AFTER THE FINAL CONFESSION

Good and gracious Lord, as you give me grace to acknowledge my sins, so give me grace in both word and heart to repent them and utterly forsake them. And forgive me those sins which my pride blinds me from discerning.

Glorious God, give me your grace to turn my back on the things of this world, and to fix my heart solely on you.

Give me your grace to amend my life, so that I can approach death without resentment, knowing that in you it is the gateway to eternal riches.

Glorious God, take from me all sinful fear, all sinful sorrow and self-pity, all sinful hope and all sinful desire. Instead give me such fear, such sorrow, such pity, such hope and such desire as may be profitable for my soul.

Good Lord, give me this grace, in all my fear and agony, to find strength in that great fear and agony which you, sweet Saviour, had on the Mount of Olives before your bitter passion.

Almighty God, take from me all desire for worldly praise, and all emotions of anger and revenge. Give me a humble, lowly, quiet, peaceable, patient, generous, kind, tender and compassionate mind.

Grant me, good Lord, a full faith, a firm hope and a fervent love, that I may desire only that which gives you pleasure and conforms to your will.

And, above all, look upon me with your love and your favour.

Mozarabic Sacramentary
3rd Century

From the earliest times the Iberian peninsular had its own liturgical form, which included special prayers for the various spiritual and moral virtues. This liturgy continued to be used throughout the period of Muslim rule, but when Spain was reconquered by Christian forces in the eleventh-century the Roman rite was imposed.

1.

FOR GUIDANCE

Plant in our hearts, Lord, such fear of your power, that we may always strive to live according to your laws. Let us always remember that through you alone comes joy and happiness, and that without you there is only misery and despair. And thus may we learn to obey you in all things.

2.

FOR HUMILITY

O God, since you created everything we can see, hear and touch, may we constantly acknowledge your bounty. And since you sustain everything we can see, hear and touch, may we always be mindful of your strength. Thus may we walk the path of life with a spirit of humility, knowing that in all things we depend on you.

3.

FOR FAITH

O Lord, we know that if we put faith in our own powers, we are building our lives on a foundation of sand, and we shall be blown over by the words of evil passions. May we put our faith in you and you alone, building our lives on the rock of your gospel, that we may withstand even the fiercest gales of temptation.

4.   FOR HOPE

Lord, when we think only of our own wants and desires, we are impatient to have them satisfied, yet in our hearts we know that such satisfaction will crumble to dust. Give us that spirit of hope which can enable us to want what you want, and to wait patiently on your time, in the knowledge that in you alone comes true and lasting pleasure.

5.   FOR LOVE

O Lord, you have brought all your faithful people into a single, universal family, stretching across heaven and earth. Bind us together with a spiritual love which is stronger than any human love, that in serving one another we may neither count the cost nor seek reward, but think only of the common good.

6.   FOR PEACE

O God, through the death of your Son you reconciled us one to another, drawing us together in the bond of peace. In times of trouble and adversity, may your peace sustain us, calming our fretful and anxious hearts, and saving us from all hateful and violent activities.

7.   FOR PURITY

Make us, O Lord, flourish like pure, white lilies in the courts of your house, giving forth the sweet fragrance of your love to all who pass.

8.   FOR MERCY

O God, in revealing to us the perfect spiritual beauty of your Son, you have shown the grotesque ugliness of our depravity, and so filled us with remorse. We beg you, Lord, to reach down to us in your mercy, re-creating us in the image of your Son, that we may be fit to live with him in your heavenly kingdom.

Thomas Münzer
c.1490–1525

An ordained priest, he followed Luther in breaking with Rome, and became a fiery Protestant preacher. But he fell out with Luther over baptism, believing that only adult believers should be baptized, and began an independent church. He joined the Peasants Revolt in which the rural poor of Germany rose up in violent revolution. When the Revolt failed he was captured and executed. His prayers, however, give no hint of his stormy life, but express with succinct eloquence his Protestant faith.

1.

FAITHFUL GOD

Faithful God, now that we have made a covenant with you, stay close beside us and guide us away from any sin or corruption. May the gentle flesh and the costly blood of your son Jesus Christ, symbolized in the bread and wine of Communion, be the seals of that covenant which can never be broken.

2.

LOVING GOD

Loving God, we give thanks for the birth of your son Jesus Christ, both in human form in Bethlehem and in spiritual form in our hearts. May he reign as king within every human heart, so that every town and village can live according to his joyful law of love.

3.   PEACEFUL GOD

Peaceful God, you allowed your son to die at Calvary, taking upon himself the punishment for our sins, that we may be reconciled to you. May our sinful selves die with him on the cross, that we may rise to that life of perfect joy and grace which he promises to all his faithful peoples.

4.   MERCIFUL GOD

Merciful God, we know that we deserve to have your anger poured out upon us; yet in your infinite love you have chosen instead to pour out the grace of your Holy Spirit. May your Spirit so enlighten our hearts, that we may show the same merciful love to others that you have shown to us.

5.   MEDITATION OF THE EUCHARIST

Just as a grain of wheat must die in the earth in order to bring forth a rich harvest, so your Son died on the cross to bring a rich harvest of love. Just as the harvest of wheat must be ground into flour to make bread, so the suffering of your Son brings us the bread of life. Just as bread gives our bodies strength for our daily work, so the risen body of your Son gives us strength to obey your laws.

Nanak
1469–1538

The founder of the Sikh religion in north-west India, he sought to reconcile Hinduism and Islam, whose rivalry was causing much misery and bloodshed. He combined the monotheism of Islam with the tolerance and mysticism of the Hindu tradition.

1.

THE LOWLIEST OF THE LOW

There is no counting the number of fools,
No counting the thieves and fraudsters,
No counting those who shed innocent blood,
No counting the adulterers and the traitors,
No counting the liars who take pleasure in deceit,
No counting those who spread malice and hatred.

I do not put myself above any of those people,
I am the lowliest of the low.
I have nothing to offer you, O Lord.
My life is not even worth sacrificing to you.
All I can do is try to obey your will.
All I want is to abide in your peace.

2.

WORDS AND MUSIC

Countless are your names, countless your dwelling-places;
The breadth of your kingdom is beyond our imagination.
Even to try and imagine your kingdom is foolish.

Yet through words and through music
We speak your name and sing your praise.
Words are the only tools we have to proclaim your greatness,
And music our only means of echoing your virtue.

You put words in our hearts and minds.
With words we can describe the glory of your creation,
And so our words can reflect your glory.
You put music in our hearts and minds.
With music we can echo the beauty of heaven,
And so our music can express our deepest wish.

How can someone as insignificant as me
Express the vastness and wonder of your creation?
How can someone as sinful as me
Dare to hope for a place in heaven?

My only answer lies in the words and the music
Which you yourself have given me.

3.   DIVINE VIRTUE

By the grace of your name
May humanity find itself lifted higher and higher.
In your dispensation, O Lord,
Let virtue reign in every human heart.

John Henry Newman
1801–1890

---

*As one of the founders of the Oxford Movement,
he urged the Church of England to return to its
Catholic roots. Then after his conversion to Roman
Catholicism, he urged many Protestant ideas on to
his adopted church. But, despite being so often in
the eye of ecclesiastical storms, he was at heart a
man of prayer, striving to work out his theology
through a rigorous daily discipline of worship and
meditation. This marriage of theology and prayer
is most clearly expressed in his* Meditations on
Christian Doctrine. *His most famous piece is the
poetic prayer,* Lead, Kindly Light, *which in his
lifetime became an outstanding popular hymn. It
was written while returning home from a trip to
Italy, where he had almost died from a viral
infection.*

1.
FOR A LOVING HEART

O most tender and gentle Lord Jesus, when will my heart have a portion of thy perfections? When will my hard and stony heart, my proud heart, my unbelieving, my impure heart, my narrow selfish heart, be melted and conformed to thine? O teach me so to contemplate thee that I may become like thee, and to love thee sincerely and simply as thou hast loved me.

2.
FOR THE GIFT OF MEDITATION

My God, how far am I from acting according to what I know so well! I confess it, my heart goes after shadows. I love anything better than communion with thee. I am ever eager to get away from thee. Often I find it difficult even to say my prayers. There is hardly any amusement I would not rather take up than set myself to think of thee. Give me grace, O my Father, to be utterly ashamed of my own reluctance! Rouse me from sloth and coldness, and make me desire thee with my whole heart. Teach me to love meditation, sacred reading, and prayer. Teach me to love that which must engage my mind for all eternity.

3.
FOR SPIRITUAL SIGHT

My God, thou knowest infinitely better than I, how little I love thee. I should not love thee at all, except for thy grace. It is thy grace which has opened the eyes of my mind, and enabled them to see thy glory. It is thy grace which has touched my heart, and brought upon it the influence of what is so wonderfully beautiful and fair. O my God, whatever is nearer to me than thou, things of this earth, and things more naturally pleasing to me, will be sure to interrupt the sight of thee, unless thy grace interfere. Keep thou my eyes, my ears, my heart, from any such miserable tyranny. Break my bonds – raise my heart. Keep my whole being fixed on thee. Let me never lose sight of thee; and, while I gaze on thee, let my love of thee grow more and more every day.

4.   FOR THE LIGHT OF TRUTH

O my God, I confess that thou canst enlighten my darkness. I confess that thou alone canst. I wish my darkness to be enlightened. I do not know whether thou wilt: but that thou canst and that I wish, are sufficient reasons for me to ask what thou at least hast not forbidden my asking. I hereby promise that by thy grace which I am asking, I will embrace whatever I at length feel certain is the truth, if ever I come to be certain. And by thy grace I will guard against all self-deceit which may lead me to take what nature would have, rather than what reason approves.

5.   FOR A HAPPY DEATH

O, my Lord and Saviour, support me in that hour in the strong arms of thy sacraments, and by the fresh fragrance of thy consolations. Let the absolving words be said over me, and the holy oil sign and seal me, and thy own Body be my food, and thy Blood my sprinkling; and let my sweet Mother, Mary, breathe on me, and my Angel whisper peace to me, and my glorious Saints smile upon me: that in them all, and through them all, I may receive the gift of perseverance, and die, as I desire to live, in thy faith, in thy Church, in thy service, and in thy love.

6.   LEAD, KINDLY LIGHT

Lead, kindly light, amid the encircling gloom,
Lead thou me on;
The night is dark, and I am far from home;
Lead thou me on.
Keep thou my feet; I do not ask to see
The distant scene: one step enough for me.

I was not ever thus, nor prayed that thou
Shouldst lead me on;
I loved to choose and see my path; but now
Lead thou me on.
I loved the garish day, and, spite of fears,
Pride ruled my will: remember not past years.

So long thy power hath blest me, sure it still
Will lead me on
O'er moor and fen, o'er crag and torrent, till
The night is gone,
And with the morn those angel faces smile
Which I have loved long since, and lost awhile.

Reinhold Niebuhr
1892–1971

For most of his working life he was Professor of Applied Christianity at the Union Theological Seminary in New York. In both his theology and his spirituality his primary concern was the relationship between the revelation of God in the Bible and the political and social problems which beset mankind. The shadow of world war looms over many of his prayers.

1.   FOR BROTHERHOOD

O God, who has ordained that all men should live and work together as brethren, remove, we humbly beseech you, from those who are now at variance, all spirit of strife and all occasion for bitterness that, seeking only what is just and equal, they may ever continue in brotherly union and concord. Lead us out of the night of this conflict into the day of justice. Give us grace to be instruments of the kingdom of love and justice in the affairs of mankind; and patience in dealing with all the sins and selfishness of men, and humility in recognizing our own, that we may judge wisely between a man and his brother, between nations and peoples; and, by composing their differences, build them up into a true community of nations.

2.   FOR THE NATIONS

Look with mercy upon the peoples of the world, so full both of pride and confusion, so sure of their righteousness and so deeply involved in unrighteousness, so confident of their power and so imprisoned by their fears of each other. Have mercy upon our own nation. Purge us of the vainglory which confuses our counsels, and give our leaders and our people the wisdom of humility and charity. Help us to recognize our own affinity with whatever truculence or malice confronts us, that we may not add to the world's woe by the fury of our own resentments. Give your Church the grace in this time to be as a saving remnant among the nations, reminding all peoples of the divine majesty under whose judgement they stand, and of the divine mercy of which they and we have a common need.

3.   FOR VICTIMS AND TYRANTS

We pray to you this day mindful of the sorry confusion of our world. Look with mercy upon this generation of your children so steeped in misery of their own contriving, so far strayed from your ways and so blinded by passions. We pray for the victims of tyranny, that they may resist oppression with courage and may preserve their integrity by a hope which defies the terror of the moment. We pray for wicked and cruel men, whose arrogance reveals to us what the sin of our own hearts is like when it has conceived and brought forth its final fruit. O God, who resists the proud and gives grace to the humble, bring down the mighty from their seats.

4.   FOR VISION

We pray for all who have some vision of your will, despite the confusions and betrayals of human sin, that they may humbly and resolutely plan for and fashion the foundations of a just peace between men, even while they seek to preserve what is fair and just among us against the threat of malignant power. Grant us grace to see what we can do, but also to know what are the limits of our powers, so that courage may feed on trust in you, who are able to rule and overrule the angry passions of men and to make the wrath of men to praise you.

5.   FOR GRATITUDE

We thank you, our Father, for all the provisions made for the needs of the bodies and souls of men, for the ordered course of nature and for the miracle of the harvest by which our life is sustained. Teach us to distribute to all according to their need what you have intended for their sustenance. We thank you for our physical life, with its strength and gladness, and for the glimpses of the eternal which shine through human joys and woes. We praise you for the human mind and its power to survey the world in its length and breadth, and for the infinities of thought and truth which carry our imagination beyond our comprehension. We thank you, too, that the world which exceeds our comprehension is not lost in mystery, but that through seers and saints, and finally Jesus Christ, we have been given light upon the meaning of the mystery which surrounds you. Grant us grace to walk in humility and gratitude before you.

6.   FOR OURSELVES

We pray for ourselves who live in peace and quietness, that we may not regard our good fortune as proof of our virtue, or rest content to have our ease at the price of other men's sorrow and tribulation.

Henri Nouwen
1932–

A priest, a prolific author, a university lecturer and a peace campaigner, he has exercised a wide influence on contemporary spirituality, seeking to combine vigorous activity in social and political affairs with the firm discipline of contemplative prayer.

1.   EBB AND FLOW

Dear Lord, today I thought of the words of Vincent van Gogh: "It is true there is an ebb and flow, but the sea remains the sea". You are the sea. Although I experience many ups and downs in my emotions and often feel great shifts and changes in my inner life, you remain the same. Your sameness is not the sameness of a rock, but the sameness of a faithful lover. Out of your love I came to life; by your love I am sustained, and to your love I am always called back. There are days of sadness and days of joy; there are feelings of guilt and feelings of gratitude; there are moments of failure and moments of success; but all of them are embraced by your unwavering love.

My only real temptation is to doubt in your love, to think of myself as beyond the reach of your love, to remove myself from the healing radiance of your love. To do these things is to move into the darkness of despair.

O Lord, sea of love and goodness, let me not fear too much the storms and winds of my daily life, and let me know that there is ebb and flow but that the sea remains the sea.

2.   SERPENT AND DOVE

Dear Lord, you have sent me into this world to preach your word. So often the problems of the world seem so complex and intricate that your word strikes me as embarrassingly simple. Many times I feel tongue-tied in the company of people who are dealing with the world's social and economic problems.

But you, O Lord, said, "Be clever as serpents and innocent as doves". Let me retain innocence and simplicity in the midst of this complex world. I realize that I have to be informed, that I have to study the many aspects of the problems facing the world, and that I have to try to understand as well as possible the dynamics of our contemporary society. But what really counts is that all this information, knowledge, and insight allows me to speak more clearly and unambiguously your truthful word. Do not allow evil powers to seduce me with the complexities of the world's problems, but give me the strength to think clearly, speak freely, and act boldly in your service. Give me the courage to show the dove in a world so full of serpents.

3. WAR AND PEACE

Dear Lord, awaken the people of the earth and their leaders to the realization of the madness of the nuclear arms race. Today we mourn the dead of past wars, but will there be anyone to mourn the dead of the next one? O Lord, turn us away from our foolish race to self-destruction; let us see that more and more weaponry indeed means more of a chance to use it. Please, Lord, let the great talents you have given to your creatures not fall into the hands of the powers and principalities for whom death is the means as well as the goal. Let us see that the resources hidden in your earth are for feeding each other, healing each other, offering shelter to each other, making this world a place where men, women, and children of all races and nations can live together in peace.

Give us new prophets who can speak openly, directly, convincingly, and lovingly to kings, presidents, senators, church leaders, and all men and women of good will, prophets who can make us wage peace instead of war. Lord, make haste to help us. Do not come too late!

4. LIGHT AND DARK

Dear Lord, help me keep my eyes on you. You are the incarnation of Divine Love, you are the expression of God's infinite compassion, you are the visible manifestation of the Father's holiness. You are beauty, goodness, gentleness, forgiveness, and mercy. In you all can be found. Outside of you nothing can be found. Why should I look elsewhere or go elsewhere? You have the words of eternal life, you are food and drink, you are the Way, the Truth, and the Life. You are the light that shines in the darkness, the lamp on the lampstand, the house on the hilltop. You are the perfect

Icon of God. In and through you I can see and find my way to the
Heavenly Father. O Holy One, Beautiful One, Glorious One, be
my Lord, my Saviour, my Redeemer, my Guide, my Consoler, my
Comforter, my Hope, my Joy, and my Peace. To you I want to
give all that I am. Let me be generous, not stingy or hesitant. Let
me give you all – all I have, think, do, and feel. It is yours, O Lord.
Please accept it and make it fully your own.

Huub Oosterhuis
1933–

*A Jesuit priest, his ministry has mainly been to
the student community of Amsterdam. He played a
major role in the renewal of the Dutch liturgy. In*
Your Word is Near *he expresses through prayer
his conviction that God is active in every aspect
of human life, and that the task of the Christian
community is to be open and sensitive to this divine
action.*

1.   YOU WAIT FOR US

You wait for us
until we are open to you.
We wait for your word
To make us receptive.
Attune us to your voice,
to your silence,
speak and bring your son to us –
Jesus, the word of your peace.
Your word is near,
O Lord our God,
your grace is near.
Come to us, then,

with mildness and power.
Do not let us be deaf to you,
but make us receptive and open
to Jesus Christ your Son,
who will come to look for us and save us
today and every day
for ever and ever.

2.
YOU ARE NO STRANGER

How many times, God, have we been told
that you are no stranger,
remote from those who call upon you
in prayer!
O let us see, God,
and know in our lives now
that those words are true.
Give us faith
and give us the joy
of recognizing your son,
Jesus Christ,
our Saviour, in our midst.
Make us receptive and open,
and may we accept your kingdom
like children taking bread
from the hands of their father.
Let us live in your peace,
at home with you
all the days of our lives.

3.
WE ARE DEPENDENT ON YOUR LOVE

We can expect nothing, God,
from ourselves
and everything that we have
comes from you.
We are dependent on your love
and your kindness.

Treat us well –
do not measure out your grace,
but give us your own power of life,
your Son Jesus Christ,
mercy and faithfulness
more than we can imagine
today and all the days
of our lives.
We are the work of your hands, O God.
You, Lord, have made us and love us.
All our life is your gift,
all your power was in
our creation
and thus you will go on giving to us
grace upon grace.
What more need we hope for
from you?
This certainty – God –
is good enough for us.

4.   YOU ARE MERCIFUL

God, you are merciful to us
in all our doings, good and bad.
You do not insist on your right
but acquit us
and accept us –
everything is possible with you.
Give us the spirit
to follow you,
make us merciful to each other
so that the world may know
who you are:
nothing but love, our Father,
God.
You watch over your creation,
a shepherd
with whom all living things are safe.

You know us all
and keep us
wherever we move.
O God, do this,
we ask you,
all the days of our lives –
may we never want
and may we enter your rest
and know your peace.
Today and every day
of our lives.

5.   YOU ARE EVERYWHERE

God, you are everywhere
present invisible
near to us speaking –
the silence awaits you
mankind exists for you
men see and know you.

Men made of flesh and bone
men of light and of stone
men of hard stone and blood
a flow unstaunchable
mankind your people
your city on earth.

Earth is all that we are
dust is all that we make,
breathe into us, open us,
make us your earth
your heaven new made
your peace upon earth.

Origen
c.185–c.254

A brilliant theologian and biblical scholar, he also possessed an intense and uncompromising faith which frequently brought him into conflict with the institutional church. He taught that the Bible should be understood on three levels, literal, moral, and allegorical; and this attitude to Scripture is reflected in his short, simple prayers.

1.   NOAH'S FLOOD

Lord, you can do everything. We beg you to take pity on us, making us not merely listen to what you say, but put it into practice also. Send the flood of your waters over our souls, destroying within us what should be destroyed, and giving life to that which should live.

2.   ABRAHAM'S CIRCUMCISION

Lord, grant that we may believe in our hearts, declare with our mouths, and prove by our deeds that his covenant with mankind may be sealed in our flesh. May our spiritual circumcision be visible to all among whom we live, that they may praise you for our good works.

3.   THE OPENING OF AGAR'S EYES

Lord, put your hands on our eyes, that we shall be able to see not only that which is visible, but also that which is invisible. Let our eyes be focused not only on that which is present, but also on that which is to come. Unseal the heart's vision, that we may gaze on God in his glory.

4. KNOWLEDGE OF SCRIPTURE

Lord, inspire us to read your Scriptures and meditate upon them day and night. We beg you to give us real understanding of what we need, that we in turn may put its precepts into practice. Yet we know that understanding and good intentions are worthless, unless rooted in your graceful love. So we ask that the words of Scriptures may also be not just signs on a page, but channels of grace into our hearts.

Prayers from Papyri

Since the nineteenth-century a great number of Christian texts, written on papyrus, have been brought to light by archaeological excavation. For the most part they are mere fragments, but some entire scrolls have been found. They include some of the earliest Christian prayers. The precise date of composition is impossible to determine, but they probably date from between the second and fourth centuries.

1. HELPER OF MEN

Helper of men who turn to you,
Light of men in the dark,
Creator of all that grows from seed,
Promoter of all spiritual growth,
Have mercy, Lord, on me.
And make me a temple fit for you.
Do not look too closely at my sins,
For if you are quick to notice my faults
I shall not dare to appear before you.
In your great mercy,

In your boundless love,
Wash away my sins
By the hand of Jesus Christ,
Your only child, the chief healer of souls.

2.   HOLY GOD

Holy God, you have shown me light and life.
You are stronger than any natural power.
Accept the words from my heart
That struggle to reach you.
Accept the silent thoughts and feelings
That are offered to you.
Clear my mind of the clutter of useless facts.
Bend down to me, and lift me in your arms.
Make me holy as you are holy.
Give me a voice to sing of your love to others.

3.   GIVE US STRENGTH

Give us strength to do your will.
Do not dwell on the sins we have committed,
Or on the sins we shall commit.
Put out of your mind our many failings.
Keep no record of our wrongs.
Both those which were deliberate,
And those which we could not help.
Remember, Lord, that men are apt to slip,
That we are a weak and spineless race,
Apt to blunder and fall.
Our skins may seem clear and fresh,
But beneath the surface are festering spiritual sores.

O God, we know you are well disposed to us,
So give us your strength and support.
Help us to live by the precepts of our faith,
Fill our minds with the light of your love.
We have heard the holy teachings of your Son.

Let us not be content merely to hear him,
But give us the desire to obey him.
Teach us always to look upwards.
Seeking to probe with our prayers the mystery of
   heaven.
May the vision of your heavenly kingdom
Guide our actions on earth.

Blaise Pascal
1623–1662

---

*In his time he was famous as a mathematician
and scientist, but today he is remembered for his
religious reflections. A tense and inhibited young
man, subject to bouts of depression, at the age of
thirty-one he had a spiritual experience in which
for two hours he was ecstatic with joy. Immediately
afterwards he wrote down his* Memorial, *pouring
out his emotions. He sewed this passionate prayer
into the lining of his jacket next to his heart, where
it was found at his death. For the remaining eight
years of his life he was beset by ill-health, but he
came to regard sickness as a blessing through which
God draws the human heart closer to himself.*

1.   MEMORIAL

"God of Abraham, God of Isaac, God of Jacob," not of the
   philosophers and scholars.
Certainty. Certainty. Emotion. Joy. Peace.
God of Jesus Christ.
"My God and your God."
Your God shall be my God.
Forgetting the world and all things, except only God.
He can be found only by the ways taught in the Gospel.

Greatness of the human soul.
Righteous Father, the world has not known you, but I have known
    you.
Joy, joy, joy, tears of joy.
I have cut myself off from him.
"They have forsaken me, the fountain of living water."
"My God, will you forsake me?"
May I not be cut off from him forever!
"This is life eternal, that they know you, the only true God, and
    Jesus Christ, whom you have sent."
Jesus Christ
Jesus Christ.
I have cut myself off from him, shunned him, decried him,
    crucified him.
Let me never be cut off from him!
We cling to him only by the ways taught in the Gospel.
Sweet and total renunciation.
Total submission to Jesus Christ and to my director,
Eternal joy in return for one day's trial on earth.
"I will not forget your word."

2.   MEDITATIONS ON THE GOOD USE OF SICKNESS

Lord, you are good and gentle in all your ways; and your mercy is
so great that not only the blessings but also the misfortunes of your
people are channels of your compassion. Grant that I may turn to
you as a Father in my present condition since the change in my
own state from health to sickness brings no change to you. You are
always the same, and you are my loving Father in times of trouble
and in times of joy alike.

You gave me health that I might serve you; and so often I failed to
use my good health in your service. Now you send me sickness in
order to correct me. My health was full of pride and selfish ambition
when I was healthy. Now please let sickness destroy that pride and
ambition. Render me incapable of enjoying any worldly pleasures,
that I may take delight in you alone. Grant that I may adore you
in the lonely silence of my sick bed. And grant that, having ignored

the things of the spirit when my body was vigorous, I may now enjoy spiritual sweetness while my body groans with pain.

How happy is the heart, O God, that can love an object so pleasing as yourself, the heart that can find its peace is an object so beautiful. How secure and durable is the happiness that is found in you since you endure for ever. Neither life nor death can separate such happiness from its object. Move my heart, O God, to repentance for all my faults, for all the many times I have looked elsewhere for happiness. Let the disorder in my body be the means through which my soul is put into order. I can now find no happiness in physical things; let me find happiness only in you.

You can see me, Lord, as I truly am; and surely you can find nothing pleasing to you in me. I can see in myself, Lord, nothing but my sufferings. Yet I find comfort in the knowledge that, in a small way, these resemble your sufferings. Look down, Lord, on the pains that I suffer, on the illness that afflicts me. Look down, blessed Saviour, on the wounds that your hand has made. You did love your own sufferings, even though they ended in death itself. You became man that you might suffer more than any man has done, in order to save man. In your body you embraced all bodily suffering. Look with favour upon my body, look with love upon my pain. Let my sorrows be my invitation to you to visit me on my sick bed.

Uproot in me, Lord, the self-pity on which self-love feeds. Let me not dwell with self-pity on my own sufferings. Let me not regret the loss of worldly pleasures; remind me that such pleasures can never satisfy the heart. Clothe my heart in the sorrow that clothed your heart on the cross. Let me henceforth ask for neither health nor life, but rather let me be content to let you dispose of me as you please. Let health and sickness, life and death, be equal in my sight. Let me joyfully acknowledge you as my king, and give and take away your blessings as you wish. Let me trust in your eternal providence, receiving with equal reverence all that comes to me from you.

O my Saviour, since I share in some small way your sufferings, fill me to the brim with the glory which your sufferings won for mankind. Let me share in some small way the joy of your risen life.

Alan Paton
1903–

One of South Africa's foremost writers, his book Cry, the Beloved Country *drew him into the political struggle against racism. His religious convictions, expressed in meditations and prayers in* Instrument of Thy Peace, *taught him that self-giving love, not violence, is the only valid means of political change.*

1.   MAKE ME WILLING TO BE USED BY YOU

Lord, make me willing to be used by you. May my knowledge of my unworthiness never make me resist being used by you. May the need of others always be remembered by me, so that I may ever be willing to be used by you.

And open my eyes and my heart that I may this coming day be able to do some work of peace for you.

2.   MAY I UNDERSTAND MORE CLEARLY YOUR NATURE

O God, Creator of mankind, I do not aspire to comprehend you or your creation, nor to understand pain or suffering. I aspire only to relieve the pain and suffering of others, and I trust that in doing so, I may understand more clearly your nature, that you are the Father of all mankind, and that the hairs of my head are numbered.

And help me this coming day to do some work of peace for you.

3.   TAKE ALL HATE FROM MY HEART

Take all hate from my heart, O God, and teach me how to take it from the hearts of others. Open my eyes and show me what things in our society make it easy for hatred to flourish and hard for us to conquer it. Then help me to try to change these things.

And so open my eyes and my ears that I may this coming day be able to do some work of peace for you.

4.   HELP ME TO BE MORE LOVING

Help me, O Lord, to be more loving. Help me, O Lord, not to be afraid to love the outcast, the leper, the unmarried pregnant woman, the traitor to the State, the man out of prison. Help me by my love to restore the faith of the disillusioned, the disappointed, the early bereaved. Help me by my love to be the witness of your love.

And may I this coming day be able to do some work of peace for you.

5.   TEACH ME TO HATE DIVISION

Lord, teach me the meaning of your commandment to love our enemies, and help me to obey it. Make me the instrument of your love, which is not denied to the hungry, the sick, the prisoner, the enemy. Teach me to hate division, and not to seek after it. But teach me also to stand up for those things that I believe to be right, no matter what the consequences may be.

And help me this day to do some work of peace for you, perhaps to one whom I had thought to be my enemy.

6.   TEACH US TO HUMBLE OURSELVES

O Lord, teach us to humble ourselves before these children who live the gospel of love and drugs because we did not live the gospel of love. Teach us to humble ourselves before the problems that face our children in this generation. Especially we pray for all parents, that they may love their children steadfastly, even in the face of bewilderment and grief. Teach us to humble ourselves when we contemplate the world we have made, the millions that we have killed and maimed in the cause of justice.

And above all make us the instruments of your love, that we may love those who call out that they love us all. Even if we cannot help them, teach us to love them.

Polycarp of Smyrna
c.69–c.155

This indomitable old bishop of Smyrna was one of the most famous martyrs of the early Church. An account of his martyrdom circulated throughout the Christian world, and his dying prayers inspired many who suffered a similar fate.

1.   AT THE STAKE

Lord God almighty, we have come to know you through that dear child of yours, Jesus Christ, and he has led us to you. I bless you because you have thought me worthy of this day and hour, worthy to be numbered among the martyrs and then to drink out of the cup that Jesus has drunk from; so with him you have counted me worthy to rise and live for ever.

May I be admitted to your presence today, a satisfactory and welcome sacrifice. You have made my life a preparation for this. You showed me that this was my destiny, and now, true to your word, you have brought it about. For this and all your blessings I praise you and give you glory.

2.   AS THE FLAMES ROSE

Lord Jesus Christ, receive my soul.
Blessings to you, Lord Jesus Christ, that you have thought me fit to share this fate with you, sinner that I am.
Lord, Lord, Lord, come to my help; I turn to you for refuge.

Book of Psalms

The Psalms are traditionally attributed to King David, but were not collected into their present form until the rebuilding of the temple in Jerusalem, where they were used as hymns. Their strength is that they express to God the whole range of human emotions, from love and gratitude, to anger and jealousy. Thus they are models of honest prayer.

1.
FOR HELP

Lord, do not rebuke me in your anger, nor punish me in your wrath. Have pity on me, O Lord, for I am worn out. Give me strength, for my body is exhausted and my soul is deeply troubled. How long, O Lord, will it be before you help me?

Turn, O Lord, and save me; in your mercy rescue me from death. In the world of the dead you are not remembered, so no one can praise you there.

I am worn out with grief. Every night I flood my bed with tears; my pillow is drenched with my weeping. My eyes are so swollen that I can hardly see.

2.
FOR JUSTICE

Why do you stand far off, O Lord? Why do you hide yourself in times of trouble? In their arrogance the wicked exploit the poor, catching them in schemes which they have devised. These wicked men are proud of their evil desires, and those who are greedy curse and reject you. So the helpless victims lie crushed, while those who have defeated them by their brute strength say to themselves: "God does not care; he has closed his eyes and will never see me".

O Lord, punish those wicked men, and give help to their victims. How can you allow the wicked men to despise you, saying "God will not call me to account". You do see what is happening. You do take notice of trouble and suffering, and are always ready to help. Those who are weak put their trust in you, because in times past you have protected them.

You will listen, O Lord, to the prayers of the lowly, and give them courage. You will hear the cries of the oppressed and the orphaned, and give them justice.

3.   ANGUISHED HOPE

My God, my God, why have you forsaken me? I have cried in desperation for help, but still it does not come. By day I call on you, O my God, but you do not answer; I call at night, but get no rest. Yet you are enthroned as the Holy One, on whom the praises of Israel are lavished. Our ancestors put their trust in you, and you saved them. They cried to you and were saved; they trusted in you, and were not disappointed.

I am no longer a man, but a worm. I am scorned and despised by everyone. All who see me jeer at me: they stick out their tongues and shake their heads. "You relied on the Lord", they say; "Let him rescue you. If the Lord likes you, why doesn't he help you?"

It was you who brought me from my mother's womb, and you who kept me safe on my mother's breasts. I have depended on you since the day I was born, and you have always been my God. Do not stay away from me. Trouble is near, and there is no one to help.

Many enemies surround me like fierce bulls from the land of Bashan. They open their mouths like lions, roaring and tearing at me. My strength is gone, spilt like water on to the ground. My bones are out of joint, and my heart is like melted wax. My throat is as dry as dust, and my tongue sticks to the roof of my mouth. You have left me for dead in the dust.

A gang of evil men is round me. Like a pack of wolves they close in on me, tearing at my hands and feet. All my bones can be seen.

My enemies look at me and stare, and they gamble for my clothes, dividing them among themselves.

O Lord, do not stay away from me. Come quickly to my rescue. Save me from the sword; deliver me from these dogs; rescue me from these lions; I am helpless before these wild bulls.

I will tell my people what you have done. I will praise you in their assembly. "Praise him you servants of the Lord! Honour him, descendants of Jacob. Worship him, people of Israel. He does not neglect the poor or ignore their suffering. He does not turn away from them, but answers when they call for help."

4.   JOYFUL CONFIDENCE

You, Lord, are all that I have, and you give me all that I need; my future is in your hands. How wonderful are your gifts to me; how good they are.

I bless you, Lord, because you guide me. In the night also you instruct my heart. I am constantly aware of your presence; and, knowing that you are near, I cannot be shaken from my faith.

So my soul is joyful, and I feel completely secure, under your protection. I am confident that you shall never abandon me. You show me the path of life, which leads to eternal bliss.

5.   IN PRAISE OF THE CREATOR

O Lord my God, how great you are! You are clothed with honour and majesty; you cover yourself with light. You stretch out the heavens like a tent, and build your home on the waters above. You make the clouds your chariots, and you ride on the wings of the wind. The winds are your messengers, and flashes of lightning your servants.

You set the earth firmly on its foundations, so that it could never be moved. You placed the oceans over it like a robe, and the waters covered the mountains. At your rebuke the waters fled, flowing over the mountains and into the valleys to the place you had made for them. You marked a boundary which they should not pass, to keep them from covering the earth again.

You make springs gush forth in the valleys, and rivers run

between the hills. They provide water for wild animals to drink. In the trees nearby the birds make their nests and sing. From the sky you send rain on the hills, and the earth is filled with your blessings.

You make the grass grow for the cattle, and plants for man to cultivate, so that he can bring food from the earth, wine to gladden his heart, olive oil to make his face shine, and bread to give him strength.

You created the moon to mark the months; the sun knows the time for setting. You made the night when all the beasts of the forest creep out. The young lions roar while they hunt, looking for the food which God provides. When the sun rises they go back and lie down in their den. Then the people go out to work, labouring until evening.

Lord, you have made so many things, fashioning them with such wisdom. The earth is filled with your creatures, and the oceans teem with countless fish.

All depend on you to give them food when they need it. You give it to them, and they eat it; you provide food, and they are satisfied. When you turn away they are afraid. When you take away their breath they die, and go back to the dust from which they came. But when you give them breath, they are created, and you renew the face of the earth.

E. B. Pusey
1800–1882

With Newman and Keble he led the Oxford Movement which sought to restore Catholic doctrine and practice to the Church of England. His particular contribution was to inspire the renewal of monastic life, and to reawaken Anglicans to the medieval tradition of spirituality. His prayers are invariably intimate and personal and to modern taste can border on the sentimental.

1.   LONELINESS

Good Jesu, Father of the fatherless, God of the lonely;
Teach me through loneliness to be alone with thee.

Good Jesu, who speakest to the secret heart;
Let loneliness be thy presence in my soul.

2.   WEAKNESS

Good Jesu, thou hast made me and remade me;
Thou knowest my weakness, who hast made me.
I am dry, heavy, desolate, lonely, desponding;
Forgive me all my sins, heal all my infirmities;
Give me the comfort of thy help,
Or strengthen me in my weariness.
Let my soul gasp for thee, like the parched ground,
And gasping for thee, receive thee.

3.   TOO LATE HAVE I LOVED THEE

Good Jesu, too late have I loved thee,
Nor ever yet have I wholly followed thee;
Make me now at last wholly to love thee,
And out of the fullness of thine infinite love
Give me all the love I might have had, had I always loved
    thee.

O dearest Lord, too late have I loved thee,
Too late have I loved thee,
Too late is it always,
Not always to have loved thee wholly.
Now, too, I cannot love thee as I would.
O dearest Lord, who art love
Give me of thine own love,
That therewith I may wholly love thee.

4.　　　　　　　　　AT CHRISTMAS

Good Jesu, born as at this time,
A little child for love of us;
Be thou born in me, that I may
Be a little child in love of thee;
And hang on thy love as on my
Mother's bosom,
Trustfully, lovingly, peacefully;
Hushing all my cares in love of thee.

Good Jesu, sweeten every thought of mine
With the sweetness of thy love.
Good Jesu, give me a deep love for thee,
That nothing may be too hard for me
To bear for love of thee.

5.　　　　　　　　　DURING HOLY WEEK

Good Jesu, my God and my all,
Be thou all to me,
Be thou all in me,
That I may be all thine,
And all thy will mine.

Make me cheerful under every cross,
For love of thy Cross;
Take from me all which displeases thee,
Or hinders thy love in me,
That I may deeply love thee.
Melt me with thy love,
That I may be all love,
And with my whole being love thee.

Good Jesu, who gavest thyself for me,
Give me of the fullness of thy love,
That for all thy love,
With thy love, I may love thee.

6.   AT ASCENSION-TIDE

Good Jesu, exalted above the highest heavens,
But dwelling with the lowly,
Make me as a little lowly child,
Suspecting nothing,
Fearing nothing,
Mistrusting nothing;
But trusting my whole self with thee.
I am not worthy to kiss the hem of thy garment,
But do thou take me up in thy arms and bless me.

7.   AT PENTECOST

Good Jesu, fountain of love: fill me with thy love,
Absorb me into thy love, compass me with thy love,
That I may see all things in the light of thy love,
Receive all things as tokens of thy love,
Speak of all things in words breathing of thy love,
Win through thy love others to thy love,
Be kindled, day by day, with a new glow of thy love,
Until I be fitted to enter into thine everlasting love,
To adore thy love and love to adore thee, my God and my all.
    Even so, come, Lord Jesu!

Michel Quoist
1921–

*His earthy and often witty meditations, arising out
of ordinary scenes and events, have brought prayer
within reach of countless people who imagined
themselves too worldly for religion. Ordained a
priest in 1947, he served for many years in Le
Havre.*

1.   THE BRICK

The bricklayer laid a brick on the bed of cement.
Then, with a precise stroke of his trowel spread another layer
And without a by-your-leave, laid on another brick.
The foundations grew visibly,
The building rose, tall and strong, to shelter men.

I thought, Lord, of that brick buried in the darkness at the base
     of the big building.
No one sees it, but it accomplishes its task, and the other bricks
     need it.
Lord, what difference whether I am on the roof-top or in the
     foundations of your building, as long as I stand faithfully at the
     right place?

2.   POSTERS

They are loud.
I cannot avoid them, for they crowd together on the wall,
     alluring and tempting.
Their violent colours hurt my eyes
And I can't rid myself of their distasteful presence.

Lord, in the same way too often I draw attention to myself.
Grant that I may be more humble and unobtrusive,
And above all keep me from trying to impress others through
     showy display,
For it is your light only, Lord, that must draw all men.

3.   THE WIRE FENCE

The wires are holding hands around the holes;
To avoid breaking the ring, they hold tight the neighbouring
     wrist,
And it's thus that with holes they make a fence.

Lord, there are lots of holes in my life.
There are some in the lives of my neighbours.

But if you wish we shall hold hands
We shall hold very tight
And together we shall make a fine roll of fence to adorn
    Paradise.

4.   THE TELEPHONE

I have just hung up; why did he telephone?
I don't know ... O! I get it ...
I talked a lot and listened very little.

Forgive me, Lord, it was a monologue and not a dialogue.
I explained my idea and did not get his;
Since I didn't listen, I learned nothing,
Since I didn't listen, I didn't help,
Since I didn't listen, we didn't communicate.

Forgive me, Lord, for we were connected,
and now we are cut off.

Rabbula of Edessa
d.435

A leading figure in the Syrian Church, he trans-
lated The New Testament *into his native tongue.*
He wrote a prayer to be used by penitents when
confessing their sins.

1.   HAVE PITY ON ME

You are rich, Lord, in grace and mercy, willing to cleanse all sinners
from their guilt. Cleanse me with hyssop, have pity on me. In your
mercy spare me, as you spared the publican and the prodigal son.
You take the sinfulness from sinners, O Christ, and when we repent

you make us welcome beside you. Redeemer of the human race, in your mercy, have pity on me.

If your salvation is hard for even the righteous to obtain, what will become of me, sinner that I am. I have not borne the day's burden or the sun's heat; I am one of those workmen who come at the eleventh hour. Save me, have pity on me.

My sins have bowed me to the ground, casting me down from the heights of power and authority which I enjoyed. I could not have done more to achieve my own ruin if I had rushed over a precipice. Who but you can restore me to the beauty in which you created me? Who but you can remake me in the image of yourself? In your mercy, Lord, deliver me; have pity on me.

My thoughts confuse and cloud my mind. I am in despair because my guilt is vaster than the ocean and my sins more numerous than the waves of the sea. When I remember how I have fallen, I tremble at the thought of your justice. I dare not look upwards, because my sins reach as high as the heavens. The mere sight of the earth is an accusation to me, for my offences exceed the number of its inhabitants. Have pity on me, Lord.

What will become of me, Lord? How will I explain myself when I must confess that there is nothing to show for the talents you bestowed on me. Have pity.

I am determined that the fire of hell will not consume me, since you have given your body and blood to feed me. I refuse to be carried off to eternal damnation, for you have clothed me with the garment of baptism.

Grant me the dew of your grace, Lord. Forgive my sins. But above all, may the glory belong to you.

Karl Rahner
1904–1984

---

*A Jesuit theologian, he exerted a major influence
on the Second Vatican Council which transformed*

the Roman Catholic Church. Yet while at the
height of his fame and power, he wrote a prayer
acknowledging to God his ignorance in the face of
the divine mystery.

1.   I FOUNDER HELPLESSLY

Without you, I should founder helplessly in my own dull and grop-
ing narrowness. I could never feel the pain of longing, not even
deliberately resign myself to being content with this world, had not
my mind again and again soared over its own limitations into the
hushed reaches which are filled by you alone, the Silent Infinite.
Where should I flee before you, when all my yearning for the
unbounded, even my bold trust in my littleness, is really a confession of you?

What a poor creature you have made me, O God! All I know
about you and about myself is that you are the eternal mystery of
my life. Lord, what a frightful puzzle man is! He belongs to you
and you are the Incomprehensible – incomprehensible in your
being and even more so in your ways and judgements. For if all
your dealings with me are acts of your freedom, quite unmerited
gifts of your grace which knows no "why", if my creation and my
whole life hang absolutely on your free decision, if all my paths are,
after all, your paths and therefore unsearchable, then, Lord,
no amount of questioning will ever fathom your depths – you
will still be the Incomprehensible, even when I see you face to
face.

But can it be that you are my true home? Are you the One who
will release me from my narrow little dungeon? Or are you merely
adding another torment to my life, when you throw open the gates
leading out upon your broad and endless plain? Are you anything
more than my own great insufficiency, if all my knowledge leads
only to your incomprehensibility? Are you merely eternal unrest
for the restless soul? Must every question fall dumb before you,
unanswered? Is your only response the mute "I will have it so" that
so coldly smothers my burning desire to understand?

But I am rambling on like a fool – excuse me, O God. You have
told me through your Son that you are the God of my love, and

you have commanded me to love you. Your commands are often hard because they enjoin the opposite of what my own inclinations would lead me to do, but when you bid me love you, you are ordering something that my own inclinations would never even dare to suggest: to love you, to come intimately close to you, to love your very life. You ask me to lose myself in you, knowing that you will take me to your Heart, where I may speak on loving, familiar terms with you, the incomprehensible mystery of my life. And all this because you are Love itself.

But when I love you, when I manage to break out of the narrow circle of self and leave behind the restless agony of unanswered questions, when my blinded eyes no longer look merely from afar and from the outside upon your unapproachable brightness, and much more when you yourself, O Incomprehensible One, have become through love the inmost centre of my life, then I can bury myself entirely in you, O mysterious God, and with myself all my questions.

Rahulabhadra

2nd century

Within the Buddhism of Tibet and China, Perfect Wisdom came to be perceived as the supreme God who created and sustains the universe. This prayer to Perfect Wisdom was frequently used as a preface to theological texts.

1.   TO PERFECT WISDOM

Let all homage be given to you, Perfect Wisdom.
You are boundless, you are above all human thought.
You are faultless, you are without blemish.
You are spotless, you are greater than space itself.

As the moonlight depends on the moon,
So all wisdom depends on your wisdom.
As the sunlight depends on the sun,
So all virtue depends on your virtue.

Those who always seek to be guided by you
Attain joy and peace with ease.
Those whose greatest desire is to gaze upon you
Find purity of heart.

Those who are constantly concerned with the welfare
    of others
Are blessed by you in their efforts.
You are like a mother to the soul,
Giving birth to love, and nourishing virtue.

As the stars dance round the moon,
So righteous souls dance round your throne.
As white clouds encircle the sun,
So pure souls encircle your throne.

As the drops of dew evaporate
When the hot rays of the sun appear,
So all evil and falsehood evaporate
Under the warmth of your love and truth.

There are some who have no affection for you,
And some who look upon you with hatred.
You do not condemn or destroy them,
But they condemn themselves to hopeless misery.

Never to look upon your brightness,
Never to hear your eternal music,
Never to feel your softness,
Is to live without pleasure or joy.

Those who are devoted to you
Are slaves to your power.
Yet in obeying your commands of love,
The soul finds perfect freedom.

Those who are cold and indifferent to you
Imagine they enjoy perfect freedom.
Yet they are slaves to their own desires,
Bound in chains by their bodily wants.

You are the only path to salvation,
There is no other way but you.
You are the saviour of the world,
The world is lost without you.

No words can properly describe you,
The soul alone can know you.
The silent love of the soul
Is the true chorus of praise.

Brother Ramon
1935–

---

*A member of the Anglican Society of St Francis,
he now lives as a hermit. He compiled a personal
retreat programme,* Heaven on Earth, *based on
his experience of leading retreats. His prayers are
rich in vivid metaphors.*

1.   EARTH AND SEASONS

Lord of the elements and changing seasons, keep me in the hollow
of your hand. When I am tossed to and fro with the winds of
adversity and the blasts of sickness and misunderstanding, still my
racing heart, quieten my troubled mind.

Bring me at last through the storms and tribulations of this mortal
life into the calm evening of your unchanging love; and grant that
in the midst of my present perplexities and confusion I may experience your peace which passes human understanding.

2. POTTER AND CLAY

Have your own way, Lord, have your own way,
You are the Potter, I am the clay;
Mould me and make me after your will,
As I am waiting, yielded and still.

3. SUN AND MOON

Heavenly Father: you have set sun, moon and stars in their places
and the music of the spheres sings your praise; as I reflect upon
their glory and your handiwork, grant me a greater awareness of
the wonder of your being and a deeper appreciation of your tender
love.

4. SEA AND RIVERS

O God, whose love is without measure: out of the depths of my
own creatureliness and yearning I call to you. Out of your own
immense depths of power and mystery you call to me. Enable me
to enter into the beginnings of the secrets of your love, and let the
poor stream of my life flow into the immensity of your Being.

5. TREES AND ANIMALS

Today, my Father, let me be like a tree planted by the river, bringing forth fruit in its season. Let the sap of your Holy Spirit rise
within me. Let me not become dry and barren but rich in abundance
and fertility. May many weary ones find refreshment in the shadow
of my branches.

6. SABBATH AND PARADISE

God of creation and Lord of the sabbath: you created the heavens
and the earth and rested on the seventh day. You commanded your
ancient people to cease from their work and rest in your love. Save
us from our frenetic religious activities and enable us to let go our

neurotic anxieties. Reveal to us your glory that we may gaze upon your beauty and be filled with your love.

Walter Rauschenbusch
1861–1918

A Baptist minister and a professor of theology, he was the leading exponent of the social gospel movement in America, which regarded social and economic justice as central to Christ's message. His book For God and People: Prayers for Social Awakening *demonstrated the spiritual implications of the social gospel.*

1.   FOR THE WORLD

O God, we thank thee for this universe, our great home; for its vastness and its riches, and for the manifoldness of the life which teems upon it and of which we are part. We praise thee for the arching sky and the blessed winds, for the driving clouds, and the constellations on high. We praise thee for the salt sea and the running water, for the everlasting hills, for the trees, and for the grass under our feet. We thank thee for our senses by which we can see the splendour of the morning, and hear the jubilant songs of love, and smell the breath of the springtime. Grant us, we pray thee, a heart wide open to all this joy and beauty, and save our souls from being so steeped in care or so darkened by passion that we pass heedless and unseeing when even the thornbush by the wayside is aflame with the glory of God.

Enlarge within us the sense of fellowship with all the living things, our little brothers, to whom thou hast given this earth as their home in common with us. We remember with shame that in the past we have exercised the high dominion of man with ruthless cruelty, so that the voice of the Earth, which should have gone up to thee in song, has been a groan of travail. May we realize that they live, not for us alone, but for themselves and for thee, and that they love the sweetness of life, even as we, and serve thee in their place better than we in ours.

When our use of this world is over and we make room for others, may we not leave anything ravished by our greed or spoiled by our ignorance, but may we hand on our common heritage fairer and sweeter through our use of it, undiminished in fertility and joy, that so our bodies may return in peace to the great mother who nourished them and our spirits may round the circle of a perfect life in thee.

2.   FOR PROPHETS AND PIONEERS

We praise thee, Almighty God, for thine elect, the prophets and martyrs of humanity, who gave their thoughts and prayers and agonies for the truth of God and the freedom of the people. We praise thee that amid loneliness and the contempt of men, in poverty and imprisonment, when they were condemned by the laws of the mighty and buffeted on the scaffold, thou didst uphold them by thy spirit in loyalty to thy holy cause.

Grant us rather that we too may be counted in the chosen band of those who have given their life as a ransom for the many. Send us forth with the pathfinders of humanity to lead thy people another day's march toward the land of promise.

3.   FOR DISCOVERERS AND INVENTORS

We praise thee, O Lord, for that mysterious spark of thy light within us, the intellect of man, for thou hast kindled it in the beginning and by the breath of thy Spirit it has grown to flaming power in our race.

We rejoice in the men of genius and intellectual vision who discern the undiscovered applications of thy laws and dig the deeper springs through which the hidden forces of thy world may well up to the light of day. We claim them as our own in thee, as members with us in the common body of humanity, of which thou art the all-pervading life and inspirer. Grant them, we pray thee, the divine humility of thine elect souls, to realize that they are sent of thee as brothers and helpers of men and that the powers within them are but part of the vast equipment of humanity, entrusted to them for the common use.

4.   FOR ARTISTS

O thou who art the all-pervading glory of the world, we bless thee for the power of beauty to gladden our hearts. We praise thee that even the least of us may feel a thrill of thy creative joy when we give form and substance to our thoughts and, beholding our handiwork, find it good and fair.

We praise thee for our brothers, the masters of form and colour and sound, who have power to unlock for us the vaster spaces of emotion and to lead us by their hand into the reaches of nobler passions. We rejoice in their gifts and pray thee to save them from the temptations which beset their powers. Kindle in their hearts a passionate pity for the joyless lives of the people, and make them rejoice if they are found worthy to hold the cup of beauty to lips that are athirst. Make them the reverent interpreters of God to man, who see thy face and hear thy voice in all things, that so they may unveil for us the beauties of nature which we have passed unseeing, and the sadness and sweetness of humanity to which our selfishness has made us blind.

5.   FOR LOVERS

We invoke thy gentlest blessings, our Father, on all true lovers. We praise thee for the great longing that draws the soul of man and maid together and bids them leave all the dear bonds of the past to cleave to one another. We thank thee for the revealing power of love which divines in one beloved the mystic beauty and glory of humanity. We thank thee for the transfiguring power of love which ripens and ennobles our nature, calling forth the hidden stores of tenderness and strength and overcoming the selfishness of youth by the passion of self-surrender.

Grant them with sober eyes to look beyond these sweet days of friendship to the generations yet to come and to realize that the home for which they long will be part of the sacred tissue of the body of humanity in which thou art to dwell, that so they may reverence themselves and drink the cup of joy with awe.

Richard Rolle
c.1300–1349

Despite his poor background, he won a place at Oxford to study for the priesthood. But he hated the intellectual approach to God of his theological teachers, and went to live as a hermit on the Yorkshire moors. There he came to experience God as a lover, whose warmth and sweetness overwhelmed him. He composed prayers and songs, which expressed in simple, vivid phrases his spiritual joy. He began touring the country, singing to the people he met and praying with them. The church authorities regarded him with suspicion, but he was universally popular amongst ordinary people.

1.   A WORTHY BRIDE

My God, my love, pour yourself over me,
Like the sweetest honey poured over a bitter fruit.
Let your sweetness penetrate my soul,
Let your delicious love heal my spiritual wounds.
My poor heart desires only you;
My soul pants for you;
My whole being thirsts for you.
Yet you will not reveal yourself to me.
You shun me, you look away, you pass me by.
You even laugh at my innocent sufferings.
Those whom you choose as your lovers
You lift high above all worldly desires.

You make them capable of loving you,
You teach them how to sing your praises
You give them the joy of knowing your sweetness.
Come to me, dear God; make me your lover.
I have sacrificed everything for your love.
I have turned my heart into a home for you.
Let me welcome you into myself.
Make me a worthy bride.

2.   REPENTANCE

Lord God, take pity on me.
During my infancy I ignored you;
During my boyhood I had no interest in you.
During my adolescence I pursued vain pleasures.
But now, Lord Jesus, I crave your mercy.
I want to know you,
I want to understand your truth,
I want to feel your joy.

3.   THE INVISIBLE BARRIER

Jesus, when I am with you, I burn with joy.
And when the heat of love surges within my breast,
I want to embrace you, to clasp you to myself.
Yet, my Beloved, my love is frustrated
By a strange, invisible barrier
That seems to stand between me and you.
If only you would break down that barrier,
And so let me rush to your arms.
I can see you clearly,
And I beg you to allow me to come to you.
I am in prison, beating my fists against the wall
That divides me from you.
But in the meantime I can sing your praises,
And in prayer I can speak with you.
So I will enjoy such blessings for the present,
In the hope of being united fully in the future.

4.   FRUSTRATED DESIRE

My love, my honey, my harp,
Playing sweet music in my soul!
When are you going to heal my grief?
When are you coming to revive my spirit
Which is constantly yearning for you?
Your beauty stimulates my desire,
But when I realize the great distance between us,
My desire is frustrated, and I sink in gloom.
Will you give me some grounds for hope
That one day my desire will be satisfied?
Will you assure me that one day
My joy will be complete?

5.   HEAVENLY MUSIC

Jesus, my joy in you is great
I want to praise you always.
When I was down and out
You stooped down to embrace me
Filling my soul with sweet, heavenly music.
Now you have silenced the ugly noise of sin within me
So I too can sing sweet spiritual songs,
Serenading your eternal love.
And as the melody of love springs forth from my soul
I realize that it is no more
Than the feeble echo of your perfect songs
With which you enchant the angels in heaven.

6.   A LOVER'S CODE

I ask you, Lord Jesus,
To inspire within me, your lover,
An affection that is unbounded,
A desire that is unrestrained,
A yearning that throws discretion to the winds.
May reason not hold my love in check.

May fear not inhibit my devotion,
May decorum not temper my fervour.

7.   EARTHLY JOYS AND HEAVENLY SWEETNESS

Just as the wealth of a lord in his castle
Vastly exceeds that of humble peasants,
So the sweetness of your love, my Beloved,
Vastly exceeds the pleasure of any earthly joys.
Those who lust after the things of this world
Are ignorant of the delight of your love.
If they have a single taste of your sweetness,
They too would become your lovers.

8.   WIND, MELODY, SWEETNESS AND LIGHT

No one can untie the knot
By which I bind myself to you, sweet Jesus.
Like the wind blowing away the autumn leaves,
Your Spirit blows away my sorrow.
Like a lullaby soothing a troubled child,
Your melody of love comforts my soul.
Like honey giving taste to dull food,
Your sweetness fills me with pleasure.
Like a lamp shining in a dark night,
Your light guides me through the dark confusion of life.

9.   GOD'S FRIENDSHIP

Your friendship, Lord, is my glory.
When I began to love you,
Your hand, Lord, held up my heart,
And I found myself wanting nothing and no one
Except you.
In you and through you I felt I could suffer
Any pain, any indignity, without anguish.
Your warmth melted my stubborn pride,
And your sweetness overwhelmed my sadness.

So I could put my whole trust in you,
Knowing that in you I would always be happy.

10.   THE MOMENT OF DEATH

Come, my Saviour, comfort my soul!
Make me steadfast in my love for you,
So that my love never falters.
When the moment of my death approaches,
Take from me any fear or grief;
Rather let me rejoice and be glad
That soon I shall enter your presence.
My mind is ablaze with love for you,
And my heart burns with desire to see you.
Therefore I endure earthly poverty,
And I despise earthly dignity,
Knowing that in heaven alone
Shall I find true wealth and true glory.

Christina Rossetti
1830–1894

An invalid for most of her life, she was a prolific poet, composing ballads for the young, love lyrics, and religious verses. Her most famous poem, In the Bleak Midwinter, *has been set to music and is now a popular Christmas hymn. Towards the end of her life she wrote a devotional commentary on the Book of Revelations called* The Face of the Deep, *in which reflections on the biblical texts are interspersed with prayers.*

1.

MAKE ME PURE

Lord, make me pure:
Only the pure shall see thee as thou art,
And shall endure.
Lord, bring me low;
For thou wert lowly in thy blessed heart:
Lord, keep me so.

2.

I CANNOT PLEAD MY LOVE

O Lord, I cannot plead my love of thee:
I plead thy love of me; –
The shallow conduit hails the unfathomed sea.

3.

WE ARE RIVERS

Lord, we are rivers running to thy sea,
Our waves and ripples all derived from thee:
A nothing we should have, a nothing be,
Except for thee.

Sweet are the waters of thy shoreless sea,
Make sweet our waters that make haste to thee;
Pour in thy sweetness, that ourselves may be
Sweetness to thee.

4.

GRANT US EYES

Lord, grant us eyes to see
Within the seed a tree,
Within the glowing egg a bird,
Within the shroud a butterfly:
Till taught by such, we see
Beyond all creatures thee,
And hearken for thy tender word
And hear it, "Fear not: it is I".

5.   FULFIL THY WILL

O Lord, fulfil thy Will
Be the days few or many, good or ill:
Prolong them, to suffice
For offering up ourselves thy sacrifice;
Shorten them if thou wilt,
To make in righteousness an end of guilt,
Yea, they will not be long
To souls who learn to sing a patient song:
Yea, short they will not be
To souls on tiptoe to flee home to thee.
O Lord, fulfil thy Will:
Make thy Will ours, and keep us patient still
Be the days few or many, good or ill.

Roger Schutz
1915–

In 1940 he acquired a house in the village of Taizé in south-east France where he sheltered Jews and other refugees. By 1944 six other young men had joined him, and they formed a monastic community. While the founders were all Protestants, subsequent members have been drawn from all Christian traditions, and the community has become an ecumenical focus of spiritual renewal, attracting tens of thousands of visitors. Brother Roger drew up the community's rule, and has written a large number of prayers and meditations which express a faith which is both joyful and robust.

1.

IF WE HAD FAITH

Lord Christ, if we had faith
that could move mountains,
yet without living charity,
what would we be?
You love us.
Without your Holy Spirit
who lives in our hearts,
what would we be?
You love us.
Taking everything on you,
you open for us a way towards faith,
towards trust in God,
who wants neither suffering
nor human distress.
Spirit of the Risen Christ,
Spirit of compassion,
Spirit of praise,
your love for each one of us
will never go away.

2.

YOU WERE IN ME

You were in me, Christ,
you were always there,
and I was not seeking you.
When I had found you, so often
I forgot you. But you continued
to love me. From the depths of my being,
a fire was rising to take hold of me.
I was burning for you to be everything
in my life. I was calling you:
You, the Christ, are the only way,
I have no other.

3. WITHIN US THERE ARE WOUNDS

Although within us there are wounds,
Lord Christ, above all there is
the miracle of your mysterious presence.
Thus, made lighter or even set free,
we are going with you, the Christ,
from one discovery to another.

John Sergieff
1829–1908

---

*The son of a poor village deacon in northern Russia,
he managed to gain a place at St Petersburg seminary,
where he trained for the priesthood. He then
married and was appointed to a remote rural
parish, where he remained for the rest of his life.
He became renowned for his concern for the poor,
collecting huge sums for their support, and for the
prayers he composed which ordinary people could
adapt and use for themselves.*

1. YOUR DWELLING-PLACE

Lord, grant me a simple, kind, open, believing, loving and generous
heart, worthy of being your dwelling-place.

2. I AM YOUR SHIP

Lord, I am your ship.
Fill me with the gifts of your Holy Spirit.
Without you I am empty of every blessing,
And full of every sin.

Lord, I am your ship.
Fill me with a cargo of good works.
Without you, I am empty of every joy,
And full of vain pleasures.

Lord, I am your ship.
Fill me with love for you.

3.   GLORIFYING THE TRINITY

Father, grant that I may always turn to you in prayer for every need
– for my needs, for the needs of your Church, and for the needs of
your world.

Jesus, grant I may always meditate on your love – manifest within
my heart, manifest in your Church, and manifest throughout your
world.

Spirit, grant that I may always be a channel of your grace – grace
within my own thought and emotions, grace within your Church,
and grace within your world.

Holy Trinity, grant that I may glorify you in all my actions –
privately in my home, and publicly in your Church and your world.

4.   HOW MANY TIMES

How many times, Lord Jesus, have you renewed my nature! How
many times have you saved me from the furnace of evil passions
burning within me! O Lord, in truth there is no number and no
measure of your mercies to me. May I for my part be faithful to
you. May I be humble, not proud; meek, not irritable; industrious,
not lazy; merciful, not judgemental; generous, not mean; and obedient, not wilful.

5.   THE SPIRIT'S CAPTIVE

Take me captive, Lord, in the sweet captivity of your Holy Spirit.
May I be a prisoner of your Spirit's impulses. Let the actions that
I perform, the words that I speak, and my innermost thoughts and
feelings, be under your Spirit's compulsions. I want only to see

what your Spirit lets me see, and go where your Spirit allows. I am a joyful, willing captive!

6.   DOING GOD'S WILL

Do not allow me, Lord, even for an instant, to do the will of your enemy, the Devil. But grant that I may continually do your will, and only your will. You are the King under whose authority all kings reign. You alone are worthy of reverence and obedience. Truly I trust you, and firmly I love you.

7.   GENEROUS ACTIONS

Lord, teach me to be generous to others with a willing and joyful heart, knowing that through generous actions I gain infinitely more spiritually than I lose materially. Let me not be influenced by those who meet poverty with indifference, who blame the past for their own misfortunes. O Lord, such hard-hearted people are so common that I meet them every day. Yet in hearing their cold attitudes, may my own heart be kindled anew to serve those who are hungry, thirsty or naked. And show me how my efforts may best be directed, to give greatest help to those in need.

8.   THE MOUNTAIN OF HEAVEN

You alone, Lord, know how those who seek to imitate you must sweat. The path to heaven is steep, hard and rough, demanding every ounce of strength. We who tread that path enjoy no rest. Yet we are happy to leave all earthly pleasures far below, because they are empty and dull. And, though we can only glimpse it far above us, the beauty of the summit inspires our hearts and strengthens our souls. What peace, what bliss, what rapture, what freedom is to be found on the mountain of eternal life.

9.   FRIENDSHIP, HUMAN AND DIVINE

Dear Lord, how the love of my friends towards me rejoices my heart. Who can describe the feeling in the heart that comes from knowing people's love? It is indescribable. To be aware that there are people who love me, even as the miserable sinner that I am, fills me with hope. And the source of the hope is the knowledge that my friends' love for me is a pale shadow of God's love for me. Thus when God takes me to heaven, the present joy I have in friendship will be multiplied a thousandfold. Such bliss is worth any earthly sacrifice. Lord, your name is Love. In your love there is sweetness beyond words. Grant that I may always be faithful to my friends here on earth, that I may be worthy of your faithful love for me.

10.   THE POWER OF THE CROSS

Glory to the never-failing power of your cross, O Lord! When the enemy oppresses me with sinful thoughts and feelings, and I turn my mind and my heart to you, nailed on the cross, then my sin suddenly passes away, the aggression lifts, and I am free. Lord, let nothing carnal, nothing evil, turn me away from you. Let me always be with you. How good it is to be with you.

11.   BELONGING TO GOD

How good you are, Lord, and how near you are to us – so near that we may always talk to you, be comforted by you, breathe through you, be enlightened by you, find peace in you, and gain spiritual nourishment from you. Grant that my fellowship with you may never be polluted by malice, pride, envy, greed, gluttony or falsehood. Grant that I may belong wholly to you.

12.   MIXING WITH ALL PEOPLE

My sweetest Saviour, having come down from heaven for the service of mankind, you did not only preach in the temple, but went out into the towns and villages. You shunned no one. You visited people, even the most notorious sinners, in their own homes. You mixed and talked with everyone. Grant that I too may go out to the market square of my town, and the villages around, to share your truth. Take from me any trace of contempt; and give me instead respect for everyone, in the conviction that anyone may become your disciple, and thus my brother. Let me remember always that I am the worst of sinners, so that anyone may be saved more easily than I was.

Simeon the Theodidact
c.949–c.1022

As a young man in Constantinople he lived a dissolute, immoral life, but also spent hours each night in prayer, enthralled by the beauty of God. Finally he entered a monastery, and was soon elected abbot. He taught that all Christians could experience direct, mystical communion with God through prayer, without the need for priests and bishops to guide them. This view antagonized church leaders, and he was exiled to a remote region of Asia Minor, where he died. His two most famous prayers express his desire to see God, and then his first direct encounter with God.

1.

O LORD, LET ME SEE YOU

You possess me, Lord, and I possess you.
You have put your faith and hope in me.
And I have put my faith and hope in you.
My life, my honour, my happiness, my peace
All rest on you.
You can see me every second of my life;
Let me see you.
I pray that you will grant me a single moment
When I can look at you face to face.
Then I will be able to give you
All my heart, all my love.
Do not wait until I have died,

But let me see you even here on earth.
I know I have no right to ask this favour
Because my heart is so luke-warm, so indifferent.
Make me worthy of such a privilege;
Make my heart ready to receive you.
And my soul ready to see you.

2.   O LORD, I HAVE SEEN YOU

How shall I describe, Lord, the vision of your face?
How shall I speak of your beauty?
How can the sound of any word contain you whom the
     world cannot contain?
How can anyone express the abundance of your love for
     mankind?
Recently I was sitting comfortably, reading the Scriptures,
A candle flickering beside me,
When the candlelight seemed to embrace me.
Then suddenly I realized that it was you, Lord;
You were embracing me.
Your light and your warmth filled the room,
Your arms held me.
My room on earth had become a room in heaven.
My house had become part of your mansion.
I heard myself crying out from the bottom of my heart,
"Have mercy on me, Master, have mercy on me,
Even though I have never truly served you".
And as I cried I could feel your mercy.
You were my physician, healing my soul.
Now as I recall this visit to my room,
I fall down in adoration.
I know that on this dark, sinful earth
The light of your love is a flickering candle.
But within my soul your divine light shines brightly.
I thank you that you revealed yourself to me.
O Lord, I have seen you!
O Lord, let me see you.

Simon the Persian
died *c.*339

Little is known of this bishop of Selencia except that he died as a martyr. His final prayer in which he welcomes his fate was recorded by an onlooker.

1.

AT THE STAKE

Give me the crown of martyrdom, Lord; you know how I long for it, because I have loved you with all my heart. When I see you in heaven I shall be filled with joy, and you will give me rest. I shall no longer have to live in this world and watch my people suffering, your churches destroyed, your altars overthrown, your devoted clergy persecuted, the weak abused, those who are lukewarm in their faith turned from you, and my own flock reduced to a tiny handful through fear of arrest and martyrdom. I shall no longer have to see my friends turn against me under the pressure of persecution.

Yet I intend to remain firm in my faith, and to walk bravely along the path which you have marked out for me, so I may be an example to my brothers. As a priest I have enjoyed the first place amongst my flock during life; now I will have the first place in death. I will be the first to give my blood. Then, Lord, you will allow me to lead my brethren into that life in which there are no cares, no anxieties; where there is neither persecutors nor persecuted, neither oppressor nor oppressed, neither tyrant nor victim. No violent kings nor bullying governors will I see.

This day, the day of my death, I shall not stumble as I walk the way you have set before me, because you shall hold me up. My weary limbs will find strength in you, and the grief in my heart will be forgotten when I drink from your cup of salvation. You will wipe away the tears from my eyes, and fill me with joy.

Sioux

*In recent years the spiritual insights of the native
American tribes have been rediscovered as a source
of inspiration to the "green" movement. These two
Sioux prayers express their sense of the divinity of
all natural things.*

1.   ON A VOYAGE

You, O God, are the Lord of the mountains and the valleys. As I
travel over mountains and through valleys, I am beneath your feet.
You surround me with every kind of creature. Peacocks, pheasants,
and wild boars cross my path. Open my eyes to see their beauty,
that I may perceive them as the work of your hands.
In your power, in your thought, all things are abundant.
Tonight I will sleep beneath your feet, O Lord of the mountains
and valleys, ruler of the trees and vines. I will rest in your love,
with you protecting me as a father protects his children, with you
watching over me as a mother watches over her children. Then
tomorrow the sun will rise and I will not know where I am; but I
know that you will guide my footsteps.

2.   AT HARVEST TIME

You, O God, are the Lord of the mountains and valleys. You are
my mother and my father. You have given rain to make the corn
grow, and sunshine to ripen it. Now in your strength the harvest
begins.
I offer you the first morsels of the harvest. I know it is almost
nothing compared with the abundance of the crop. But since you
have provided the harvest, my gift to you is only a sign of what you
have given to me.

You alone know how many suns and moons it will take to finish reaping. You alone know how heavy the crop will be. If I work too hard and too fast I forget about you, who gave me the harvest. So I will work steadily and slowly, remembering that each ear of corn is a priceless gift from you.

Rita Snowden
1907–

A deaconess in the New Zealand Methodist Church,
she is a prolific author for both adults and children.
In her prayers for women, she strives to see God's
grace in every aspect of female life.

1.   EXPECTING A BABY

O God, it might seem odd to some to pray for someone not yet born – but not to you and not to me. In these nine months of womanly patience, I have learned more than ever to marvel at your creative plans – and our part in them. I rejoice that the fashioning of a baby, and the founding of a family, requires the gifts of body, mind and spirit you have given to each of us. Bless these days of waiting, of preparation, of tender hope.

Let only things and thoughts that are clean and strong and glad be about us. I give you thanks that from childhood till this experience of maturity, you have made it both beautiful and natural for me to give love and to receive it. In this newest experience, hold us each safe, relaxed, and full of eager hope – even as you count each life in your presence, precious.

2.   BEING A YOUNG MOTHER

O God, I hardly have a moment to myself. As I get my husband
off, and the children bathed and clad and fed, the phone rings, or
a neighbour calls. I can't always do what I would like to do about
the house: there is the endless washing for the children – when the
weather allows – and the airing. I have the shopping to do and I
take the little ones with me for an outing – and the hours fly. In
no time I'm putting them to rest and planning the meal.

Help me to make this house a home, full of joy and security; a
home to which we will all be eager to return at the day's end, a
centre of understanding and love. Help me to make time for the
most important things; and not to become so overtired that I forget
that you have honoured me with this far-reaching, and rewarding
task. Bless our free times together – all our fun; bless our plans as
we look ahead; our relationships with friends in the community,
and in the church here, and in the wide world.

3.   LIVING ALONE

O God, I live alone like many in this city, this country. I do my
own work, I go in and out, I think my own thoughts. I am friendly
to those I know, but nobody knows me as you do, and nobody
anywhere is so close and so understanding. Bless all those I know
who live alone from choice, all who live alone following a death,
all who live alone because of estrangement, all who live alone for
financial reasons. Bless each small room I think of, each flat, each
too large old house, wherever one raises her voice to you in prayer
at any time. Bless especially, any one of us who has grown shy,
selfish, or odd, anyone who would like to change, but feels she
can't; anyone ill, or frail. Some of us are young still and we enjoy
freedom, we go out and we come in – we visit and have visitors; we
are happy to surround ourselves with beauty; we enjoy our meals,
and flowers and pretty things. Single, married, divorced – young,
middle-aged, old – we are all your children, part of your great
human family. All the time, we need courage and reassurance and
your loving care and presence. Keep us.

Solomon

10th century BC

*He succeeded his father David to become the second
king of the united nation of Judah and Israel. The
wisdom for which he prayed on his accession earned
respect throughout the ancient world. His most
important achievement was building the temple at
Jerusalem, which became the focus of Jewish loyal-
ties and aspirations.*

1.   BECOMING KING

You always showed great love for my father David, for he was good,
honest and loyal towards you. And you have continued to show him
your great and constant love by giving him a son who today sits on
his throne. O Lord God, you have let me succeed my father as
king, although I am still young and have little knowledge of worldly
affairs. Here I am, among the people you have chosen to be your
own, a people who are so numerous they cannot be counted. Give
me the wisdom to rule your people with justice, discerning the
difference between good and evil. Otherwise how could I ever be
able to rule this great people of yours?

2.   DEDICATION OF THE TEMPLE

Lord God of Israel, there is no god like you in heaven above or on
earth below! You keep your covenant with your people, showing
steadfast love to those who obey you with all their heart. You have
kept the promise which you made to my father David; today every
word has been fulfilled. And now, Lord God of Israel, I pray that
you will also keep the other promise which you made to my father,
when you said that always one of his descendants would rule as king

of Israel, provided they obeyed you with the same care as he did. So let everything come true, O God of Israel, that you promised to my father David, your servant.

But can you, O God, really live on earth? Not even all heaven is large enough to hold you, so how can this temple I have built contain you? Lord my God, I am your servant. Listen to the prayers which I offer to you this day. Watch over this place, where you have chosen to be worshipped, day and night. Hear me when I face this temple and pray. Hear my prayers and the prayers of your people when they turn to this place and pray. Hear us in your home in heaven; and when you hear, forgive us.

When a person is accused of doing wrong to another, and is brought before the altar of this temple, judge your servants, punishing the guilty and acquitting the innocent.

When your people of Israel are defeated by their enemies because they have sinned against you, and then they come to you at this Temple, humbly praying to you for forgiveness, have mercy upon them and restore them to their land.

When you hold back the rain because your people have sinned against you, and they face you in the temple, have mercy upon them and teach them to do what is right. Then send rain to this land of yours.

When there is famine, or an epidemic, or scorching winds, or swarms of locusts which destroy the crops, listen to their prayers. If any of your people, in heartfelt sorrow, stretch out their hands in prayer towards this temple, hear their prayer. Listen to them in your home in heaven, forgive them and help them. You alone know the secrets of each human heart. Deal with each person as he deserves, so that your people may learn to obey you, and live peacefully in the land which you gave to our ancestors.

Charles Haddon Spurgeon
1834–1892

At the age of seventeen, after an intense conversion experience, he travelled from his native Cambridgeshire village to London where he became minister of a small, demoralized Baptist congregation. His fiery, yet often humorous, sermons were so popular that within a decade he had built the largest chapel in Britain, able to hold six thousand people. He constantly urged his congregation to adopt a strict discipline of private prayer. And as an aid he composed a series of morning and evening meditations for every day of the year, based on a verse of Scripture. Each meditation ends with a simple prayer, the first of which is for the morning of New Year's Day.

1.　　　　WE WILL BE GLAD, AND REJOICE IN THEE

O sweet Lord Jesus, thou art the present portion of thy people, favour us this year with such a sense of thy preciousness, that from its first to its last day we may be glad and rejoice in thee. Let January open with joy in the Lord, and December close with gladness in Jesus.

2.　　　　FOR ME TO LIVE IN CHRIST

Lord, accept me; I here present myself, praying to live only in thee and to thee. Let me be as the bullock which stands between the plough and the altar, to work or to be sacrificed; and let my motto be, "Ready for either".

3.   WE WILL REMEMBER THY LOVE MORE THAN WINE

We remember thy love, O Jesus, as it was manifest to us in thy holy life, from the manger of Bethlehem to the garden of Gethsemane. We track thee from the cradle to the grave – for every word and deed of thine was love – and we rejoice in thy love, which death did not exhaust; thy love which shone resplendent in thy resurrection. We remember that burning fire of love which will never let thee hold thy peace until thy chosen ones be all safely housed.

4.   THOU HAST LEFT THY FIRST LOVE

O Lord, after thou hast so richly blessed us, shall we be ungrateful and become indifferent to thy good cause and work? O quicken us that we may return to our first love, and do our first works! Send us a genial spring, O Son of Righteousness.

5.   TO HIM BE GLORY, BOTH NOW AND FOR EVER

Lord, help me to glorify thee. I am poor, help me to glorify thee by contentment. I am sick, help me to give thee honour by patience. I have talents, help me to extol thee by spending them for thee. I have time, Lord, help me to redeem it, that I may serve thee. I have a heart to feel, Lord, let that heart feel no love but thine, and glow with no flame but affection for thee. I have a head to think, Lord, help me to think of thee and for thee. Thou hast put me in this world for something, Lord; show me what that is, and help me to work out my life-purpose.

6.   RISE UP MY LOVE, MY FAIR ONE, AND COME AWAY

To come to thee is to come home from exile, to come to land out of the raging storm, to come to rest after long labour, to come to the goal of my desires and the summit of my wishes. But Lord, how can a stone rise, how can a lump of clay come away from the horrible pit? O raise me, draw me. Thy grace can do it. Send forth thy Holy Spirit to kindle sacred flames of love in my heart, and I will continue to rise until I leave life and time behind me, and indeed come away.

7. EPHRAIM IS A CAKE NOT TURNED

Turn my unsanctified nature to the fire of thy love and let it feel the sacred glow, and let my burnt side cool a little while I learn my own weakness and want of heat when I am removed from thy heavenly flame. Let me not be found a double-minded man, but one entirely under the powerful influence of reigning grace; for well I know if I am left like a cake unturned, and am not on both sides the subject of thy grace, I must be consumed for ever amid everlasting burnings.

8. CANST THOU BIND THE INFLUENCES OF PLEIADES, OR LOOSE THE BANDS OF ORION?

Lord, end my winter, and let my spring begin. I cannot with all my longings raise my soul out of her death and dullness, but all things are possible with thee. I need celestial influences, the clear shinings of thy love, the beams of thy grace, the light of thy countenance; these are the Pleiades to me. I suffer much from sin and temptation, these are my wintry signs, my terrible Orion. Lord, work wonders in me, and for me.

Johann Starck
1680–1756

A leading member of the Pietist movement, which sought to infuse new spiritual life in the Lutheran Church, he wrote numerous prayers and hymns. These were collected under the title, A Daily Handbook for Days of Joy and Sorrow, *and it remained popular throughout Germany for about*

two centuries. It contains prayers for every situ-
ation, as well as a weekly pattern of devotion.

1.   ON THE SABBATH DAY

Gracious God, I praise and thank you that you have preserved me
during the past week, and blessed the work of my hands. You have
through each day helped me to build a temple of prayer in my
heart, so that even in the midst of my labours, I may rejoice in you.
And now on the day of rest, I may devote all my attention to you.
Let the joy of this day be a foretaste of the joy of paradise. Let this
day of worship be a sign of the constant and everlasting worship
around your heavenly throne.

Gracious God, help me this day to listen to your teachings, that
my mind may be re-fashioned according to your love. Let me turn
a deaf ear to all idle and malicious gossip, and let me turn a blind
eye to all temptation. Make of me a new man, alert only to your
truth, and alive only to your grace. And thus let me celebrate Sunday
after Sunday, and Sabbath after Sabbath, with unstinting devotion,
until you shall admit me to the unceasing celebrations of heaven,
the eternal sabbath.

2.   AT THE START OF THE WEEK

O loving and merciful God, you alone know what will transpire in
the coming week. I am ignorant and uncertain, fearful of misfortune, and hopeful of good fortune. My efforts are vain unless they
are blessed by you. My hands are clumsy unless they are guided by
you. May your Holy Spirit bless and guide me, that all my work
may be done according to your will. Protect me from all danger
and injury. Guard my house against robbers and vandals. Lead me
away from any temptations, physical and spiritual. Fill my heart
with the desire to serve only you. Grant this week that I grow in
holiness, that I increase in the knowledge of truth, and that I deepen
in prayer. In this way let me reflect more closely the image of your
beloved Son, our saviour, Jesus Christ.

3. A TEST OF FAITH

My God, you have plunged me into such sorrow and anguish that my eyes are swollen with tears, and even the beat of my heart is hard and irregular. Was I not happy once? Did I not enjoy peace and rest? I used to look to you for comfort and consolation. I used to flee into your arms when I was afraid. But now you yourself hurl me down; you yourself reject me. Indeed your rejection is the source of my anguish. At first I thought it was only my human friends who had turned against me; and I innocently believed that you would remain by my side. But then I found that you, my Divine Friend, are cold and indifferent. I tried to pray, but could feel no response. I cried out in pain, but my cries were lost in the empty sky. Come back to me, Lord. I will endure any earthly suffering if I can know your love. Assure me that the present rejection is only a test of my faith, and that soon you will decide the test is over. Yes, I am faithful. Yes, I will pass the test. But end it now, and raise me up.

4. FOR A BABY

O Lord my God, shed the light of your love on my child. Keep him safe from all illness and all injury. Enter his tiny soul, and comfort him with your peace and joy. He is too young to speak to me, and to my ears his cries and gurgles are meaningless nonsense. But to your ears they are prayers. His cries are cries for your blessing. His gurgles are gurgles of delight at your grace. Let him as a child learn the way of your commandments. As an adult let him live the full span of life, serving your kingdom on earth. And finally in his old age, let him die in the sure and certain knowledge of your salvation. I do not ask that he be wealthy, powerful or famous. Rather I ask that he be poor in spirit, humble in action, and devout in worship. Dear Lord, smile upon him.

5. AT THE TIME OF DEATH

I know, O God, that the time appointed by you for my death is almost here. I know now that soon I shall appear before you to be judged. And I know that I am a great sinner. I have broken all your holy commandments. I have frequently failed to love you, and strayed from the footsteps of Jesus. I have at times closed my heart to the guidance of the Holy Spirit. I have often missed opportunities to help my neighbour, because I have been so preoccupied with my own wants and desires.

Yet at this hour of crisis I feel bold enough to beg your forgiveness. Yes, I am fearful of your judgement. But I am also confident of your mercy. In that confidence I ask you to blot out my sinfulness, and remember only those times – few as they are – when I have been faithful to you, obeying your commandments and following the teachings of your Son. Lord, I know I am not fit for heaven; make me fit.

Robert Louis Stevenson
1850–1894

At the age of thirty-eight he went with his wife to live in Samoa. He was already a famous novelist in Britain, and amongst the Samoans he soon gained a reputation as a "Tunsitale" or "Story-teller". He also composed prayers to be said each evening in his household. After his sudden death, his widow published them to illustrate how his literary genius could be turned to spiritual purposes.

1.   FOR SUCCESS

Lord, behold our family here assembled. We thank thee for this place in which we dwell; for the love that unites us; for the peace accorded us this day; for the hope with which we expect the morrow; for the health, the work, the food and the bright skies, that make our lives delightful; for our friends in all parts of the earth, and our friendly helpers in this foreign isle. Let peace abound in our small company. Purge out of every heart the lurking grudge.

Give us grace and strength to forbear and to persevere. Offenders ourselves, give us the grace to accept and to forgive offenders. Forgetful ourselves, help us to bear cheerfully the forgetfulness of others. Give us courage and gaiety and a quiet mind. Spare to us our friends, soften to us our enemies. Bless us, if it may be, in all our innocent endeavours. If it may not, give us the strength to encounter that which is to come, that we be brave in peril, constant in tribulation, temperate in wrath, and in all changes of fortune, and, down to the gates of death, loyal and loving one to another. As the clay to the potter, as the windmill to the wind, as children of their sire, we beseech of thee this help and mercy.

2.   FOR SELF-BLAME

Lord, enlighten us to see the beam that is in our own eye, and blind us to the mote that is in our brother's. Let us feel our offences with our hands, make them great and bright before us like the sun, make us eat them and drink them for our diet. Blind us to the offences of our beloved, cleanse them from our memories, take them out of our mouths for ever. Help us at the same time with the grace of courage, that we be none of us cast down when we sit lamenting amid the ruins of our happiness or our integrity. Touch us with fire from the altar, that we may be up and doing to rebuild our city.

3.   IN TIME OF RAIN

We thank thee, Lord, for the glory of the late days and the excellent face of thy sun. We thank thee for good news received. We thank thee for the pleasures we have enjoyed and for those we have been able to confer. And now, when the clouds gather and the rain impends over the forest and our house, permit us not to be cast down. Let us not lose the savour of past mercies and past pleasures; but, like the voice of a bird singing in the rain, let grateful memory survive in the hour of darkness. If there be in front of us any painful duty, strengthen us with the grace of courage; if any act of mercy, teach us tenderness and patience.

4.   BEFORE A TEMPORARY SEPARATION

Today we go forth separate, some of us to pleasure, some of us to
worship, some upon duty. Go with us, our guide and angel; hold
thou before us in our divided paths the mark of our low calling,
still to be true to what small best we can attain to. Help us in that,
our maker, the dispenser of events – thou, of the vast designs, in
which we blindly labour, suffer us to be so far constant to ourselves
and our beloved.

5.   FOR GRACE

Grant that we here before thee may be set free from the fear of
vicissitude and the fear of death, may finish what remains before us
of our course without dishonour to ourselves or hurt to others; and,
when the day comes, may die in peace. Deliver us from fear and
favour: from mean hopes and cheap pleasures. Have mercy on each
in his deficiency; let him be not cast down. Support the stumbling
on the way, and give at last rest to the weary.

Henry Suso
c.1295–1366

---

*Having joined the Dominicans at the age of thir-
teen, he endured fifteen years of depression when
prayer seemed a meaningless ritual. Then he experienced an intense mystical experience in which
his own mind seemed to be taken up into the wisdom
of God. He continued to suffer periods of depression,
but even at their worst he now felt able to communicate with God. His spiritual autobiography records
his dialogue with God, both in joy and in sadness.*

1.   IN LOVE WITH GOD

Ah Lord, you can show yourself to us as so beautiful and tender, that our hearts cannot help but fall in love with you. We yearn to be close to you. As we read the pages of Scripture, it is as if you are whispering sweet words of affection in our ears. So overwhelming is your love that it leaves no space for mortal love between men and women. O my dear Lord, my soul sighs for you. And when I cannot hear you speak my heart is heavy with sadness. Unless you are close beside me, I cannot rest or sleep. Let me lie beside you, my head on your bosom.

2.   LIKE A WILD FLOWER

Lord, you are like a wild flower. You spring up in places where we least expect you. The bright colour of your grace dazzles us. When we reach down to pluck you, hoping to possess you for our own, you blow away in the wind. And if we tried to destroy you, by stamping on you and kicking you, you would come back to life. Lord, may we come to expect you anywhere and everywhere. May we rejoice in your beauty. Far from trying to possess you, may you possess us. And may you forgive us for all the times when we have sinned against you.

3.   A FAITHLESS LOVER

I have gone astray. I have failed you. My heart shrinks with shame when I hear your sweet, forgiving words. When your clear, pure eyes look at me, I turn my face away. There was never a soul so hard, a heart so cold as mine. And yet I can feel your soft love causing my soul to crumble and my heart to melt. Dear Lord, I have pursued false desires, I have put my trust in worldly wisdom. I have been besotted with the shallow pleasures. I have been a faithless lover. I cannot understand why you do not punish me, beating me until my flesh is raw and bloody. Instead you forgive me, beckoning me back to your side. Yes, I will come. I will always be true. I will always trust in your wisdom. I will find pleasure only in your grace.

4.　　　　　　　　UNBEARABLE SUFFERING

Lord, it may well be that suffering brings great good, provided that it is limited, and that it is not too dreadful and overwhelming. You alone know all things, seen and unseen, and you know the weight, the number and the size of things. So you know that my sufferings are without limit, that they are wholly beyond my power of endurance, that I am quite overwhelmed with pain. Lord, is there anyone in the world who suffers more constantly and more deeply than I? If you would just send me ordinary sufferings, I could bear them. But I do not see how I can endure such extraordinary sufferings as these – sufferings which so oppress my heart and soul that you alone can understand them.

5.　　　　　　　　SUFFERING AS DISCIPLINE

Lord, I can see plainly that you are the only and the true source of wisdom, since you alone can restore faith and hope to a doubting and despairing soul. In your Son, Jesus, you have shown me that even the most terrible suffering can be beautiful, if it is in obedience to your will. And so the knowledge of your Son has enabled me to find joy in my own suffering. Lord, my dear Father, I kneel before you this day, and praise you fervently for my present sufferings, and give thanks for the measureless sufferings of the past. I now realize that all these sufferings are part of your paternal love, in which you chastise and purify me. And through that discipline I now look at you without shame and terror, because I know that you are preparing me for your eternal kingdom.

Rabindranath Tagore
1861–1941

A Bengali poet and mystic, he sought to combine the best in the Western and Hindu traditions. He translated his most famous collection of spiritual verses, Gitanjali, *into English, and won the Nobel Prize.*

1.

THOU HAST MADE ME ENDLESS

Thou hast made me endless, such is thy pleasure. This frail vessel thou emptiest again and again, and fillest it ever with fresh life. This little flute of a reed thou hast carried over hills and dales, and hast breathed through it melodies eternally new. At the immortal touch of thy hands my little heart loses its limits in joy and gives birth to utterance ineffable. Thy infinite gifts come to me only on these very small hands of mine. Ages pass, and still thou pourest, and still there is room to fill.

2.

WHEN THOU COMMANDEST ME TO SING

When thou commandest me to sing it seems that my heart would break with pride; and I look to thy face, and tears come to my eyes. All that is harsh and dissonant in my life melts into one sweet harmony – and my adoration spreads wings like a glad bird on its flight across the sea. I know thou takest pleasure in my singing. I know that only as a singer I come before thy presence. I touch, by the edge of the far spreading wing of my song, thy feet which I could never aspire to reach. Drunk with the joy of singing I forget myself and call thee friend who art my lord.

3.

LET ONLY THAT LITTLE BE LEFT OF ME

Let only that little be left of me whereby I may name thee my all. Let only that little be left of my will whereby I may feel thee on every side, and come to thee in everything, and offer to thee my love every moment. Let only that little be left of me whereby I may never hide thee. Let only that little of my fetters be left whereby I am bound with thy will, and thy purpose is carried out in my life – and that is the fetter of thy love.

4. THIS IS MY PRAYER

This is my prayer to thee, my Lord – strike, strike at the root of penury in my heart. Give me the strength lightly to bear my joys and sorrows. Give me the strength to make my love fruitful in service. Give me the strength never to disown the poor or bend my knees before insolent might. Give me the strength to raise my mind high above daily trifles. And give me the strength to surrender my strength to thy will with love.

5. I WANT THEE, ONLY THEE

That I want thee, only thee – let my heart repeat without end. All desires that distract me, day and night, are false and empty to the core. As the night keeps hidden in its gloom the petition for light, even thus in the depth of my unconsciousness rings the cry – I want thee, only thee. As the storm still seeks its end in peace when it strikes against peace with all its might, even thus my rebellion strikes against thy love and still its cry is – I want thee, only thee.

Jeremy Taylor
1613–1667

His eloquent preaching and elegant appearance attracted the attention of King Charles I who appointed him as his chaplain. He revelled in the pomp and ceremony of royal worship and the luxury of court life. After the king's defeat at Cromwell's hand, he escaped to Wales where he became domestic chaplain at a small country house. His extravagant tastes gradually gave way to a deep mystical awareness of God's presence in every event and object, however small and insignificant. He wrote Rules and Exercises for Holy Living *in which he sets*

out a pattern of prayer and morality by which ordi-
nary people can discern God in all things.

1.   THE DIVINE PRESENCE

O Almighty God, infinite and eternal, thou art in the consciences
of all men. Teach me to walk always as in thy presence, to fear thy
majesty, to reverence thy wisdom: that I may never dare to commit
any indecency in the eye of my Lord and my Judge; that I, expressing the belief of thy presence here, may feel the effects of it in
eternal glory.

2.   FOR WIFE OR HUSBAND

Bless thy servant (my wife or husband) with health of body and of
spirit. Let the hand of thy blessing be upon his head, night and day,
and support him in all necessities, strengthen him in all temptations,
comfort him in all his sorrows, and let him be thy servant in all
changes; and make us both to dwell with thee for ever in thy favour,
in the light of thy countenance, and in thy glory.

3.   FOR OUR CHILDREN

Bless my children with healthful bodies, with good understandings,
with the graces and gifts of thy Spirit, with sweet dispositions and
holy habits; and sanctify them throughout in their bodies, and souls,
and spirits, and keep them unblamable to the coming of the Lord
Jesus.

4.   FOR FRIENDS

Be pleased, O Lord, to remember my friends, all that have prayed
for me, and all that have done me good. Do thou good to them,
and return all their kindness double into their own bosom,
rewarding them with blessings, and sanctifying them with thy
graces, and bringing them to glory.

5.   FOR CONTENTMENT

O Almighty God, Father and Lord of all the creatures, by secret and undiscernible ways bringing good out of evil: give me wisdom from above; teach me to be content in all changes of person and condition, to be temperate in prosperity, and in adversity to be meek, patient, and resigned; and to look through the cloud, in the meantime doing my duty with an unwearied diligence, and an undisturbed resolution.

6.   FOR TEMPERANCE

O Almighty God who fillest all things with plenty, teach me to use thy creatures soberly and temperately, that I may not, with loads of meat or drinks, make my spirit unapt for the performance of my duty, or my body healthless, or my affections sensual and unholy. In the strength of thy provisions may I cheerfully and actively and diligently serve thee; that I may worthily feast at thy table here, and through thy grace, be admitted to thy table hereafter.

7.   AN ACT OF DESIRE

Lord Jesus, come quickly; my heart is desirous of thy presence, and would entertain thee, not as a guest, but as an inhabitant, as the Lord of all my faculties. Enter in and take possession, and dwell with me for ever, that I also may dwell in the heart of my dearest Lord, which was opened for me with a spear and love.

8.   AN ACT OF FAITH

Thou didst take upon thee my nature, and thou didst suffer to deliver me from my sins that I might serve thee in holiness and righteousness all my days. Lord, I am as sure thou didst the great work of redemption for me and all mankind, as that I am alive. This is my hope, the strength of my spirit, my joy and my confidence; and do thou never let the spirit of unbelief enter into me and take me from this rock. Here I dwell, for I have a delight therein; here I will live, and here I desire to die.

9.   AN ACT OF LOVE

O eternal God, helper of the helpless, comforter of the comfortless, hope of the afflicted, bread of the hungry, drink of the thirsty, and Saviour of all them that wait upon thee: I bless and glorify thy name, and adore thy goodness, and delight in thy love. Take from me all affection to sin or vanity; let my affections soar upwards to the element of love, that I may hunger and thirst for the bread of life, and the wine of elect souls, and know no love but the love of God.

Teilhard de Chardin
1881–1955

A French Jesuit theologian, he worked for many years as a palaeontologist in China, where his extraordinary cosmic vision, combining science and religion, was formed. In The Divine Milieu *he reflects on the forces which both attract the soul to, and repel it from, God; and at times these reflections lead him into a direct conversation with God. In* The Cosmic Life *he perceives God as the utmost fulfilment of the evolutionary process, and also as the consummation of all human desire.*

1.   THE DIVINE MILIEU

Lord, it is you who, through the imperceptible goadings of sense-beauty, penetrated my heart in order to make its life flow out into yourself. You came down into me by means of a tiny scrap of created reality; and then, suddenly, you unfurled your immensity before my eyes and displayed yourself to me as Universal Being. Lord, in this first image, so close at hand and so concrete, let me savour you at length, in all that quickens and all that fills to overflowing, in all that penetrates and all that envelops – in sweetness of scent, in light, and love, and space.

I have thought to hear it said, Lord, that among those who serve you there are some who take fright when they see a heart that feels too acutely (just as they dread to see a mind that thinks too much). I cannot believe that such a fear can be justified; since, Lord, if a man closes his soul against the summons of the immanent Godhead, from what substance will he draw nourishment to keep alive the processes by which he claims to sustain his prayer?

When your presence bathed me in its light, I sought to find in it the supreme tangible reality.

Now that I hold you, sovereign consistence, and feel that I am carried along by you, I realize that hidden away beneath my yearnings was an unspoken longing not to embrace but to be possessed.

It is not in the form of a ray of light or of a tenuous matter, but as fire that I desire you; and it was as fire that I felt your presence, in the intuition of my first contact. I shall never, I know well, find rest, unless some active force pours down from you, to cover and transform me.

I pray you, divine milieu, already decked with the spoils of quantity and space, show yourself to me as the focus of all energies; and, that you may do so, make yourself known to me in your true essence, which is creative action.

It is impossible for me, Lord – impossible for any man who has acquired even the smallest understanding of you – to look on your face without seeing in it the radiance of every reality and every goodness. In the mystery of your mystical body – your cosmic body – you sought to feel the echo of every joy and every fear that moves each single one of all the countless cells that make up mankind. And correspondingly, we cannot contemplate you and adhere to you without your being, for all its supreme simplicity, transmuting itself as we grasp it into the re-structured multitude of all that you love upon earth.

And the result of this astonishing synthesis of all perfection and all growth that you effect in yourself, is that the act by which I possess you combines, in its strict simplicity, more attitudes and more insights than I have spoken of here, and more than I could ever express. When I think of you, Lord, I cannot say whether it is in this place that I find you more, or in that place – whether you are to me friend or strength or matter – whether I am contemplating you or whether I am suffering – whether I rue my faults or find union – whether it is you I love or the whole sum of others. Every affection, every desire, every possession, every light, every depth, every harmony, and every ardour glitters with equal brilliance, at one and the same time, in the inexpressible relationship that is being set up between me and you.

2.   COSMIC LIFE

Lord Jesus Christ, you truly contain within your gentleness, within your humanity, all the unyielding immensity and grandeur of the world. And it is because of this, it is because there exists in you this ineffable synthesis of what our human thought and experience would never have dared join together in order to adore them, element and totality, the one and the many, mind and matter, the infinite and the personal; it is because of the indefinable contours which this complexity gives to your appearance and to your activity, that my heart, enamoured of cosmic reality, gives itself passionately to you.

I love you, Lord Jesus, because of the multitude who shelter within you and whom, if one clings closely to you, one can hear with all the other beings murmuring, praying, weeping.

I love you because of the transcendent and inexorable fixity of your purposes, which causes your sweet friendship to be coloured by an intransigent determinism and to gather us all ruthlessly into the folds of its will.

I love you as the source, the activating and life-giving ambience, the term and consummation, of the world, even of the natural world, and of its process of becoming.

You the centre at which all things meet and which stretches out over all things so as to draw them back into itself: I love you for the extensions of your body and soul to the farthest corners of creation through grace, through life, and through matter.

Lord Jesus, you who are as gentle as the human heart, as fiery as the forces of nature, as intimate as life itself, you in whom I can melt away and with whom I must have mastery and freedom: I love you as a world, as this world which has captivated my heart; and it is you, I now realize, that my brother-men, even those who do not believe, sense and seek throughout the magic immensities of the cosmos.

Lord Jesus, you are the centre towards which all things are moving: if it be possible, make a place for us all in the company of those elect and holy ones whom your loving care has liberated one by one from the chaos of our present existence and who now are being slowly incorporated into you in the unity of the new earth.

Teresa of Ávila
1515–1582

An unruly child, she was sent by her despairing father to a convent school in Ávila. There she went to the other extreme, devouring spiritual books and striving to imitate the saints. Against her father's wishes she joined the Carmelite monastery in the town, but almost immediately her spiritual enthusiasm faded, and she suffered both physical and mental torment. At the age of forty, however, her endurance was rewarded with a series of ecstatic experiences, which she interpreted as a mystical marriage to Christ. Thereafter she combined an intense spiritual life with tireless administrative activity, founding, with John of the Cross, a new order of Carmelites in which the primitive rule was followed with uncompromising rigour. Her spiritual journey is reflected in a series of prayers, which appear in her Book of God's Mercies. *She also*

composed towards the end of her life a number of
poetic prayers.

1.
BE QUICK, BE CLEAN

O my Lord, since it seems you are determined to save me, I ask that you may do so quickly. And since you have decided to dwell within me, I ask that you clean your house, wiping away all the grime of sin.

2.
STUBBORNNESS

Although I have often abandoned you, O Lord, you have never abandoned me. Your hand of love is always outstretched towards me, even when I stubbornly look the other way. And your gentle voice constantly calls me, even when I obstinately refuse to listen.

3.
FAILING ONESELF

When the sins in my soul are increasing, I lose the taste for virtuous things. Yet even at such moments, Lord, I know I am failing you – and failing myself. You alone can restore my taste for virtue. There are so many false friends willing to encourage sin. But your friendship alone can give the strength of mind to resist and defeat sin.

4.
A SEED OF LOVE

What a good friend you are, Lord! You are so patient, willing to wait as long as necessary for me to turn to you. You rejoice at the times when I love you, but you do not hold against me the times when I ignore you.

Your patience is beyond my understanding. Even when I pray, my mind fills with worldly concerns and vain daydreams. Yet you are happy if I give only a single second of honest prayer, turning that second into a seed of love. O Lord, I enjoy your friendship so much, why is it not possible for me to think of you constantly?

5.   A GARDEN OF FLOWERS

O Lord my God! I cannot speak to you at present without both tears
of sadness and also overwhelming joy. You desire constantly to be
present within me; and for that my soul is filled with gladness. Yet
despite your wonderful love, I still so often do things which offend
and upset you. Is it possible, Lord, for a soul which has received such
blessings as you have bestowed on my soul, still to remain so hard and
stubborn? Yes, I know it is possible, because I so frequently rebuff
your advances and reject your blessings. Perhaps I am the only person
alive who treats you so badly. I hope so, because I cannot bear the
thought of others offending you in the same measure.

Teach me, Lord, to sing of your mercies. Turn my soul into a
garden, where the flowers dance in the gentle breeze, praising you
with their beauty. Let my soul be filled with beautiful virtues; let
me be inspired by your Holy Spirit; let me praise you always.

6.   DIVINE MADNESS

Lord, I am mad. I have become mad from your love. It is a holy,
heavenly madness which overwhelms me, deriving from your goodness and mercy. And I try to turn everyone to whom I speak equally
mad. I am an apostle of divine madness! O Lord, ensure that I need
pay no more attention to the things of this world, and also take
me out of this world. My mad spirit could not deal with worldly
concerns.

O Lord, how delicate and how heavy is the cross which you
have prepared for those who have reached this state of madness.
"Delicate" because it is so sweet and enjoyable; "heavy" because
there are times when it is impossible to bear. Yet I do not want to
be freed from this madness. Rather I want to be as mad as you
want, knowing that you will bear my burdens.

7.   WHAT ARE YOU DOING?

Lord, look what you are doing! Do not forget so quickly my great
wickedness. In order to forgive me you seem to have blotted out
my sins. Yet I ask you to remember them, in order to put a limit

on the favours you bestow upon me. Do not pour such precious wine into a broken bottle; you have already seen how often I spill and waste it. Do not put such treasure into a rubbish heap; you have already seen how often I ignore it. Do not give the keys of your castle to a coward who will unlock the gates at the first attack of the enemy. Do not risk your jewels with such a wretch.

Yes, I would like to drink the wine of your love to the full; I would like to understand the greatness of your glory; I would like to guard your truth; I would like to enjoy your beauty. But my soul is so crippled that I can do none of these things. My spiritual talents are not only hidden, but buried in the most vile earth.

Yet I would willingly and joyfully lose the greatest earthly possession to receive the smallest of your blessings.

8.   AT THE PEAK OF ECSTASY

May you be blessed, Lord, that from such filthy mud as I, you make water so clear that it can be served at your table. May you be praised for having raised up a worm so vile.

With what skill you have re-fashioned my soul from miserable ugliness to divine beauty! With what gentle coaxing you have lured me from the false pleasures of sin to the true joy of your love! And yet with what force you have snapped the chains of sin, and freed my soul to adore you!

9.   BUILDING A CONVENT

My Lord, how is it that you command things that seem impossible? As a woman, I am constrained on every side in my ambition to serve you. I want to build a convent that truly reflects your glory. But I lack money and I lack the means to raise it. What can I do?

10.   THE ROYAL ROAD

O my Lord, how obvious it is that you are almighty! There is no need to understand the reasons for your commands. So long as we love and obey you, we can be certain that you will direct us on to the right path. And as we tread that path, we will know that it is your power and love that has put us there.

It is said that the path which leads to you is narrow and rough, with steep cliffs on either side plunging down into dark valleys. Yet the path on which you have put me is a royal road, broad and smooth. It is safe for anyone who chooses to take it. And your Son holds the hand of all who walk on it. If we become tired or discouraged, we need only look up to see your smiling face in the distance, inviting us to share your joy.

11.   A BUSY FRANTIC LIFE

How is it, my God, that you have given me this hectic busy life when I have so little time to enjoy your presence. Throughout the day people are waiting to speak with me, and even at meals I have to continue talking to people about their needs and problems. During sleep itself I am still thinking and dreaming about the multitude of concerns that surround me. I do all this not for my own sake, but for yours. To me my present pattern of life is a torment; I only hope that for you it is truly a sacrifice of love. I know that you are constantly beside me, yet I am usually so busy that I ignore you. If you want me to remain so busy, please force me to think about and love you even in the midst of such hectic activity. If you do not want me so busy, please release me from it, showing how others can take over my responsibilities.

12.   RECEIVING COMMUNION

When I approached the altar to receive you in the blessed sacrament, my hair stood on end. Then my legs went weak, and I felt as if I were about to collapse under the weight of your majesty. In the tiny piece of bread you revealed to me your grandeur and your purity. Since I am so wretched and so filthy, I should have felt terrified of your presence. But instead I felt comforted and reassured by the knowledge that you, the King of kings, were about to give yourself in love to me.

13. KNOCKING IN GRACE

Dear Lord, you give so much, while I give so little. I should give up everything for you, trusting you to care for my every need. Yet I fail, I fail, I fail – I could say it a thousand times – I fail to give up everything for you. I hate even to continue living in the shame of my failure, because I know that the only purpose in life is to offer back to you all that you have given to us. How many imperfections I see in myself! I would like to be knocked unconscious so that I am no longer aware of my wickedness. Lord, knock your grace into me, that I may truly be good.

14. MAY YOU BE BLESSED FOREVER

May you be blessed forever, Lord, for not abandoning me when I abandoned you.
May you be blessed forever, Lord, for offering your hand of love in my darkest, most lonely moment.
May you be blessed forever, Lord, for putting up with such a stubborn soul as mine.
May you be blessed forever, Lord, for loving me more than I love myself.
May you be blessed forever, Lord, for continuing to pour out your blessings upon me, even though I respond so poorly.
May you be blessed forever, Lord, for drawing out the goodness in all people, even including me.
May you be blessed forever, Lord, for repaying our sin with your love.
May you be blessed forever, Lord, for being constant and unchanging, amidst all the changes of the world.
May you be blessed forever, Lord, for your countless blessings on me and on all your creatures.

15. A LOVE SONG

Majestic sovereign, timeless wisdom,
Your kindness melts my hard, cold soul.
Handsome lover, selfless giver,
Your beauty fills my dull, sad eyes.

I am yours, you made me.
I am yours, you called me.
I am yours, you saved me.
I am yours, you loved me.
I will never leave your presence.

Give me death, give me life.
Give me sickness, give me health.
Give me honour, give me shame.
Give me weakness, give me strength.
I will have whatever you give.

16.   LIVING WITHOUT YOU

My God, how sad it is
To live without you.
I long to see you,
But if I cannot see you
I want to die.

Master, my soul
Cries out in vain for you,
My eyes have never seen you,
My ears have never heard you,
My hands have never touched you,
My nose has never smelt you.

My God, when at last
You enter my heart,
I want you to stay.
But if you cannot stay there
I want to die.

17.   FINAL WORDS

My Lord, it is time to move on. Well then, may your will be done.
O my Lord and my Spouse, the hour that I have longed for has
come. It is time for us to meet one another.

Mother Teresa
1910–

The daughter of an Albanian grocer, she became a
nun and travelled to India at the age of seventeen.
For twenty years she taught in a convent school,
but in 1948 she left to work amongst the sick and
dying in the slums of Calcutta. She founded the
Missionaries of Charity, which now has over two
hundred branches worldwide. Her simple prayers
reflect her radiant love.

1.   LORD, OPEN OUR EYES

Lord, open our eyes,
That we may see you in our brothers and sisters.
Lord, open our ears,
That we may hear the cries of the hungry, the cold,
the frightened, the oppressed.
Lord, open our hearts,
That we may love each other as you love us.
Renew in us your spirit
Lord, free us and make us one.

2.   LORD, SHAKE AWAY MY INDIFFERENCE

Lord, shake away my indifference and insensitivity to the plight of
the poor. When I meet you hungry, thirsty or as a stranger, show
me how I can give you food or quench your thirst or receive you
in my home – and in my heart. Show me how I can serve you in
the least of your brothers.

3.   TAKE, O LORD, AND RECEIVE

Take, O Lord, and receive
All my liberty, my memory,
my understanding and my will,
all that I have and possess.
You have given them to me;
To you, O Lord, I restore them.
All things are yours:
Dispose of them according to your will.
Give me your love and your grace,
For this is enough for me.

4.   LORD BY THY GRACE

Lord by thy grace,
Let the poor seeing me be drawn to Christ and invite him to enter
their homes and their lives.
Let the sick and the suffering find in me a real angel of comfort
and consolation.
Let the little ones of the streets cling to me because I remind them
of him, the friend of all little ones.

5.   HERE I AM, LORD

Here I am, Lord – body, heart and soul.
Grant that with your love,
I may be big enough to reach the world,
And small enough to be at one with you.

6.   DELIVER ME FROM MYSELF

Lord, when I think that my heart is overflowing with love and
realize in a moment's honesty that it is only myself that I love in
the loved one,
Deliver me from myself.
Lord, when I think that I have given all that I have to give and
realize in a moment's honesty that it is I who am the recipient,

Deliver me from myself.
Lord, when I have convinced myself that I am poor and realize in
a moment's honesty that I am rich in pride and envy,
Deliver me from myself.
And, Lord, when the Kingdom of Heaven merges
deceptively with the kingdoms of this world,
Let nothing satisfy me but God.

7.   DAILY SELF-OFFERING

O beloved sick,
How doubly dear you are to me
when you personify Christ;
and what a privilege is mine
to be allowed to tend you.

Sweetest Lord,
Make me appreciative of the dignity of my high
    vocation
And its many responsibilities.
Never permit me to disgrace it
by giving way to coldness,
unkindness,
or impatience.

And O God,
While you are Jesus,
My Patient,
deign also to be to me a patient Jesus,
bearing with my faults,
looking only to my intention
which is to love and serve you
in the person of each of your sick.

Lord,
Increase my faith,
bless my efforts and work,
now and for evermore.

Thérèse of Lisieux
1873–1897

*Brought up in a devout and devoted family, she
and two of her sisters entered the Carmelite convent
of Lisieux in Normandy. Though her outward life
was uneventful, her interior spiritual life was so
intense that she was asked by her superior to write
her autobiography,* Story of a Soul. *She described
a "little way" by which people in every walk of life
can reach God through small acts of charity and
spontaneous prayer. After her early death her autobiography was published, and the child-like holiness
which shines through her words has made her one
of the most popular saints of all times. While most
of the book is addressed to her mother superior, from
time to time, often in the middle of a paragraph,
she turns to speak to God.*

1.   TOO YOUNG TO BE A NUN

Lord, I am not going to hurry you. I am ready to wait to become
a nun for as long as you want me to. But I want to ensure that it is
not through any fault of mine that this union between us is delayed.
So in the meantime I'll work hard to prepare myself, like a bride
preparing her wedding dress. And when you see that I am ready, I
know that nothing in heaven or on earth will prevent you from
coming to me, and making me, once and for ever, your bride.

2.   ON BECOMING A NUN

Jesus, my heavenly bridegroom, never may I lose this robe of purity.
Take me to yourself before I commit any wilful fault, however
slight. May I look for nothing and find nothing except you and only
you. May the things of this world mean nothing to me, because
you, Jesus, are everything to me. May earthly desires have no power
to disturb the peace of my soul. Your peace and your love are all
that I ask of you – love that is infinite, love that has eyes only for
your beauty. Jesus I would like to die as a martyr for your sake, in
soul or in body – better still, in both. Give me grace to keep my
vows of poverty, chastity and obedience in their entirety. Make me
understand what is expected of one who is your bride. Let me never
be a burden to the community, nor demand anyone's attention. I
want everyone to regard me as no better than a grain of sand,
trampled under foot and forgotten for your sake. May your will be
perfectly fulfilled in me, till I reach the place in heaven which you
have prepared for me. Jesus, may I be the means of saving many
souls, may no soul be lost due to my failings. Pardon me, Jesus, if
I am saying more than I have a right to say; I am thinking only of
your pleasure, of your contentment.

3.   THE FIRE OF LOVE

My God, everywhere your love is misunderstood and cast aside.
The hearts upon which you are ready to lavish your love turn away
towards earthly pleasures instead, as if happiness could be found in
more material attachments. They refuse to throw themselves into
your arms and accept the gift of your infinite love. Must this rejected
love of yours remain shut up in your own heart? If only you could
find yourself souls ready to offer themselves as victims, to be burnt
up in the fire of your love! You would lose no time in satisfying
their desire. Thus you would find a welcome outlet for the pent-up
force of your great devotion.

   Jesus, grant me the happiness of being such a victim, burnt up in
the fire of your divine love.

4.   THE SUNSHINE OF YOUR GRACE

Jesus, my beloved, how considerate you are in your treatment of
my worthless soul. Storms rage all around me, yet suddenly the
sunshine of your grace peeps out.

5.   DESIRE FOR HEROISM

To be betrothed to you, dear Jesus, as a nun, should be enough for
anybody. Yet not for me. I seem to have so many other vocations
as well. I feel as if I am called to be a fighter, a priest, an apostle,
a theologian, a martyr – as if I could never be satisfied without
performing for your sake every kind of heroic action at once. I feel
as if I have the courage to be a crusader, dying on the battlefield in
defence of the Church. And at the same time I want to be a priest,
carrying you in my hands to bestow on men's souls. And yet I have
nothing but admiration for St Francis of Assisi who in his humility
refused the honour of the priesthood. Dear Jesus, how am I to
reconcile these conflicting ambitions? How am I to give substance
to these dreams?

Insignificant as I am, I long to enlighten men's minds as the
prophets and theologians did. I feel the call to be an apostle. I'd
like to travel all over the world, making your name known and
planting your cross on heathen soil. But I wouldn't be content with
a single mission; I would want to be preaching the gospel on all
five continents at once. And even then I would not be satisfied.
Instead of being a missionary for a limited number of years, I should
want to go on preaching the gospel till the world came to an end.

Dear Jesus, what are you going to say to all these silly dreams of
a soul so unimportant, so ineffective as mine? The truth is that, in
my simple life in the convent, you are already fulfilling my deepest
needs.

6.   A DISTRACTED BIRD

Jesus, you have been very patient with me until now, and it is true
that I have never strayed far from you. But I know, and you know,
how often in my wretched imperfection I allow myself to be dis-

tracted, when I should be looking steadily at the sun which claims all my attention. I am like a bird, picking up a piece of grain first on this side, then on that side, running off to catch a worm, coming across a pond and wetting its feathers there, and even having a look at some pretty flowers it passes. Since I cannot compete with the eagles, I am more ready to occupy my mind with the trifles of earth.

But, dear Jesus, after all these infidelities, I don't rush away into a corner and weep. I turn back to the sun which is the centre of my love and dry my bedraggled wings in its rays. I tell the Father all about my faults, down to the last details. I throw myself recklessly on him, as the best way to regain control of myself, and so win a greater measure of your love. After all, haven't you told us that you came to call sinners, not the righteous?

7.   OCEAN OF LOVE

Your love, Jesus, is an ocean with no shore to bound it. And if I plunge into it, I carry with me all the possessions I have. You know, Lord, what these possessions are – the souls you have seen fit to link with mine.

8.   CHASM OF LOVE

My God, you know that the only thing I've ever wanted is to love you. I have no ambition for any other glory except that. In my childhood your love was there waiting for me. As I grew up, it grew with me. And now it is like a great chasm too deep to be plumbed. Love creates love. And my love for you, Jesus, wants to grow and expand until it fills that chasm which you have made for it. But it's no good. In truth my love is less than a drop of dew lost in the ocean. Can I love you as much as you love me? The only way to do that is to come to you for the loan of your own love; I could not content myself with anything less.

Dear Jesus, I can have no certainty about this, but I do not see how you could have squandered more love on a human soul than you have on mine. That is why I venture to ask that the souls which you have entrusted to me, that I might pray for them, may experience your love as I have. One day, perhaps, in heaven I shall

find out that you love them better than me. And I shall be glad of
that – glad to think that these people earned your love better than
I ever did. But here on earth I cannot imagine a greater wealth of
love than the love you have squandered on me, without my doing
anything to earn it.

Thomas à Kempis
c.1380–1471

---

*Born near Cologne, he was educated at a school run
by the brethren of the Common Life, whose intense
devotion to the person of Christ deeply influenced
him. He took vows as a monk in 1406, and spent
the rest of his long life transcribing manuscripts –
including an entire Bible – and writing politically.
His most famous work,* The Imitation of Christ,
has unjustly overshadowed Meditations on the
Life of Christ, *which is a collection of prayers
arising out of his profound reflection on the gospels.*

1.   HOW CAN I ENDURE?

Lord, how can I endure this life of sorrow, unless you strengthen
me with your mercy and grace? Do not turn your face from me.
Do not withdraw your consolation from me, lest my soul becomes
like a waterless desert. Teach me, O Lord, to do your will, and to
live humbly. You alone know me perfectly, seeing into my soul.
You alone can give lasting peace and joy.

2.   I AM NOTHING

I will presume to speak to you, my Lord, though I am mere dust
and ashes. If I imagined myself to be anything more, you would
confront me with my sins, which bear witness against me. But if I

humble myself and acknowledge my nothingness, if I cast away all self-esteem and reduce myself to dust, then your grace will come to me, and your light will enter my heart. So let the last trace of pride be swallowed up in the depths of my own nothingness and perish forever. Let me see myself for what I am and what I have been, as mere nothingness.

Now, Lord, look upon me. Your gaze can turn my nothingness into newness, my darkness into light, my misery into joy, my death into life. When I become nothing, I discover both myself and you. When I admit I deserve only punishment, you shower me with blessings. You are my salvation, my power, my strength.

3.   PLUNGING INTO GOD'S LOVE

As yet my love is weak, my heart imperfect, and so I have great need of your strength and comfort. Visit me often, I pray, and instruct me in the way of your laws. Set me free from all evil passions, and heal my heart from all immoral desires. And thus, healed and cleansed in spirit, may I learn how blissful it is to plunge into the depths of your love.

Let your love dissolve my hard heart. Let your love raise me above myself. Let your love reveal to me joy beyond imagination. Let my soul exhaust itself in singing the praises of your love. Let me love you more than I love myself, and let me love myself only for your sake. And let me see your love shining in the hearts of all people, that I may love them as I love you.

4.   CLINGING TO THE GOSPEL

How can we love life, when it holds so much bitterness and brings so much sorrow? Indeed, how can we call the daily struggle true life, when it brings physical pain and spiritual sadness in equal measure? Yet people cling to sinful activities as a source of comfort. They grasp desperately at the passing pleasures and vanities of the world. They do not readily abandon the desires of the body and the lusts of the eye.

Lord, strengthen me with heavenly courage, that I may fight against pleasures and vanities that harm the soul. I do not expect or ask that trials and sorrows should cease. I ask only that, in your strength, I resist the temptation to seek consolation in sin. For I know that only by clinging to the gospel of righteousness, and by grasping at your eternal grace, can I ever experience true and lasting joy.

5. GOD'S JUDGEMENT

Lord, your judgements roll like thunder against me. My limbs tremble and shake with fear, and my soul is filled with terror. Since even the heavens are not pure in your sight, what can be my fate? If even the stars can fall and the heavens come under your judgement, what hope is there for me? Men whose deeds seemed righteous and praiseworthy were condemned by you as sinners; so how can such a feeble and helpless creature as me expect mercy?

The truth, Lord, is that you are the only source of holiness. Righteousness is mere dust unless it comes from you. No wisdom can direct us, unless you are the guide. No courage can sustain us, unless you are our defence. No vigilance can protect us, unless you watch over all that we do. But if you come to visit us, you raise us above the highest heavens. You turn our sin into purity, and so make us worthy of your love.

6. I MUST SPEAK

Lord, I must speak; I cannot remain silent. I want to cry out, praising you for the great joy you bestow upon those who trust you. Simply to think about you brings sweetness beyond words. Out of your love you created me; out of your love you led me back when I went astray, out of your love you teach me your love of love.

O fount of eternal love, what can I say to you that is worthy of you? What can I offer you that you did not first give to me? What faith do I possess that does not come from your faith in me? What service can I render to you who serves me night and day? With all my heart I want to praise you, sacrifice myself to you, trust you in all things, and labour only for your kingdom.

7. A CONSTANT PRAYER

Lord, may my desires change to your desires. Lord, if a desire is good and profitable, give me grace to fulfil it to your glory. But if it be hurtful and injurious to my soul's health, then remove it from my mind.

8. GIVE ME WINGS

Lord Jesus, you are the source of all holiness and beauty: and yet you are holier and more beautiful than we could ever imagine. You are the source of knowledge and skill: and yet your knowledge of truth and your skill in creation far exceeds our greatest visions. You are the source of glory and honour, power and dignity, joy and gladness, fame and praise; yet we have only the dimmest under-standing of these many blessings, which you bestow upon us with such generosity. Above all, you are the source of sweetness and consolation, which bring true joy amidst the greatest sorrows.

O Lord Jesus Christ, spouse of my soul, lover of purity, Lord of creation, give me wings that I may fly to you. Set me free from all sin, that I may taste your sweetness.

Embrace every thought in my mind and feeling in my heart, turning me into your perfect bride.

9. GOD'S BLESSINGS

My God and my All! What greater blessing can I receive than your love? What greater wealth can I possess than your grace? What greater pleasure can I enjoy than your presence? What greater sweetness can I taste than your body and blood? What greater wisdom can I know than your gospel?

Your wisdom is so simple that even fools like myself can under-stand it. Your holy communion is so generously given that even sinners like me are allowed to receive it. Your presence is every-where so that even someone with such a dull mind as I have can find you. Your grace is such a constant source of reassurance that I can trust you completely for all my spiritual and material needs. And your love is so warm and so forgiving that even a cold, hard heart like my own is melted.

10.   LIGHT EVERLASTING

O Light everlasting, surpassing all created light! Pour forth from
heaven the glorious rays of your light, and pierce the dark depths
of my soul. Purify, gladden and enlighten my soul, that it may turn
to you in joy. I know that the shadow of sin still hangs over me. I
know that I fight against your light, preferring the gloom of worldly
pride to the bright sunshine of true humility. Yet you, who can
make the raging sea calm, can bring peace to my soul. You, who
turn night into day, can bring gladness to my miserable soul. Act
now! Banish darkness at this very moment! Inspire my soul with
your love at the next breath I take!

Thomas Aquinas
c.1225–1274

---

*The most influential theologian of the medieval
period, he came to regard theology as valueless, compared with the direct encounter with God through
prayer. Educated by the monks at Monte Cassino,
he joined the Dominican order in 1244, and spent
the bulk of his life teaching in Paris. His prayers
are scattered throughout his work, especially in his
biblical commentaries.*

1.   GOD'S ORDER

Most merciful God, order my day so that I may know what you
want me to do, and then help me to do it. Let me not be elated by
success or depressed by failure. I want only to take pleasure in what
pleases you, and only to grieve at what displeases you. For the sake
of your love I would willingly forgo all temporal comforts. May all
the joys in which you have no part weary me. May all the work
which you do not prompt be tedious to me. Let my thoughts fre-

quently turn to you, that I may be obedient to you without complaint, patient without grumbling, cheerful without self-indulgence, contrite without dejection, and serious without solemnity. Let me hold you in awe without feeling terrified of you, and let me be an example to others without any trace of pride.

2. BEFORE HOLY COMMUNION

All-powerful, everlasting God, I came to you as a man sick, in need of life-giving medicine; as useless, to bathe under your fountain of mercy; as blind, seeking your eternal light; as a beggar, pleading for your spiritual treasure. I implore you in your abundant kindness to cure my sickness, cleanse my impurity, enlighten my blindness, and enrich my poverty. May this bread and wine be not only signs of such grace, but also the true source of grace. In receiving the body of your Son, let me become a member of your mystical body. And grant that, while on earth I must see him under the veil of food and drink, in heaven I may behold him face to face.

3. AFTER HOLY COMMUNION

Thank you, all-powerful and eternal Father, for allowing me to receive the precious body and blood of your Son. May this wonderful gift not bring judgement on my sinfulness, but be the means of reconciliation with you and with my fellow men. May it be the armour of faith and the shield of good will, protecting me from all evil desires. May it be the food which nourishes virtue and love within my soul. And may it be a foretaste of the heavenly banquet in which I may sit at table with all those who love you, sharing your perfect peace and joy.

4. BEFORE WRITING OR PREACHING

O Creator of the universe, who has set the stars in the heavens and causes the sun to rise and set, shed the light of your wisdom into the darkness of my mind. Fill my thoughts with the loving knowledge of you, that I may bring your light to others. Just as you can make even babies speak your truth, instruct my tongue and guide my pen to convey the wonderful glory of the gospel. Make my intellect sharp, my memory clear, and my words eloquent, so that I may faithfully interpret the mysteries which you have revealed.

5. FOR ALL GOOD THINGS

Loving God, who sees in us nothing that you have not given yourself, make my body healthy and agile, my mind sharp and clear, my heart joyful and contented, my soul faithful and loving. And surround me with the company of men and angels who share my devotion to you. Above all let me live in your presence, for with you all fear is banished, and there is only harmony and peace. Let every day combine the beauty of spring, the brightness of summer, the abundance of autumn, and the repose of winter. And at the end of my life on earth, grant that I may come to see and know you in the fullness of your glory.

6. HEARING YOU AND SEEING YOU

With all my heart I worship you, O hidden God.
You who hide yourself behind the things of your creation.
My heart submits to you, and so does my mind.
Compared with contemplating you, all else is nothing.
I cannot touch you, taste you, see you.
All senses are cheated of you – except the ear.
Your Son has spoken, and I believe.
Nothing has truth beyond the word I hear.
On the cross your divinity was hidden,
And now on earth your humanity is hidden.
But I acknowledge you and cry to you,
As did the thief who died beside you.
I do not gaze, like Thomas, on your wounds,
But I confess that you are God.
Give me a stronger faith, a surer hope,
And a deeper love for you, my Lord.
You gave us a memorial of your dying
In the living Bread that gives life to men.
As I eat your bread, may you live in me.

And may I always turn to you for strength.
O Christ, who gave your heart for all men,
Cleanse my sin in your blood which was spilt.
A single drop of it would save the world,
Cleansing every man from his foul guilt.
A veil is over your face, I cannot see you.
I cry to you to show me yourself,
To let me see you face to face.
With that vision my soul will be at peace.

Frank Topping
1937–

He has enjoyed a varied life as a sailor, song-writer, actor and Methodist minister. His meditations, composed in simple, colloquial English, have frequently been broadcast on radio.

1.   LISTENING

How often do I nod,
as if I were listening,
to words I cannot hear,
because I'm thinking about something else,
because I'm planning what I intend to say.
Yet there are those who are good listeners:
a good conversationalist listens,
a good counsellor or adviser listens,
a good doctor listens, a good judge,
a good friend.
And you, my Lord,
you listen even to my thoughts.
Teach me to listen,
that I may hear when you speak

in the wind, in music,
and in love.

2.   RESTING

Lord,
teach me to rest in you.
Teach me to see the sky
and to think of nothing else
but the joy of it.
Teach me to look
at field and flower
and be soothed
by colours and seasons.
Teach me to close my eyes
and to rest
in the Love that has supported me
all my days.
Teach me, Lord,
to rest in you.

3.   PRAISING

You were praised, Lord.
When you entered Jerusalem
people shouted, "Hosanna",
and strewed your path with palms;
and yet within days
their shouts of praise rang hollow.
Lord, help me to praise God
for all the goodness
that has been shown to me.
I have sung his praises with delight.
Help me, in darker days,
when others mock or deride,
not to be silent,
but continue to be loyal
in love and praise.

4.   LIVING

Lord, you came to give us life,
and life that was more abundant.
Help me not to run away from life,
but to follow your spirit,
to accept the thorn
as well as the flower
and to be grateful
for the gift of life.

Thomas Traherne
1637–1674

---

*An Anglican priest, he was blessed with a cheerful
and optimistic temperament. He saw the purpose of
life as the attainment of holiness, and he could see
the marks of divine holiness in all living things.
His most famous work,* Centuries of Meditations,
*was discovered and published over two hundred
years after his death. Its short reflections and
prayers sparkle with hope and love.*

1.   THE MIND OF CHRIST IN ME

Let the same mind be in me that is in Christ Jesus. For he that is
not led by the spirit of Christ is none of his. Holy Jesus I admire
thy love unto me also. O that I could see it through all those
wounds! O that I could feel it in those stripes! O that I could hear
it in all those groans! O that I could taste it beneath the gall and
vinegar! O that I could smell the savour of thy sweet ointments,
even in this Golgotha, or place of a skull. I pray thee teach me first
thy love unto me, and then unto mankind! But in thy love unto
mankind I am beloved.

2.   THE FREEDOM OF THY BOUNTY

What, O my Lord, could I desire to be which thou hast not made
me! If thou hast expressed thy love in furnishing the house, how
gloriously doth it shine in the possessor! My limbs and members
when rightly prized, are comparable to the fine gold, but that they
exceed it. The topaz of Ethiopia and the gold of Ophir are not to
be compared to them. What diamonds are equal to my eyes; what
labyrinths to my ears; what gates of ivory, or ruby leaves to the
double portal of my lips and teeth? Is not sight a jewel? Is not
hearing a treasure? Is not speech a glory? O my Lord, pardon my
ingratitude, and pity my dullness who am not sensible of these gifts.
The freedom of thy bounty hath deceived me. These things were
too near to be considered. Thou presentedst me with thy blessings,
and I was not aware. But now I give thanks and adore and praise
thee for thine inestimable favours.

3.   I IN ALL, AND ALL IN ME

O adorable Trinity! What hast thou done for me? Thou hast made
me the end of all things, and all the end of me. I in all, and all in
me. In every soul whom thou hast created, thou hast given me the
similitude of thyself to enjoy! Could my desires have aspired unto
such treasures? Could my wisdom have devised such sublime enjoyments? O thou hast done more for us than we could ask or think.
I praise and admire, and rejoice in thee: who are infinitely infinite
in all thy doings.

4.   A FREE AGENT

O adorable and eternal God! Hast thou made me a free agent? And
enabled me if I please to offend thee infinitely? What other end
couldst thou intend by this, but that I might please thee infinitely?
That having the power of pleasing or displeasing, I might be the
friend of God? Of all exaltations in all worlds this is the greatest.
To make a world for me was much, to command angels and men
to love me was much, to prepare eternal joys for me was more. But
to give me a power to displease thee, or to set a sin before thy face,

which thou infinitely hatest, to profane eternity, or to defile thy works, is more stupendous than all these. What other couldst thou intend by it but that I might infinitely please thee? And having the power of pleasing or displeasing, might please thee and myself infinitely, in being pleasing!

5.   AN OFFSPRING OF PLEASURE

Replenish our actions with amiableness and beauty, that they may be answerable to thine, and like unto thine in sweetness and value. That as thou in all thy works art pleasing to us, we in all our works may be so to thee; our own actions as they are pleasing to thee being an offspring of pleasures sweeter than all.

Tychon of Zadonsk
1724–1783

In a period when Western ideas and attitudes were being eagerly embraced by Russian aristocrats and church leaders, he sought to remain loyal to the Russian mystical tradition. He was a gruff and unkempt monk who preferred the company of peasants and workers to that of priests and lords. Firmly rejecting the fashionable nationalist philosophy of the West, he believed that prayer, in which the individual soul wrestles with God, should be the basis of all thought and action.

1.   YOU CAME FOR ME

Since you came into the world for all people, O Saviour, therefore you came for me, for I am one of the people. Since you came into the world to save sinners, therefore you came to save me, for I am one of the sinners. Since you came to find those who are lost, therefore you came to find me, for I am one of the lost. O Lord my God, I should have come to you, I should have cast myself before you as a miserable sinner, I should have tried to find you. But I was so proud and so stubborn that you had to come to me. You had to come down to earth as a tiny baby, enduring poverty, discomfort and danger, in order to reach me. You had to walk dusty lanes, enduring insults and persecution, in order to reach me. You had to suffer and die on a cross, in order to reach me. Forgive me my stubborn pride that I have put you to such trouble and such pain on my behalf.

2.   WHY DO YOU BOTHER WITH ME?

Shepherds search for their lost sheep, but for their own profit. Men seek their lost property, but out of self-interest. Travellers visit foreign countries, but for their own benefit. Kings offer ransoms for prisoners, but out of political calculation. But why have you searched for me? Why have you sought me out? Why have you visited this hostile earth where I live? Why have you ransomed me with your blood? I am not worthy of such effort. Indeed in my sin I have wilfully tried to escape from you, so you would not find me. I have wanted to become a god myself, deciding for myself what is good and bad according to my own whims and lusts. I have provoked you and insulted you. Why do you bother with me?

3.   I STAND BEFORE YOU

I stand before you – I for whose sake you came to earth. Look upon me, and you will see nothing but my need for salvation. Look upon me, and you may choose to condemn me to everlasting hell. Indeed, I would have no grounds for complaint if you sent me to hell, because it is what I deserve. Yet if that was your intention, you would not have come. Your presence tells me that you are merciful, that you are ready to forgive me, that you want to save me from hell and prepare me for heaven. You love me, though I have given you no cause to love. You love me, though so often I have hated you. I stand before you now, to beg your mercy. Grant that, as you look upon me, I may look upon you with the eyes of faith, gazing upon your infinite beauty.

4.   HOW CAN I REPAY YOU?

How shall I repay your generosity, O my Lover? How shall I repay you for all you have given me? If I had died a thousand times for your sake, it would be as nothing. You are my Lord, and I am just clay and ashes, a worthless sinner, who deserves to die thousands upon thousands of deaths. How shall I thank you, who suffered dishonour, insult, mockery, scourging, and death for my sake? How shall I, who has nothing, reward you who gave everything? I have ruined my own soul, which was given by you. And now the only merit my soul possesses is that which you have bestowed, in your forgiving love. The only thing I can return to you is my prayer, that time I devote each day speaking and listening to you. Receive my prayer, as a tiny token of my enormous gratitude.

5.   MAKE ME HOLY

You have accomplished a deed so sublime that my mind cannot grasp it. You have come down to earth and saved me. It is the wonder of all wonders, the miracle of all miracles. I believe in you, I confess your name, I preach to others your gospel of salvation, I marvel that you have shown such love towards me, and I want others to receive such love for themselves. O Lover of men, my Lover, I implore you to grant me one more favour. Yes, you have saved me. Yes, you have promised me a place in heaven. Yet I am still a sinner, I am still distorted by evil thoughts and feelings. Do not delay. Redeem your promise now. Make me fit for heaven, even while I live on earth. Make me holy, as you are holy, that I may glorify you in every thought, every feeling, and every action.

Manikka Vasahar
8th century

He was chief minister of southern India, renowned for his gentleness. His famous prayers, still used amongst Tamil-speaking people, were uttered on a visit to the temple at Perundurai, when he was suddenly seized by intense religious emotion.

1.   I CLING AND I BOW TO YOU

King of heaven, you have revealed your wonder even to someone as vile as me. You have taken from me the false joy of earthly pleasures, and given me instead the true joy of your heavenly love. You have taken me into your heavenly family, treating me as a beloved child. And I cling to you as a small child clings to its mother. I will never let go; I will always stay in your presence.

King of heaven, you have showered your wealth even onto someone as undeserving as me. You have taken from me any desire for the perishable riches of earth, and given me instead only the desire for the imperishable wealth of heaven. You have taken me into your royal court, treating me as the chief steward of your spiritual treasures. I bow before you as a servant bows to his master. I will never cease to adore you; I will always strive to serve you.

2.   I DESIRE ONLY YOU

I do not ask for fame, for a high position in society, for a palace in which to live. I do not ask for the company of clever and witty people. Such ambitions mean nothing to me. I desire only you, Lord of life. Your love makes my heart melt like butter. Your grace gives a taste like honey on my tongue. Your goodness is as soft as silk upon my skin. Your beauty makes my eyes sparkle with joy. I want nothing but you.

3.   YOU ARE LIKE A TIGER

You are like a tiger, compelling in your beauty, yet terrifying in your strength.

You are like a honey-comb on the branch of a tree; I can see the sweet honey, but the branch is too high for me to climb.

You are like a gold fish swimming in a pond, only an arm's length from the bank; yet if I try to catch you in my hand, you slip from my grasp.

You are like a snake, your skin dazzling in its bright colours, yet your tongue able to destroy a man with a single prick.

Be merciful to me, O Lord. Give me life, not death. Reach out to me, and hold me in your arms. Come down to me, and lift me up to heaven. Sustain my feeble soul with your power.

Henry Vaughan
1622–1695

A medical doctor in Wales, he suffered a serious illness himself which triggered a profound spiritual experience. The fruit of this was a series of religious poems, in which the whole range of human emotions is offered to God. In both the style and the substance of his poetry he acknowledged his debt to George Herbert.

1.

ANGUISH

My God and King! to thee
I bow my knee,
I bow my troubled soul, and greet
With my foul heart thy holy feet.
Cast it, or tread it! It shall do
Even what thou wilt, and praise thee too.

My God, could I weep blood,
Gladly I would;
Or if thou wilt give me that art,
Which through the eyes pours out the heart,
I will exhaust it all, and make
Myself all tears, a weeping lake.

O! 'tis an easy thing
To write and sing;
But to write true, unfeigned verse
Is very hard! O God, disperse
These weights, and give my spirit leave
To act as well as to conceive!

O my God, hear my cry;
Or let me die!

2.

CHEERFULNESS

Lord, with what courage and delight
I do each thing
When thy least breath sustains my wing!
I shine and move
Like those above,
And (with much gladness
Quitting sadness)
Make me fair days of every night.

Affliction thus, mere pleasure is,
  And hap what will,
If thou be in't, 'tis welcome still;
  But since thy rays
  In sunny days
  Thou dost thus lend
  And freely spend,
Ah! what shall I return for this?

O that I were all Soul! that thou
  Wouldst make each part
Of this poor, sinful frame pure heart!
  Then would I drown
  My single one
  And to thy praise
  A consort raise
Of Hallelujahs here below.

3.

THE PURSUIT

Lord! what a busy restless thing
  Hast thou made man!
Each day and hour he is on wing,
  Rests not a span;
Then having lost the sun and light
  By clouds surprised
He keeps a commerce in the night
  With air disguised;
Hadst thou given to this active dust
  A state untired,
The lost son had not left the husk
  Nor home desired;
That was thy secret, and it is
  Thy mercy too,
For when all fails to bring to bliss,
  Then, this must do.
Ah! Lord! and what a purchase will that be
To take us sick, that sound would not take thee!

4.

DRESSING

O thou that lovest a pure and whitened soul!
That feed'st among the lilies, till the day
Break, and the shadows flee; touch with one coal
My frozen heart; and with thy secret key

Open my desolate rooms; my gloomy breast
With thy clear fire refine, burning to dust
These dark confusions, that within me nest,
And soil thy Temple with a sinful rust.

Thou holy, harmless, undefiled high-priest!
The perfect, full oblation for all sin,
Whose glorious conquest nothing can resist,
But even in babes dost triumph still and win.

Atharva Veda
c.1500 BC

The most ancient sacred texts of Hinduism, the
Vedas, *are a collection of hymns and verses, origin-*
ally transmitted orally, but eventually written
down. Many are of outstanding literary value. The
fourth veda, the Atharva Veda, *includes a number*
of prayers. Although many deities are mentioned
in the Vedas, *these prayers suggest a belief in a*
single supreme power.

1.

TO THE BREATH OF LIFE

Homage to you, Breath of Life, for the whole universe obeys you.
You are the ruler of all things on earth, and the foundation of the
earth itself.

Homage to you, Breath of Life, in the crashes of thunder and in the flashes of lightning. The rain you send gives food to the plants and drink to the animals.

Homage to you, Breath of Life, in the changing seasons, in the hot dry sunshine and the cold rain. There is comfort and beauty in every kind of weather.

The plants themselves rejoice in your bounty, praising you in the sweet smell of their blossom. The cattle rejoice, praising you in the pure white milk they give.

Homage to you, Breath of Life, in our breathing out and breathing in. At every moment, whatever we are doing, we owe you praise and thanksgiving.

Homage to you, Breath of Life, in our birth and in our death. In the whole cycle of life you sustain and inspire us.

Homage to you, Breath of Life, in the love and friendship we enjoy. When we love one another, we reflect your infinite love.

Men and women rejoice in your bounty, praising you in poem and song. The little children rejoice, praising you in their innocent shrieks of laughter.

2.   DIVINE BLESSING

Almighty Lord, if we offer you a devoted mind and heart, you will offer to us every blessing on earth and in heaven.

You grant our deepest wishes. You give food to the body and peace to the soul. You look upon us with the love of a mother for her children.

You created this beautiful earth all around us. And in every plant and animal, every tree and bird, your spirit dwells.

You have revealed yourself to me, infusing my soul with the knowledge that you are the source of all blessing.

And so I sing your praises day and night. I who am feeble, glorify you who are powerful. I who am nothing, devote myself to you who are everything.

Jean-Baptiste Marie Vianney
1786–1859

*Popularly known as Curé d'Ars, he served that
parish for over forty years. His reputation as a
confessor and spiritual director drew people from
throughout France.*

1.   HOW GOOD IT IS TO LOVE YOU

My Jesus, from all eternity you were pleased to give yourself to us
in love. And you planted within us a deep spiritual desire that can
only be satisfied by yourself.

I may go from here to the other end of the world, from one
country to another, from riches to greater riches, from pleasure to
pleasure, and still I shall not be content. All the world cannot satisfy
the immortal soul. It would be like trying to feed a starving man
with a single grain of wheat.

We can only be satisfied by setting our hearts, imperfect as they
are, on you. We are made to love you; you created us as your lovers.

It sometimes happens that the more we know a neighbour, the
less we love him. But with you it is quite the opposite. The more
we know you, the more we love you. Knowledge of you kindles
such a fire in our souls that we have no energy left for worldly
desires.

My Jesus, how good it is to love you. Let me be like your disciples
on Mount Tabor, seeing nothing else but you. Let us be like two
bosom friends, neither of whom can ever bear to offend the other.

Wapokomo

This tribe, who inhabit land to the west of Lake Tana, never succumbed to the power and Christian faith of the Ethiopians to their east. But, as their prayers illustrate, they were deeply influenced by the Christian spirit.

1.   GIVE US PEACE

O God, give us peace, give us contentment, give us good fortune.

Let no one curse us. Let no one have evil thoughts about us. Let all think well of us.

Give us rain when we sow our crops. Give us sunshine when we harvest our crops.

Let those who are sick be healed. Let those who are ready to die go in peace.

2.   YOU ARE IMMORTAL

O God, you are immortal. You do not know death. You live always. You never know that cold sleep from which a man never wakes. Your children never gather round your death-bed.

O God, you are the immortal father of our people. Your health never fails. Your benign shadow is cast over all our actions.

You are powerful, were are powerless. You are strong, we are weak. Hear us when we call upon you. Accept the sacrifices we offer. We belong to you. Protect us as your own.

Mary Ward
1585–1645

As a devout Roman Catholic in Protestant Eng-
land, she lived in continuous fear of being arrested
for her faith. And as the founder of a religious
order for women, she was hounded, and at one point
imprisoned, by her church for asserting that women
are intellectually equal to men, and should therefore
play an equal part in educating the young.

1. ON FIRST ENTERING A CONVENT, AGED NINETEEN

O Parent of parents, and Friend of all friends, thou tookest me into thy care, and by degrees led me from all else that at length I might see and settle my love in thee. What had I ever done to please thee? Or what was there in me wherewith to serve thee? Much less could I ever deserve to be chosen by thee. O happy begun freedom, the beginning of all my good, and more worth to me at that time than the whole world besides. Had I never since hindered thy will and working in me, what degrees of grace should I now have had. It is more than nineteen years since, and where as yet am I? My Jesus, forgive me, remember what thou hast done for me, and whither thou hast brought me, and for this excess of goodness and love let me no more hinder thy will in me.

2. WHEN FOUNDING HER OWN RELIGIOUS COMMUNITY

O my God, how liberal you are and how rich are they to whom you will vouchsafe to be a friend.

In your will I only found quiet rest.

The most forcible motive of all to me to leave sin is that you forbid it, whom I love.

If I ever see myself favoured by you, I cry out continually: "You alone are important, I am nothing." I will not take credit from you, to build myself up. Take me, all that I am, and do what you want with me. Without you I am nothing.

3.   AT A TIME OF PERSECUTION

Neither life nor death, my God, but thy holy will be ever done in me. What pleaseth thee best, that do. Only this, let me no more offend thee, nor leave to do what thou wouldst have me.

Leslie Weatherhead
1883–1975

As pastor of the Congregationalist City Temple in London for nearly thirty years, he built up a reputation both as an eloquent preacher and as a sympathetic pastor. It was in the latter role, responding to numerous requests for guidance in personal prayer, that he wrote The House of Prayer. *He depicts the pattern of daily prayer as moving through seven rooms in a house; and he gives sample prayers that can be said in each room.*

1.   ROOM 1   AFFIRMATION OF GOD'S PRESENCE

As I bow in the quiet room I have made in my heart, O Lord, let the hush of thy presence fall upon me.

2.   ROOM 2   ADORATION AND PRAISE

I turn my thoughts quietly, O God, away from self to thee. I adore thee. I praise thee. I thank thee. I here turn from this feverish life to think of thy holiness – thy love – thy serenity – thy joy – thy mighty purposefulness – thy wisdom – thy beauty – thy truth – thy final omnipotence. Slowly I murmur these great words about thee and let their feeling and significance sink into the deep places of my mind.

3.   ROOM 3   CONFESSION AND FORGIVENESS

Dear Lord, forgive me in that so much of my religion is concerned with myself. I want harmony with thee. I want peace of mind. I want health of body – and so I pray.

Forgive me, for I have made thee the means and myself the end.

I know it will take long to wean me from this terrible self-concern, but O God, help me, for hell can be nothing else but a life on which self is the centre.

Can I ever abandon self as men a sinking ship, only to find that the waves will bear them up and a divine hand will rescue them? My salvation can come only from thee, O Lord. Leave me not.

Forgive and uphold me and make me truly thine in utter commit-tal to thee.

4.   ROOM 4   RELAXATION

Help me now to be quiet, relaxed and receptive, accepting the thought of thy healing grace at work, deep within my nature.

5.   ROOM 5   PETITION

I pray, O Lord, that today I may know with keener awareness that I am in thy hands; well or ill, happy or sad, at work or at play, with others or alone, may I become increasingly conscious that I dwell within thy purposeful providence.

Illness does not mean punishment or thy disfavour. Fun is not "secular". The trifles of my life do not forfeit thine interest in me.

Grant me the sense of thy presence, born of thine indwelling and of thine enfolding love, and let me increasingly pause to recollect that, in every circumstance, I live within thy life and am always the object of thy care.

6.

ROOM 6   INTERCESSION

I lift up my heart, O God, for all who are the prey of anxious fears, who cannot get their minds off themselves and for whom every demand made on them fills them with foreboding, and with the feeling that they cannot cope with all that is required of them.

Give them the comfort of knowing that this feeling is illness, not cowardice; that millions have felt as they feel, that there is a way through this dark valley, and light at the end of it.

Lead them to those who can help them and understand them and show them the pathway to health and happiness. Comfort and sustain them by the loving presence of the Saviour who knows and understands all our woe and fear, and give them enough courage to face each day, and rest their minds in the thought that thou wilt see them through.

7.

ROOM 7   MEDITATION

Come, in this quiet moment of meditation; call me again, lead me in thy way for me, let the assurance of thy friendship take away my fears. Let every shadow make me look up into thy blessed face. Let me rise up now and follow thee.

Charles Wesley
1707–1788

The younger brother of John, he was blessed with a more tranquil temperament which enabled him to enjoy a happy home life. His main contribution to his brother's mission was to write hymns which could be sung at open air evangelical meetings to the popular tunes of the day. Their simple, memorable phrases, and their pleasing rhymes and rhythms have made his hymns vehicles by which people of

many Christian traditions express their love for
God.

1.

JESU, LOVER OF MY SOUL

Jesu, Lover of my soul,
    Let me to thy bosom fly,
While the nearer waters roll,
    While the tempest still is high:
Hide me, O my Saviour, hide,
    Till the storm of life be past!
Safe into the haven guide,
    O, receive my soul at last!

Other refuge have I none,
    Hangs my helpless soul on thee;
Leave, ah! leave me not alone,
    Still support and comfort me:
All my trust on thee is stayed,
    All my help from thee I bring;
Cover my defenceless head
    With the shadow of thy wing.

Thou, O Christ, art all I want
    More than all in thee I find!
Raise the fallen, cheer the faint,
    Heal the sick, and lead the blind;
Just and holy is thy name,
    I am all unrighteousness;
False and full of sin I am
    Thou art full of truth and grace.

Plenteous grace with thee is found,
    Grace to cover all my sin,
Let the healing streams abound;
    Make and keep me pure within:
Thou of life the fountain art,
    Freely let me take of thee,

Spring thou up within my heart,
Rise to all eternity.

2. TALK WITH US, LORD

Talk with us, Lord, thyself reveal
While here o'er earth we rove;
Speak to our hearts, and let us feel
The kindling of thy love.

With thee conversing we forget
All time, and toil, and care:
Labour is rest, and pain is sweet
If thou, my God, art here.

Here then, my God, vouchsafe to stay,
And bid my heart rejoice;
My bounding heart shall own thy sway,
And echo to thy voice.

Thou callest me to seek thy face –
'Tis all I wish to seek;
To attend the whispers of thy grace,
And hear thee inly speak.

Let this my every hour employ,
Till I thy glory see,
Enter into my Master's joy,
And find my heaven in thee.

3. O THOU WHO CAMEST FROM ABOVE

O thou who camest from above
The pure celestial fire t'impart,
Kindle a flame of sacred love
On the mean altar of my heart!

There let it for thy glory burn
With inextinguishable blaze,

And trembling to its source return
   In humble love, and fervent praise.

Jesu, confirm my heart's desire
   To work, and speak, and think for thee;
Still let me guard the holy fire,
   And still stir up thy gift in me;

Ready for all thy perfect will,
   My acts of faith and love repeat,
Till death thy endless mercies seal
   And make the sacrifice complete.

4.   CHRIST, MY LIFE, MY ONLY TREASURE

Christ, my life, my only treasure,
   Thou alone
   Mould thine own,
After thy good pleasure.

Thou, who paidst my price, direct me!
   Thine I am,
   Holy Lamb,
Save, and always save me.

Order thou my whole condition,
   Choose my state,
   Fix my fate
By thy wise decision.

From all earthly expectation
   Set me free,
   Seize for thee
All my strength of passion.

Into absolute subjection
   Be it brought,

Every thought,
Every fond affection.

That which most my soul requires
    For thy sake
    Hold it back
Purge my best desires.

Keep from me thy loveliest creature,
    Till I prove
    Jesus' love
Infinitely sweeter;

Till with purest passion panting
    Cries my heart
    "Where thou art
Nothing more is wanting".

Blest with thine abiding spirit,
    Fully blest
    Now I rest,
All in thee inherit.

Heaven is now with Jesus given;
    Christ in me,
    Thou shalt be
Mine eternal heaven.

John Wesley
1703–1791

Founder of the Methodist movement, he was a tireless preacher, travelling in the course of his life over a quarter of a million miles on horseback and

*delivering forty thousand sermons. He urged people
to receive Jesus Christ into their hearts as their
personal saviour. He held an annual covenant service at which people could renew their commitment
to God, a practice which still continues in Methodist
churches. He encouraged a regular discipline of
daily prayer in which individuals entrust all their
needs and concerns to God, and he wrote as a guide
two simple prayers, for Sunday and for weekdays.*

1.   ANNUAL RENEWAL OF THE COVENANT

O blessed Jesus, I come to you hungry, wretched, miserable, blind,
and naked; a most loathsome, polluted wretch, a guilty, condemned
malefactor, unworthy to wash the feet of the servants of my Lord,
much more to be solemnly married to the King of Glory. But since
such is your unparalleled love, I do here, with all my power, accept
you, and take you for my Head and Husband, for better, for worse,
for richer, for poorer, for all times and conditions, to love, honour,
and obey you before all others, and this to the death. I embrace
you in all your offices: I renounce my own worthiness, and do
here avow you the Lord for my righteousness; I renounce my own
wisdom, and do here take you for my only guide; I renounce my
own will, and take your will for my law.

And since you have told me I must suffer if I will reign, I do here
covenant with you to take my lot, as it falls, with you, and by your
grace assisting to run all hazards with you, verily purposing that
neither life nor death shall part between you and me.

And because you have been pleased to give me your holy laws as
the Rule of my life, and the way in which I should walk to your
kingdom, I do here willingly put my neck under your yoke, and set
my shoulder to your burden, and subscribing to all your laws as
holy, just, and good, I solemnly take them as the Rule of my words,
thoughts, and actions; promising that though my flesh contradict
and rebel, I will endeavour to order and govern my whole life
according to your direction, and will not allow myself in the neglect
of any thing that I know to be my duty.

Now, Almighty God, searcher of hearts, you know that I make

this Covenant with you this day, without any known guile or reservation, beseeching you, if you espy any flaw or falsehood therein, you would discover it to me, and help me to do it aright.

2.   ON THE SABBATH MORNING

O my Father, my God, I am in your hand; and may I rejoice above all things in being so. Do with me what seems good in your sight; only let me love you with all my mind, soul and strength.

Deliver me, O God, I beseech you, from all violent passions. Deliver me, O God, from all idolatrous love of any creature. I know infinite numbers have been lost to you by loving those creatures for their own sake.

Above all, deliver me, O my God, from all idolatrous self-love. I know, O God (blessed be your infinite mercy for giving me this knowledge) that this is the root of all evil.

O let your almighty arm so stablish, strengthen, and settle me that you may ever be the ground and pillar of all my love.

3.   ON A WEEKDAY MORNING

O God, who are the giver of all good gifts, I your unworthy servant entirely desire to praise your name for all the expressions of your bounty toward me. Blessed be your love for giving your Son to die for our sins, for the means of grace, and for the hope of glory. Blessed be your love for all the temporal benefits which you have with a liberal hand poured out upon me; for my health and strength, food and raiment, and all other necessaries with which you have provided your sinful servant. I also bless you, that after all my refusals of your grace, you still have patience with me, have preserved me this night, and given me yet another day to renew and perfect my repentance.

Make yourself always present to my mind, and let your love fill and rule my soul, in all those places, and companies, and employments to which you call me this day. O you who are good and do good, who extend your loving-kindness to all mankind, the work of your hands, your image, capable of knowing and loving you eternally: suffer me to exclude none, O Lord, from my charity, who are the objects of your mercy; but let me treat all my neighbours with that tender love which is due to your servants and to your children. Let your love to me, O blessed Saviour, be the pattern of my love to them.

Preserve my parents, my brothers and sisters, my friends and relations, and all mankind, in their souls and bodies. Forgive my enemies, and in your due time make them kindly affected toward me. O grant that we, with those who are already dead in your faith and fear, may together partake of a joyful resurrection.

The Whole Duty of Man
1658

It was probably the most popular devotional treatise of its day in Britain. Its prayers and reflections seemed to transcend the wearisome conflict between Puritan and High Churchman, which had brought the nation close to ruin, and instead offered a spiritual and moral path which all could follow.

1.   FOR FAITH

O blessed Lord, whom without faith it is impossible to please; let thy Spirit, I beseech thee, work in me such a faith as may be acceptable in thy sight even such as worketh by love. O let me not rest in a dead, ineffectual faith, but grant that it may be such as may show itself by my works; that it may be that victorious faith, which may enable me to overcome the world, and conform me to the image of that Christ, on whom I believe.

2.

FOR HOPE

O Lord, who art the hope of all the ends of the earth, let me never be destitute of a well-grounded hope, nor yet possessed with a vain presumption: suffer me not to think thou wilt either be reconciled to my sins, or reject my repentance; but give me, I beseech thee, such a hope as may be answerable to the only ground of hope, thy promises, and such as may both encourage and enable me to purify myself from all filthiness, both of flesh and spirit; that so, it may indeed become to me an anchor of the soul both sure and steadfast.

3.

FOR LOVE

Lord, thou art pleased to require my heart, and thou only hast a right to it. O let me not be so sacrilegiously unjust, as to alienate any part of it, but enable me to render it up whole and entire to thee. But, O my God, if thou seest fit, be pleased to let me taste of the joys, those ravishments of thy love, wherewith thy saints have been so transported. But if in this I know not what I ask, if I may not choose my place in thy kingdom, yet, O Lord, deny me not to drink of thy cup; let me have such a sincerity and degree of love, as may make me endure anything for thy sake; such a perfect love as may cast out all fear and sloth, that nothing may seem to me too grievous to suffer, or too difficult to do, in obedience to thee.

4.

FOR SINCERITY

O Lord, I cannot deceive thee, but I may most easily deceive myself. I beseech thee, let me not rest in any such deceit, but bring me to a sight and hatred of my most hidden corruptions, that I may not cherish any darling lust. O suffer me not to speak peace to myself when there is no peace; but grant I may judge of myself as thou judgest of me, that I may never be at peace with myself till I am at perfect peace with thee.

5.   FOR TRUST

O Almighty Lord, who never failest them that trust in thee: give me grace, I beseech thee, in all my difficulties and distresses to have recourse to thee, to rest and depend on thee. Thou shalt keep him, O Lord, in perfect peace, whose mind is stayed on thee. O let me always rest on this firm pillar, and never exchange it for the broken reeds of worldly succours: suffer not my heart to be overcharged with the cares of this life, taking thought what I shall eat or drink, or wherewithal I shall be clothed; but grant, that having, by honest labour and industry, done my part, I may cheerfully commit myself to thy providence, casting all my care upon thee.

6.   FOR CONTENTMENT

O Merciful God, thy wisdom is infinite to choose, and thy love forward to dispense good things to us: O let me always fully and entirely resign myself to thy disposal, have no desires of my own, but a perfect satisfaction in thy choice for me; that so, in whatsoever state I am, I may be therein content; Lord, grant I may never look with murmuring on my own condition, nor with envy on other men's. And, to that end, I beseech thee purge my heart of all covetous affections.

William of Saint Thierry
c.1065–1148

For fifteen years he served as abbot of the Benedictine monastery of St Thierry near Reims. Then in 1135 under the influence of Bernard of Clairvaux he founded a Cistercian house in the Ardennes. Like his mentor he engaged passionately in the theological controversies of the day. But his lasting repu-

tation depends on his spiritual works, The Golden
Epistle *and* On Contemplating God.

1. ## THE GIFT OF LOVE

To be saved by you, O Lord, is to receive from you the gift of
loving you and being loved by you. This is why you willed that
your Son be called Jesus, Saviour, for he saves people from their
sins by the power of his love. He teaches us to love him by his love
for us. He shows us the mercy of love by sacrificing himself on the
cross out of his love for all mankind. By holding us so dear, he has
stirred our hearts to love him.

Thus, Lord, through your Son you expressed your infinite love
for us, that we might love you. That was not because you needed
to be loved by us. It was because we could not be what you created
us to be, except by loving you.

You, O God, our souls' creator, know that affection cannot be
forced from unwilling souls, but has to be evoked. This is because
there can be no freedom where there is compulsion. Love must
always be freely given and freely received.

We could not with justice have been saved without learning to
love you. And we love you because you evoked our love, through
the loving sacrifice of your Son. You willed that we should love
you, yet without ever constraining our freedom.

We hold as a gift more precious than gold, your love. From the
beginning of creation your Son, the eternal Word, has been tossing
about on the stormy waters of human souls, striving to bring peace
through the gift of love. Now he has breathed over the waters of
our souls, and the waves are calm. Merciful Father, we thank you.

2. ## WE CANNOT DECEIVE YOU

Pardon us, O Lord, pardon us. We beg to shift the blame for our
sins, we make excuses. But no one can hide himself from the light
of your truth, which both enlightens those who turn to it, and
exposes those who turn away. Even our blood and our bones are
visible to you, who created us out of dust.

How foolish we are to think that we can rule our own lives,

satisfying our own desires, without thought of you. How stupid we are to imagine that we can keep our sins hidden. But although we may deceive other people, we cannot deceive you. And since you see into our hearts, we cannot deceive ourselves, for your light reveals to us our own spiritual corruption.

Let us, therefore, fall down before you, weeping with tears of shame. May your judgement give new shape to our souls. May your power mould our hearts to reflect your love. May your grace infuse our minds, so that our thoughts reflect your will.

3.   REFLECTING YOUR BRIGHTNESS

Loving you, O God, brings its own reward here on earth, as well as the eternal reward of heaven. And failure to love you, even when we can offer a thousand excuses, brings its own punishment. By becoming mirrors of your love, by wearing the mask of your likeness, and by allowing you to make us perfect, we can know the joy of heaven, even while we abide here on earth. Our consciences are sullied by our many sins; cleanse them, that we may reflect your infinite brightness.

Harry Williams
1919–

After serving as Dean of Trinity College, Cambridge, in the 1960s, where he gained a reputation for his radical political and theological views, he became a monk in 1969. His sermons at Trinity College, which attracted a large student congregation, contained snippets of prayers, in which God is addressed with naked honesty.

1. COMING INTO CHURCH

Hello, it is me, your old friend and your old enemy, your loving friend who often neglects you, your complicated friend, your utterly perplexed and decidedly resentful friend, partly loving, partly hating, partly not caring. It is me.

2. BEING HONEST TO GOD

O God, I am hellishly angry; I think so-and-so is a swine; I am tortured by worry about this or that; I am pretty certain that I have missed my chances in life; this or that has left me feeling terribly depressed. But nonetheless here I am like this, feeling both bloody and bloody-minded, and I am going to stay here for ten minutes. You are most unlikely to give me anything. I know that. But I am going to stay for the ten minutes nonetheless.

Count von Zinzendorf
1700–1760

The founder of the Moravian Church, he proclaimed a "religion of the heart" based on an intimate personal relationship between God and the individual. He was opposed by the Lutheran Church in his native Germany, which was suspicious of the unbridled enthusiasm of Moravian worship. But he had a profound influence on the Evangelical revival, and John Wesley paid him the compliment of translating some of his prayers as poetry.

1.

THE MELTED HEART

Lord, when my eye confronts my heart, and I realize that you have filled my heart with your love, I am breathless with amazement. Once my heart was so small in its vision, so narrow in its compassion so weak in its zeal for truth. Then you chose to enter my heart, and now in my heart I can see you, I can love all your people, and I have courage to proclaim the truth of your gospel to anyone and everyone. Like wax before a fire, my heart has melted under the heat of your love.

2.

THE IRRESISTIBLE LOOK

My dearest Saviour! We beg of you this same blessed look, this same irresistible look, which you always fix on the souls who like to look upon you, who like to receive you, who are ready to share your wounds, and who are even prepared to die for you. May all souls on earth, high and low, rich and poor, yearn for your look. And let us for our part testify amongst those we meet to your sacrificial love, that the number of those who succumb to your look may grow and grow. Indeed we promise that we shall not rest until we are able to look upon you, and say: "Lord, we have filled every place in heaven, by bringing every soul on earth under the bright light of your love".

3.

ETERNAL DEPTH OF LOVE

Eternal depth of love divine,
   In Jesus, God with us, displayed;
How bright thy beaming glories shine!
   How wide thy healing streams are spread!

With whom dost thou delight to dwell?
   Sinners, a vile and thankless race:
O God, what tongue aright can tell
   How vast thy love, how great thy grace!

The dictates of thy sovereign will
   With joy our grateful hearts receive:

All thy delight in us fulfil;
  Lo! all we are to thee we give.

To thy sure love, thy tender care,
  Our flesh, soul, spirit, we resign:
Oh, fix thy sacred presence there,
  And seal the abode forever thine.

O King of glory, thy rich grace
  Our feeble thought surpasses far;
Yea, even our crimes, though numberless,
  Less numerous than thy mercies are.

Still, Lord, thy saving health display,
  And arm our souls with heavenly zeal;
So fearless shall we urge our way
  Through all the powers of earth and hell.

4.   ALL-SEARCHING SIGHT

O thou to whose all-searching sight
The darkness shineth as the light,
Search, prove my heart; it pants for thee;
O, burst these bonds, and set it free!

Wash out its stains, refine its dross,
Nail my affections to the Cross;
Hallow each thought; let all within
Be clean, as thou, my Lord, art clean!

If in this darksome wild I stray,
Be thou my light, be thou my way;
No foes, no violence I fear,
No fraud, while thou, my God, art near.

When rising floods my soul o'erflow,
When sinks my heart in waves of woe,

Jesus, thy timely aid impart,
And raise my head, and cheer my heart.

Saviour, where'er thy steps I see,
Dauntless, untired, I follow thee!
Oh, let thy hand support me still,
And lead me to thy holy hill!

If rough and thorny be the way,
My strength proportion to my day;
Till toil, and grief, and pain shall cease,
Where all is calm, and joy, and peace.

Zoroaster

6th Century BC

Little is known about Zoroaster himself, but his religion flourished in the Persian Empire from about 500 B.C., and had a deep influence on both Jewish and Christian thought. He taught people to worship a single God, "Ahura Mazda" which means "Wise Lord": they should pray directly to him, and strictly obey his moral laws. He saw himself not as an originator of a new faith, but as a reformer bringing together the wisdom of all the ancient religions.

1.   HOW SHOULD I PRAY?

How should I pray? Teach the art of prayer to me, that I may devote myself to you. Should I meditate upon the wonders of your creation? Should I give thanks for the wisdom of my elders? Should I praise you for your many gifts to me? Should I reflect on all the things I have done wrong? Or should I simply wait until you speak to me? Tell me truly: how should I pray?

2.   I WORSHIP YOU

I worship you in every religion that teaches your laws and praises your glory. I worship you in every plant whose beauty reflects your beauty. I worship you in every event which is caused by your goodness and kindness. I worship you in every place where you dwell. And I worship you in every man and woman who seeks to follow your way of righteousness.

3.   IF I HAVE OFFENDED YOU

If I have offended you, O Wise Lord, whether by thought or word or deed, whether intentionally or inadvertently, I earnestly seek to make amends by offering you praise. If I have reduced the honour in which you are held, I proclaim your glory with even greater fervour. May your will rule in the hearts of all your creatures. May every animal and plant, as well as every man and woman, live according to your laws, for the seed of righteousness lives in every living thing.

4.   ORDER OUR LIVES

Order our lives by your wisdom, and care for our needs by your bounty. Enable us to live in peace with one another, so that we can help each other in our work. Take from us all threat of war and famine. Make our animals fat and healthy, and make our crops grow abundantly. In each village set a man of honesty as chief, and let every person respect his authority. Above all, make us holy in all our thoughts and words and deeds.

BIBLIOGRAPHY

ADAM OF ST VICTOR, *The Liturgical Poetry*, trans. D. S. Wrangham.

AELRED OF RIEVAULX, *Prayers of St Aelred*, trans. A. Hoste.

ALCUIN OF YORK, *Life and Letters*, ed. S. Allot.

AMBROSE OF MILAN, *Early Christian Prayers*, ed. A. Hamman.

LANCELOT ANDREWES, *The Private Prayers of Lancelot Andrewes*, ed. Hugh Martin.

ANSELM OF CANTERBURY, *Prayers and Meditations*, trans. Benedict Ward.

GEORGE APPLETON, *Prayer in a Troubled World*.

JUAN ARIAS, *Prayers without Frills*.

ARJUNA, *The Bhagavad Gita*, trans. J. Mascaro.

AUGUSTINE OF HIPPO, *Confessions of Saint Augustine*, trans. E. B. Pusey.

JOHN BAILLIE, *A Diary of Private Prayer*.

AUGUSTINE BAKER, *Holy Wisdom*, ed. Abbot Sweeney.

WILLIAM BARCLAY, *A Barclay Prayer Book*.

KARL BARTH, *Call of God*, trans. A. T. Mackay.

BASIL OF CAESAREA, *The Later Christian Fathers*, trans. H. Bettenson.

RICHARD BAXTER, *The Grand Question Resolved*.

BEDE, *A History of the English Church and People*, trans. J. Stevens.

EDWARD BENSON, *Prayers Public and Private*, ed. Hugh Benson.

BERNARD OF CLAIRVAULX, *On the Christian Year*, trans. A Religious from CSMV.

JACOB BOEHME, *The Way to Christ*, trans. P. C. Erb.

BONAVENTURA, *The Tree of Life*, trans. E. Cousins.

DIETRICH BONHOEFFER, *Fiction from Prison*, trans. C. Green.

JOHN CALVIN, *The Christian Life*, trans. J. H. Leith.

HELDER CAMARA, *Into Your Hands, Lord*.

AMY CARMICHAEL, *Learning of God*, ed. Stuart and Brenda Blanch.

ELIZABETH CATEZ, *Complete Works*, ed. Conrad de Meester.

CATHERINE OF GENOA, *The Spiritual Dialogue*, trans. S. Hughes.

CATHERINE OF SIENA, *The Dialogue*, trans. S. Noffke.

JEAN-PIERRE DE CAUSSADE, *Self-Abandonment to Divine Providence*, trans. A. Thorold.

CELTIC PRAYERS, *Celtic Fire*, ed. R. Van de Weyer.

FRANÇOIS CHAGNEAU, *Stay with Us*.

RICHARD CHALLONER, *Garden of the Soul*.

REX CHAPMAN, *A Kind of Praying*.

CLEMENT OF ALEXANDRIA, *Early Christian Prayer*, ed. A. Hamman.

CLEMENT OF ROME, *Early Christian Prayers*, ed. A. Hamman.

JOHN COSIN, *A Collection of Private Devotions*, ed. P. G. Stanwood.

WILLIAM COWPER, *The Poetical Works*, ed. H. S. Milford.

THOMAS CRANMER, *The Work of Thomas Cranmer*, ed. G. D. Duffield.

RICHARD CRASHAW, *The Poems*, ed. J. R. Tutin.

CYPRIAN OF CARTHAGE, *Early Christian Prayers*, ed. A. Hamman.

DIDACHE, *Early Christian Prayers*, ed. A. Hamman.

DIMMA, *Western Liturgies*, ed. R. C. West.

JOHN DONNE, *Sermons*, ed. E. M. Simpson, *Divine Poems*, ed. Helen Gardner.

EDMUND OF ABINGDON, *The Mirror of St Edmund*, trans. F. M. Steele.

QUEEN ELIZABETH I, *A Book of Devotions*, trans. A. Fox.

EPHREM THE SYRIAN, *Hymns*, ed. K. E. McVey.

ERASMUS, *Prayers of Erasmus*, trans. C. S. Coldwell.

EXETER BOOK, *Anglo-Saxon Poetry*, trans. S. A. J. Bradley.

FENELON, *Letters to Men and Women*, trans. D. Stanford.

NICHOLAS FERRAR, *Original Sources*, ed. R. Van de Weyer and P. Saunders.

CHARLES DE FOUCAULD, *Spiritual Autobiography*, trans. Jean-François Six.

FRANCIS OF ASSISI, *The Complete Works*, trans. R. J. Armstrong and I. C. Brady.

FRANCIS OF SALES, *The Love of God*, trans. V. Ken.

JOHANN FREYLINGHAUSEN, *Spiritual Songbook*, trans. P. C. Erb.

FULBERT OF CHARTRES, *Letters and Poems*, ed. F. Behrends.

DOMINIC GAISFORD, *A Touch of God*, ed. Maria Boulding.

GEMMA GALGANI, *The Life of the Servant of God*, trans. A. M. O'Sullivan.

GELASIAN SACRAMENTARY, *Early Christian Prayers*, ed. A. Hamman.

PAUL GERES, *Prayers for Impossible Days*, trans. I. H. Hjelm.

KAHIL GIBRAN, *Jesus the Son of Man*.

ELIZABETH GOUDGE, *A Vision of God*, ed. C. Rawlins.

GREGORY OF NAZIANZUS, *Early Christian Prayers*, ed. A. Hamman.

LADY JANE GREY, *Literary Remains*, ed. N. H. Nicolas.

GUIGO THE CARTHUSIAN, *The Ladder of Monks*, trans. E. Colledge and J. Walsh.

JOSEPH HALL, *The Art of Divine Meditation*.

DAG HAMMERSKJÖLD, *Markings*, trans. W. H. Auden.

BERNARD HÄRING, *The Redemption of the World*.

GEORGE HERBERT, *Lament and Love*, ed. R. Van de Weyer and P. Saunders.

HILARY OF POITIERS, *Patrologia Latina*, ed. J. P. Mingne.

HILDEGARD OF BINGEN, *Scievias*, trans. B. Hozeski.

HIPPOLYTUS, *Early Christian Prayers*, ed. A. Hamman.

HENRY SCOTT HOLLAND, *Logic and Life*.

GERARD MANLEY HOPKINS, *Poetry and Prose*, ed. C. Phillips.

IGNATIUS OF LOYALA, *Spiritual Exercises*, trans. T. Corbishley.

JACOPONE DA TODI, *The Lauds*, trans. S. and E. Hughes.

PHILIP JEBB, *A Touch of God*, ed. Maria Boulding.

JOHN OF THE CROSS, *Complete Works*, ed. E. Allison Peers.

SAMUEL JOHNSON, *Diaries, Prayers and Annals*, ed. E. L. McAdam and M. Hyde.

BEN JONSON, *Ben Jonson and the Cavalier Poets*, ed. H. Maclean.

JULIAN OF NORWICH, *Revelations of Divine Love*, trans. C. Walters.

MARGERY KEMPE, *The Book of Margery Kempe*, trans. B. A. Windeott.

THOMAS KEN, *Directions for Prayers*.

SØREN KIERKEGAARD, *Selected Readings*, ed. R. Van de Weyer.

JOHN KNOX, *The Works*, ed. B. Laing.

WILLIAM LAUD, *Biography*, W. H. Hutton.

BROTHER LAWRENCE, *The Practice of the Presence of God*, ed. H. Martin.

LEONINE SACRAMENTARY, *Western Liturgies*, ed. R. C. West.

GEORGE MACDONALD, *An Anthology*, ed. C. S. Lewis.

GEORGE MACLEOD, *The Whole Earth Shall Cry Glory*.

FREDERICK MACNUTT, *The Prayer Manual*.

MECHTHILD OF MAGDEBURG, *The Flowing Light of the Godhead*, trans. L. Menzies.

THOMAS MERTON, *Elected Silence*.

ERIC MILNER-WHITE, *My God, My Glory*.

THOMAS MORE, *Guide to Holiness*, ed. Marilynne Bromley.

MOZARABIC SACRAMENTARY, *Western Liturgies*, ed. R. C. West.

THOMAS MÜNZER, *Collected Works*, trans. P. Matheson.

NANAK, *The Sikh Religion*, M. A. Macauliffe.

JOHN HENRY NEWMAN, *I Step, I Mount*, ed. R. Van de Weyer and P. Saunders.

REINHOLD NIEBUHR, *Justice and Mercy*, ed. U. Niebuhr.

HENRI NOUWEN, *Seeds of Hope*, ed. R. Durback.

HUUB OOSTERHUIS, *Your Word is Near*, trans. N. D. Smith.

ORIGEN, *Philokalia*, trans. G. Lewis.

PRAYERS FROM PAPYRI, *Early Christian Prayers*, ed. A. Hamman.

BLAISE PASCAL, *Selected Readings*, ed. R. Van de Weyer.

ALAN PATON, *Instrument of Thy Mercy*.

POLYCARP OF SMYRNA, *Documents of the Christian Church*, ed. H. Bettenson.

E. B. PUSEY, *Private Prayers*, ed. H. P. Liddon.

MICHEL QUOIST, *Prayers of Life*, trans. A. M. De Commaile and A. M. Forsyth.

RABBULA OF EDESSA, *Early Christian Prayers*, ed. A. Hamman.

KARL RAHNER, *Encounters with Silence*, trans. J. M. Demske.

RAHULABHADRA, *Buddhist Scriptures*, ed. E. Conze.

BROTHER RAMON, *Heaven on Earth*.

WALTER RAUSCHENBUSCH, *Prayers of Secret Awakening*.

RICHARD ROLLE, *Selected Works*, ed. G. C. Heseltine.

CHRISTINA ROSSETTI, *The Face of the Deep*.

ROGER SCHUTZ, *Life From Within*.

JOHN SERGIEFF, *My Life in Christ*, trans. E. E. Goulaeff.

SIMEON THE THEODIDACT, *Hymns of Divine Love*, trans. G. A. Maloney.

SIMON THE PERSIAN, *Early Christian Prayers*, ed. A. Hamman.

RITA SNOWDEN, *A Woman's Book of Prayers*.

CHARLES HADDON SPURGEON, *Morning and Evening*.

JOHANN STARCK, *Daily Handbook for Days of Rejoicing and Sorrow*.

ROBERT LOUIS STEVENSON, *Prayers Written at Vailima*.

HENRY SUSO, *The Exemplar*, trans. M. A. Edward.

RABINDRANATH TAGORE, *Gitanguli*, introduced by W. B. Yeats.

JEREMY TAYLOR, *The Rule and Exercise of Holy Living*.

TEILHARD DE CHARDIN, *The Prayer of the Universe*, trans. R. Hague.

TERESA OF ÁVILA, *Complete Works*, ed. A. Peers.

MOTHER TERESA, *In the Silence of the Heart*, ed. K. Spink.

THÉRÈSE OF LISIEUX, *Autobiography of a Saint*, trans. R. Knox.

THOMAS À KEMPIS, *Christ for all Seasons*, ed. P. Toon.

THOMAS AQUINAS, *An Aquinas Reader*, ed. M. T. Clark.

FRANK TOPPING, *Lord of Life*.

THOMAS TRAHERNE, *Centuries*.

TYCHON OF LADONSK, *Memoirs*, trans. H. Iswolsky.

MANIKKA VASAHAR, *Hymns of the Tamil Saints*, trans. F. Kingsbury and G. E. Phillips.

HENRY VAUGHAN, *Poems*, ed. L. Martz.

ATHARVA VEDA, *Hindu Scriptures*, trans. R. C. Zaehner.

JEAN-BAPTISTE MARIE VIANNEY, *The Cure d'Ars*, trans. E. E. Graf.

MARY WARD, *Till God Will*, ed. M. E. Orchard.

LESLIE WEATHERHEAD, *A Private House of Prayer*.

CHARLES AND JOHN WESLEY, *Selected Writings and Hymns*, ed. F. Whaling.

THE WHOLE DUTY OF MAN, ed. M. Hammond.

WILLIAM OF ST THIERRY, *The Gold Epistle*, trans. W. Shewring.

HARRY WILLIAMS, *True to Experience*, ed. E. Mable.

COUNT VON ZINZENDORF, *Hymns and Sacred Poems*, trans. J. Wesley.

ZOROASTER, *Zend-Avesta*, trans. M. Muller.

INDEX

Through the Day

1. MORNING – WAKING, RISING, DRESSING, PREPARING FOR THE DAY
Ambrose of Milan 4
John Baillie 1
Jacob Boehme 1, 2, 3
John Calvin 1
Erasmus 4
Thomas Ken 1, 2
John Knox 1
Leonine Sacramentary 1

2. DAY-TIME – WORKING, TRAVELLING, GOING TO SCHOOL
Jacob Boehme 2, 5
John Calvin 2, 3
Thomas Ken 4,5
Brother Lawrence 1
Johann Starck 2
John Wesley 3

3. EVENING – RESTING, RELAXING
John Baillie 2
Jacob Boehme 6
Celtic Prayers 4
Dinka 4
Leonine Sacramentary 2

4. NIGHT-TIME – GOING TO BED, SLEEPING, DREAMING
Alcuin of York 3
Ambrose of Milan 5
Jacob Boehme 7
John Calvin 6
Erasmus 5
Johann Freylinghausen 6, 7
Thomas Ken 6, 8
William Laud 6

5. MEAL-TIMES
Alcuin of York 1
Richard Baxter 2, 3
John Calvin 4, 5
Thomas Ken 3
John Knox 3

6. STUDYING THE SCRIPTURES
Bede 3
Gregory of Nazianzus 6
Origen

7. SABBATH
Johann Starck 1
John Wesley 2

Through the Year

1. ADVENT
Exeter Book 1
Gelasian Sacramentary 1

2. CHRISTMAS
Adam of St Victor 1
Karl Barth 1
Bernard of Clairvaux 1
Ephrem the Syrian 1, 2
Gelasian Sacramentary 2
E. B. Pusey 3

3. NEW YEAR
Karl Barth 2

4. LENT
Bernard of Clairvaux 2
Exeter Book 2
Gelasian Sacramentary

5. HOLY WEEK
Bernard of Clairvaux 3
Gelasian Sacramentary 2
E. B. Pusey

6. EASTER
Adam of St Victor 2
Karl Barth 3
Bernard of Clairvaux 4
Gelasian Sacramentary 5
Hippolytus 3

7. ASCENSION
Bernard of Clairvaux 5
Gelasian Sacramentary 6
E. B. Pusey 5

8. PENTECOST
Adam of St Victor 3
Bonaventura 7
Gelasian Sacramentary 7
Hildegard of Bingen

9. THE LORD'S RETURN
Bernard of Clairvaux 6

Personal and Corporate Devotion

1. SELF-OFFERING
Lancelot Andrewes 5
Augustine of Hippo 1–6
Amy Carmichael 2
Elizabeth Catez 1
François Chagneau 1
Richard Challoner 1
Columbanus 1
John Cosin 1–9
Edmund of Abingdon 1, 2
Queen Elizabeth I 1, 2
Fenelon 1
Charles Foucauld 1
Francis of Sales 7
Johan Freylinghausen 3
Dominic Gaisford 1
Gemma Galgani 2

Joseph Hall 2
Dag Hammarskjöld 1–6
Henry Scott Holland 1, 2
Gerard Manley Hopkins 1
Ignatius of Loyola 1, 2
Philip Jebb 2
John of the Cross 4, 5
Ben Jonson 2
Margery Kempe 9
Thomas Ken 7
William Laud 4, 5
Brother Lawrence 2
George MacDonald 2, 3
Mahayana Buddhism 2
Peter Marshall 1, 2, 3
Mechthild of Magdeburg 1–13
Eric Milner-White 1–4

Mohammed 1, 2, 3
Reinhold Niebuhr 6
Prayers from Papyri 2
Blaise Pascal 1
E. B. Pusey 1, 2
John Sergieff 1–8
Rita Snowden 1–3
Robert Louis Stevenson 1
Rabindranath Tagore 3, 4, 5
Mother Teresa 1–7
Thomas à Kempis 6, 7
Thomas Aquinas 1, 5
Frank Topping 1–4
Tychon of Zadonsk 5
Leslie Weatherhead 1, 2, 4, 7
Henry Williams 1, 2
Count von Zinzendorf 1, 2

2. BELIEF
Lancelot Andrewes 2
Anselm of Canterbury 6
Amy Carmichael 1
François Chagneau 2
Fenelon 3
George Herbert 1
Kalahari Bushmen 1

3. CONFESSION AND FORGIVENESS
Lancelot Andrewes 1
Catherine of Genoa 1
William Cowper 1
John Donne 1
Queen Elizabeth I 1
Gilbert of Hoyland 3
Henry Scott Holland 3
Philip Jebb 1
Jeremiah 2
Margery Kempe 1
Søren Kierkegaard 1, 2
George MacDonald 1
Michel Quoist 1–4
Karl Rahner 1
Robert Louis Stevenson 2

Thérèse of Lisieux 6
Tychon of Zadonsk 1–3

4. INTERCESSION
Lancelot Andrewes 3
William Barclay 1
Richard Baxter 1
Celtic Prayers 7
Clement of Rome 1, 2
Cyprian of Carthage 1
Dinka 2
Fulbert of Chartres 5
Gemma Galgani 3
Gilbert of Hoyland 1, 2
Elizabeth Goudge 2
George Herbert 2
Kalahari Bushmen 2, 3
Margery Kempe 7, 8
William Laud 1–3
Mahayana Buddhism 1
Book of Psalms 1, 2
Solomon 1, 2
Robert Louis Stevenson 3
Thomas Traherne 5
Leslie Weatherhead 5, 6

5. THANKSGIVING
Lancelot Andrewes 4
Margery Kempe 10
Thomas à Kempis 9, 10
Thomas Traherne 3, 4
Tychon of Zadonsk 4

6. COMMUNION
Anselm of Canterbury 3
Basil of Caesarea 3
Book of Common Prayer 5
Didache 1, 2
Hippolytus 1, 2
Margery Kempe 4
Thomas Münzer 5
Thomas Aquinas 2, 3
Teresa of Ávila 12

God's Care

1. CREATION
Catherine of Siena 4
Celtic Prayers 6
Francis of Assisi 4
Francis of Sales 1
George MacLeod 1–3
Huub Oosterhuis 5

Book of Psalms 5
Brother Ramon 6
Teilhard de Chardin 1, 2
Thomas Traherne 2
Atharva Veda 1

2. TRUTH AND FAITH
Aelred of Rievaulx 8
Arjuna 1, 2
Book of Common Prayer 7
Columbanus 3
Joseph Hall 1, 3
Bernard Häring 2
George Herbert 1
Hilary of Poitiers 1
Hildegard of Bingen 2
John of the Cross 1, 2
Margery Kempe 8
Søren Kierkegaard 6
George MacDonald 4, 5
Frederick Macnutt 3–5
Thomas Merton 2
Mozarabic Sacramentary 3
Thomas Münzer 1
Nanak 2
John Henry Newman 2–4
Origen 2, 3
Alan Paton 2
Rahulabhadra 1
Brother Ramon 3
Christina Rossetti 4
Simon the Theodidact 1, 2
Thomas Aquinas 6
Manikka Vasahar 3
Wapokomo 2
Whole Duty of Man 1, 2, 4, 5
William of St Thierry 2, 3
Zoroaster

3. LOVE AND COMPASSION
Alcuin of York 2
Augustine Baker 1
Amy Carmichael 3
Bernard of Clairvaux 7
Helda Camara 1, 2, 4
Catherine of Genoa 2
Catherine of Siena 2, 5, 6
Gemma Galgani 1
Elizabeth Goudge 1
Hilary of Poitiers 3
Gerard Manley Hopkins 2
John Sergieff 9
Margery Kempe 6
Frederick Macnutt 1
Mozarabic Sacramentary 5
Thomas Münzer 2
John Henry Newman 1
Brother Ramon 4
Christina Rossetti 2
Jeremy Taylor 9
Terese of Ávila 4, 6, 7, 8, 15
Thérèse of Lisieux 3

Manikka Vasahar 2
Jean-Baptiste Marie Vianney 1
Whole Duty of Man 3
William of St Thierry 1
Count von Zinzendorf 3

4. MERCY
Ambrose of Milan 6
Helder Camara 5
Catherine of Siena 1
Dietrich Bonhoeffer 1
Dimma 2
Dinka 3
John Donne 2
Gilbert of Hoyland 3
Mozarabic Sacramentary 8
Thomas Münzer 4
Huub Oosterhuis 4
Origen 1
Prayers from Papyri 1
Rabbula of Edessa 1
Teresa of Ávila 2, 3, 4

5. PEACE
Book of Common Prayer 1, 3
William Cowper 3
Cyprian of Carthage 2
Samuel Johnson 3
Frederick Macnutt 2
Mozarabic Sacramentary 6
Thomas Münzer 3
Rabindranath Tagore 2
Wapokomo 2
Whole Duty of Man 6

6. GRACE
Alcuin of York 5
Book of Common Prayer 2
Richard Crashaw 1
Bernard Häring 1
Nanak 3
Huub Oosterhuis 1, 2, 3
Brother Ramon 5
Christina Rossetti 3
Rabindranath Tagore 1
Jeremy Taylor 2–6
Teresa of Ávila 13
Manikka Vasahar 1
Atharva Veda 2

7. PROVIDENCE
Augustine Baker 2
Jean-Pierre de Coussade 1–5
Francis of Sales 6
Fulbert of Chartres 3
Gerard Manley Hopkins 3

Christina Rossetti 5
Sioux 2
Jeremy Taylor 1

8. GUIDANCE
Basil of Caesarea 1
Catherine of Siena 4
Clement of Alexandria 1
Columbanus 2
Cyprian of Carthage 3
Dinka 1
Nicholas Ferrar 3
Johann Freylinghausen 4
Fulbert of Chartres 2
Joseph Hall 4
Gerard Manley Hopkins 4
Samuel Johnson 1, 2
Leonine Sacramentary 4
Mozarabic Sacramentary 1
John Henry Newman 6
Sioux 1
Robert Louis Stevenson 4, 5

Teresa of Ávila 9–11
Whole Duty of Man 8
Count von Zinzendorf 4

9. PURITY AND HUMILITY
Book of Common Prayer 4
Clement of Rome 3
Peter Marshall 4
Mozarabic Sacramentary 2, 7
Nanak 1
Alan Paton 6
Christina Rossetti 1
Teresa of Ávila 1
Whole Duty of Man 7

10. HOLINESS
George Appleton 1
Charles de Foucauld 2
Francis of Assisi 2
Francis of Sales 4, 5
Brother Ramon 2
Zoroaster 3, 4

The Human Condition

1. DEATH AND LIFE
Ambrose of Milan 2, 3
George Appleton 5
Juan Arias 2
Bede 1
Dinka 5
Dietrich Bonhoeffer 3
Celtic Prayers 5, 8, 9
Columbanus 2
Francis of Sales 3, 8
Johann Freylinghausen 5
John of the Cross 3
Samuel Johnson 4, 5
Huub Oosterhuis 3, 4
Richard Rolle 10
Johann Starck 5

2. SUFFERING AND JOY
George Appleton 2
William Barclay 3
Catherine of Genoa 3
Richard Crashaw 2
John Donne 4, 5
Fenelon 2
Guigo the Carthusian 1, 2
George Herbert 3
Book of Psalms 4
Jacopone da Todi 1, 2

Johann Starck 3
Thomas à Kempis 2, 10

3. SIN AND RIGHTEOUSNESS
Juan Arias 1
William Cowper 2
Francis of Sales 2
Paul Geres 2, 3
Hildegard of Bingen 1, 3–6
Jeremiah 1
Thomas à Kempis 3, 5

4. STRENGTH AND WEAKNESS
Bernard Haring 3
George Herbert 4
Søren Kierkegaard 5
Leonine Sacramentary 5
Henri Nouwen
Prayers from Papyri 3
Book of Psalms 3
Thomas à Kempis 1, 4

5. YOUTH AND AGE
George Appleton 4
Amy Carmichael 4

6. SICKNESS AND HEALING
Aelred of Rievaulx 7

412　INDEX

George Appleton 3
Aztec 2
Dimma 1, 3
Erasmus 6
Nicholas Ferrar 2
Gregory Nazianzus 4, 5
Lady Jane Grey 1
Huub Oosterhuis 2
Blaise Pascal 2
Johann Starck 4
Teresa of Ávila 16, 17

7. ENMITY AND FRIENDSHIP
Alcuin of York 4
Anselm of Canterbury 4, 5
Aztec 1
Reinhold Niebuhr 1, 2
Henri Nouwen 3
Alan Paton 3, 4, 5
Walter Rauschenbusch 1, 5

8. OPPRESSION AND FREEDOM
Helder Camara 3
Dietrich Bonhoeffer 2
Michael Hollings 1–3

Reinhold Niebuhr 3, 4
Huub Oosterhuis 1

9. VOCATION
Ambrose of Milan
Edward Benson 1, 2
Catherine of Siena 3
Celtic Prayers 1, 2, 3
Paul Geres 1
Jeremiah 3
George MacDonald 7
Thomas Merton 1
Henri Nouwen 2
Alan Paton 1
Walter Rauschenbusch 2, 3, 4
Thérèse of Lisieux 1, 2, 5
Thomas Aquinas 4
Mary Ward 1, 2

10. MARTYRDOM
Thomas Cranmer 1
Thomas More 1, 2
Polycarp of Smyrna 1, 2
Simon the Persian

The Person of Jesus

Aelred of Rievaulx 1–6
Bonaventura 1–6
Rex Chapman 1–7
Clement of Alexandria 2
Richard Crashaw 3
Charles de Foucauld 3
Francis of Assisi 1, 3, 5
Johann Freylinghausen 1, 2
Kahil Gibran 1–4
Hildegard of Bingen 7, 8

John Sergieff 10, 11, 12
Søren Kierkegaard 3, 4
Richard Rolle 1–9
Roger Schutz 1, 2, 3
Charles Haddon Spurgeon 1–8
Henry Suso 1–5
Thérèsa of Lisieux 7, 8
Thomas Traherne 1
Charles Wesley 1–4

ACKNOWLEDGEMENTS

The editor and publisher are grateful to the following for permission to reproduce copyright material in this anthology.

Ateliers & Presses de Taizé (France):
Life from Within by Brother Roger of Taizé.

Burns & Oates Ltd (UK):
Elected Silence by Thomas Merton.

Cassell Plc (UK):
The Prayer Manual by F. B. Macnutt.

Christian Literature Crusade, (USA):
Candles in the Dark by Amy Carmichael.

Darton, Longman & Todd Ltd (UK):
Prayer in a Troubled World by George Appleton.
Into Your Hands, Lord by Helder Camara.
Becoming What I Am by Harry Williams.

Edward England Books (UK):
A Private House of Prayer by Leslie D. Weatherhead.

Faber & Faber Ltd (UK):
Markings by Dag Hammarskjöld, translated by Leif Sjöberg and W. H. Auden.

Fortress Press (USA):
Prayers for Impossible Days by Paul Geres, translated by Ingalill H. Hjelm.

Gill & Macmillan Ltd, Dublin (Ireland) and Andrews & McMeel, Kansas (USA):
"The Brick", "Posters", "The Wire Fence" and "The Telephone" from *Prayers of Life* by Michel Quoist.

HarperCollinsPublishers Ltd (UK):
The Prayers of Peter Marshall edited by Catherine Marshall.
Justice and Mercy by Reinhold Niebuhr, edited by Ursula M. Niebuhr.
Instrument of thy Peace by Alan Paton.

Heaven on Earth by Brother Ramon, SSF.
A Woman's Book of Prayers by Rita F. Snowden.
The Prayer of the Universe by Teilhard de Chardin, translated by René Hague.

Hodder & Stoughton Publishers Ltd (UK):
A Diary of Prayer by Elizabeth Goudge.

The Lutterworth Press (UK):
Lord of Life by Frank Topping.

McCrimmon Publishing Company Ltd (UK):
Prayers for Others by Michael Hollings and Etta Gullick.

The Mercier Press Ltd, Cork (Ireland):
Prayer without Frills by Juan Arias.

Newman Press, Maryland (USA):
Stay with us by François Chagneau.
Your Word is Near by Huub Oosterhuis, translated by N. D. Smith.
"God of my Life" from Encounters with Silence by Karl Rahner, translated by James M. Demske, S.J.

Oxford University Press (UK):
A Diary of Private Prayer by John Baillie.

St Paul Publications (UK) and Liguori Publications (USA)
The Sacred Heart of Jesus and the Redemption of the World by Bernard Häring, CSSR.

SCM Press Ltd (UK):
A Barclay Prayer Book by William Barclay.
Call of God by Karl Barth, translated by A. Mackay.
A Kind of Praying by Rex Chapman.

SPCK (UK):
On Man's Prayers by George Appleton.
"Cast your Bread upon the Waters" by Dominic Gaisford and *"Wonder is so Sudden a Gift"* by Philip Jebb from *A Touch of God* edited by Maria Boulding.
My God, My Glory by Eric Milner-White.
In the Silence of the Heart: Meditations by Mother Teresa of Calcutta compiled by Kathryn Spink.

Wild Goose Publications (UK):
The Whole Earth Shall Cry Glory by George MacLeod.

We apologise to those copyright holders whom it has proved impossible to locate.